Zondervan/Youth Specialties Books

Adventure Games
Amazing Tension Getters
Called to Care
The Complete Student Missions Handbook
Creative Socials and Special Events
Divorce Recovery for Teenagers
Feeding Your Forgotten Soul (Spiritual Growth for Youth Workers)
Get 'Em Talking
Good Clean Fun
Good Clean Fun, Volume 2
Great Games for 4th–6th Graders (Get 'Em Growing)
Great Ideas for Small Youth Groups
Greatest Skits on Earth
Greatest Skits on Earth, Volume 2
Growing Up in America
High School Ministry
High School TalkSheets
Holiday Ideas for Youth Groups (Revised Edition)
Hot Talks
Ideas for Social Action
Intensive Care: Helping Teenagers in Crisis
Junior High Ministry
Junior High TalkSheets
The Ministry of Nurture
On-Site: 40 On-Location Programs for Youth Groups
Option Plays
Organizing Your Youth Ministry
Play It! Great Games for Groups
Teaching the Bible Creatively
Teaching the Truth about Sex
Tension Getters
Tension Getters II
Unsung Heroes: How to Recruit and Train Volunteer Youth Workers
Up Close and Personal: How to Build Community in Your Youth Group
Youth Specialties Clip Art Book
Youth Specialties Clip Art Book, Volume 2

A Youth Speaker's Sourcebook

Hot Talks

Compiled & Edited by
Duffy Robbins

Youth Specialties

ZONDERVAN PUBLISHING HOUSE
Grand Rapids, Michigan

HOT TALKS

Youth Specialties Books are published by
Zondervan Publishing House
Grand Rapids, Michigan 49530

Copyright © 1987 by Youth Specialties, Inc.

Library of Congress Cataloging in Publication Data

Hot talks: a youth speaker's sourcebook / compiled and edited by Duffy Robbins.
   p. cm.
  ISBN 0-310-34841-2
  1. Youth sermons. 2. Preaching to youth. I. Robbins, Duffy.
BV4310.H56   1987   87-21469
252'.55—dc19   CIP

Edited by Lori J. Walburg
Designed by Ann Cherryman

Printed in the United States of America

92 93 94 95 96 / AK / 10 9 8 7 6

This book is dedicated to Dick Gehron, my former Young Life club leader, through whom I became a Christian, and from whom I heard some great youth talks;

and, David Seamands and Roy Putnam, two great preachers who showed me the power in preaching the Word of God;

and Tony Campolo, my friend, my colleague, and a not-too-shabby youth speaker himself!

About the YouthSource™ Publishing Group

YouthSource™ books, tapes, videos, and other resources pool the expertise of three of the finest youth-ministry resource providers in the world:

• **Campus Life Books**—publishers of the award-winning *Campus Life* magazine, who for nearly fifty years have helped high schoolers live Christian lives.

• **Youth Specialties**—serving ministers to middle-school, junior-high, and high-school youth for over twenty years through books, magazines, and training events such as the National Youth Workers Convention.

• **Zondervan Publishing House**—one of the oldest, largest, and most respected evangelical Christian publishers in the world.

Campus Life
465 Gundersen Dr.
Carol Stream, IL 60188
708-260-6200

Youth Specialties
1224 Greenfield Dr.
El Cajon, CA 92021
619-440-2333

Zondervan
1415 Lake Dr., S.E.
Grand Rapids, MI 49506
616-698-6900

Contents

Contributors to Hot Talks

Brent Bromstrup is minister to students at First Covenant Church in Minneapolis, Minnesota.

Dave Bruno is a member of the youth staff at First Evangelical Free Church in Fullerton, California.

Jim Burns is president of the National Institute of Youth Ministry in Dana Point, California. He has written several books including *Handling Your Hormones* and *High School Ministry* (co-authored with Mike Yaconelli).

Chap Clark is area director for Young Life in Denver, Colorado. He is also author of the book *Next Time I Fall in Love.*

Byron Emmert is director of Youth for Christ in Mountain Lake, Minnesota. He is also director of Youth Congress '88.

John King is youth pastor at Great Valley Presbyterian Church in Malvern, Pennsylvania.

Craig Knudsen is former area director for Young Life in San Diego, California, and is now a high-school teacher and basketball coach.

Bill MacPhee is minister of youth at Hillcrest Covenant Church in Prairie Village, Kansas.

Greg McKinnon is director of youth ministries at Central Presbyterian Church in St. Louis, Missouri.

Duffy Robbins heads the department of youth ministry at Eastern College, St. Davids, Pennsylvania, and is an associate staff member with Youth Specialties Ministries.

Barry St. Clair is director of Reach Out Ministries in Avondale Estates, Georgia, and is author of several books, including *Leadership* and *Joy Explosion.*

Susie Shellenberger is director of Sheep Factory Ministries in Bethany, Oklahoma. She is also a youth evangelist in the Church of the Nazarene.

Kim Talley is director of Young Life in Tulsa, Oklahoma.

Todd Temple is national director of Grow For It Events for Youth Specialties Ministries, El Cajon, California.

Dan Webster is youth pastor at Willow Creek Community Church in South Barrington, Illinois.

Mike Yaconelli is co-founder of Youth Specialties in El Cajon, California, and editor of *The Wittenburg Door* magazine. He is co-author of the book *High School Ministry.*

Topical Index

Foreword

A friend of mine recently resigned as the Professor of Preaching at a large Presbyterian seminary. He explained to me that he gave up his faculty position because he felt that students at the seminary no longer believed that sermons were effective instruments of communication. He told me that the seminary students that he had taught believed that young people in today's world do not listen to sermons, and that those who work with young people would spend their time better developing other modes of communication.

There are many who would agree with the negative attitudes toward preaching that were articulated by those seminarians. Some argue that the television medium has rendered all other forms of communication archaic and boring by comparison; that the consciousness which pervades the youth culture is unreceptive to any didactic style of teaching; that Soren Kierkegaard, the famous Danish existentialist, was correct when he said that the gospel cannot be heard—it can only be overheard and received in an indirect manner.

I do not agree. To those who consider preaching foolishness, I can only reiterate Scripture's teaching that it is *through* the "foolishness of preaching" that the message of God is effectively communicated. I am not suggesting that it is the only way, but I am contending that it is one of the primary ways.

A survey of any group of Christian leaders will reveal that most of them made decisions to surrender to the lordship of Christ and to go into Christian service as a result of messages delivered by effective speakers. It is true that a great deal of what is called "pre-evangelism" sets up young people for the decision-making that often results from hearing good sermons, but many young people never do make decisions for Christ because they have not been privileged to hear messages that lead them into decision-making. I believe that young people need to hear clear and powerful declarations of the gospel presented by speakers who are capable of putting the message of God into a language that both forms and is relevant to the social-psychological mindset of the youth culture.

I believe that this book gives examples of the kinds of messages that young people need to hear. Needless to say, as good as these messages are, they are inadequate unless the messengers are empowered to deliver them with the dynamism that can only be provided by the Holy Spirit.

Duffy Robbins, the man who put this book together, is a brilliant speaker, and he is particularly good with young people. Whenever he speaks at chapel at Eastern College, where both of us teach, the turnout of the students is great. They know that, in his half-hour talk, he will not only entertain and humor them, but that he will also provide them with great biblical truths. I mention the fact that Duffy is a great speaker, because I am convinced that only a great speaker is capable of understanding what goes into composing great talks for young people.

Using his critical skills, Duffy Robbins has put together a collection of some of the best talks for young people available in America. These talks represent the best products of some of the best communicators in youth ministry. They constitute a fantastic resource for those of us who are constantly looking for new material to include in our messages. But they do more than that. For anyone who studies these talks, they provide brilliant models of how talks for young people should be constructed.

Duffy has also provided useful comments preceding each of the talks that will help the readers of this book improve the style and the content of their presentations. All good speakers study the messages of other good speakers. Consequently, all good youth speakers will want to have a copy of this book.

Everything that Duffy Robbins does is first-class. At Eastern College, where he heads up the Department of Youth Ministry, he has earned the respect of his colleagues and the admiration of his students. Consequently, none of us is surprised that he has turned out a first-class book in his effort to help those who work with young people to communicate the gospel with greater effectiveness. I know you are going to enjoy what he has to offer.

Tony Campolo
Department of Sociology, Eastern College

Introduction

This book is an experiment. It's an attempt to put in written form what people in youth ministry have come to describe as "youth talks" or "youth messages"—one of those projects that sounds to everyone like a good idea, but turns out to be a lot more difficult than anyone had thought. Some people have told us that you just can't write out a "youth talk." It's like trying to send an ice cube through the mail to your friends sweltering down in Miami. By the time the thing gets delivered to the people who need it, it just doesn't seem to offer the same refreshment that it once did.

And those people may be right. But week after week, all over the country, men and women stand up before groups of teenagers to share the Christian faith through some form of youth talk. Some of these folks routinely find this task an enjoyable challenge, an exciting opportunity to take the life-changing truths of the faith and put them in a form that will get kids excited about Jesus.

But for many youth workers, the regular responsibility of trying to "do devotions" or "give a youth talk" is anticipated with all the excitement of a trip to the dentist. The purpose of this book is to make the strengths and gifts of those in that first group available to those who count themselves in the second—to lead lay and professional youth workers to discoveries of new ways to communicate the adventure of the Christian life.

For those of us who regularly find ourselves standing before a mob of teenagers entrusted with the task of talking about the Christian faith in ways that are clever, insightful, theologically profound, enlightening, provocative, challenging, creative, and lightly ironic (and to be finished in fifteen minutes!), here are some new models for presenting the "old, old story." We dare never become so comfortable and lazy in our speaking that we cease to seek out illustrations and insights that will sharpen and improve our communication of the ageless truth of the gospel.

How to Use This Book

This book is a collection of "talks"—not a collection of essays! The talks in this book are presented in an "oral" style, meaning that the grammar, pacing, sentence structure, and wording are more typical of spoken language than of written language. In fact, many of these talks were transcribed from tapes of the talks as they were originally delivered, then lightly edited for the sake of conciseness.

Our overriding goal with each message in this book is to deliver to you the best possible message that can be used in the greatest number of situations. But we've also tried to be faithful to each speaker's individual style, reflecting as much as possible the phrasing and style that each speaker intended. Obviously, dynamics like pitch, pace, and volume can't be written into a manuscript—yet none of these talks will work for you unless you pay real attention to these factors. The disadvantage of writing "talks" is that it tends to underplay the importance of eye contact, facial expressions, posture, and gestures. It is left up to those who use these talks to pray them to life, and speak them as convincingly as they were initially spoken.

Use these talks creatively. Each talk is introduced by a "description" statement to give you some idea of how each message might be used. But don't stop there! Approach each message with a critical sense of how it might be creatively changed to be more useful for your particular ministry context.

Obviously, speaking styles differ. Feel free to change each talk so that it fits your style. Add your own illustrations and emphases. Make use of your group's history and shared experiences. While each talk is designed to be usable just as it appears in this book, it might be helpful for you to think of each talk as being skeletal. Take it upon yourself to creatively add the meat on the bones! The outlines of each talk included at the end of the book will help.

Use these talks personally. We've tried, as much as possible, to preserve each speaker's individual style of delivery—but unless you want to sound artificial and strained, it's critical that you retain your own personal style in giving these talks. Don't try to be Chap Clark one week, Mike Yaconelli the next, and Barry St. Clair after that. The kids will wonder what's wrong with you. Instead, make these messages your own. Personalize them. Keep the phrases you're comfortable with and drop any ideas and phrases that make you uncomfortable.

In some cases, that's easier said than done—especially when it comes to the illustrations in some of these talks. "How can I have a sledding accident that I didn't have?" "What if I don't have a best friend named Rod?" "How can I use someone's personal experience without being dishonest?" The answer is to be flexible and creative.

If, for instance, you're using one of the talks from this book in which the speaker refers to an incident from his own experience, you can retain that illustration by using a little flexibility in how you present it. For example: In one of the talks, Chap Clark refers to a sledding accident he had one New Year's Day as he was growing up. You can introduce that illustration by simply saying, much as you would if you were telling a story, "Chap was only ten years old that New Year's Day when he was flying down a snow-covered hill in his sled. . . ." Or you could introduce the illustration by saying, "I have a friend named Chap Clark (and that's true—if you bought this book, you *are* Chap's friend!), and one New Year's Day, he was sledding. . . ."

You also have the option of thinking through your own personal experiences for a situation similar to the one described by Chap. Then, simply substitute your own experience for Chap's.

There may, of course, be some portions of some talks that contain perspectives or opinions that you don't agree with. In that case, remember: sincerity communicates. Don't try to communicate a truth you haven't practiced. Don't try to use a story or a style that isn't true for you.

Use these talks conscientiously. As Sunday school material has become easier to use, and as publishers have become better and better at producing materials that are "teacher-friendly," there has probably been an increase in the number of teachers who don't feel quite as much pressure to do personal preparation on their own. They study a little less. They "wing it" a little more. And the result is better material that produces worse lessons.

Don't allow a book full of ready, available talks keep you from setting apart adequate time for personal preparation. There is no talk in this book that will work without conscientious study and thorough preparation. The most exciting youth talk in this book will be woefully flat and boring if it is delivered without time devoted to rehearsing the delivery, reading over Bible passages with potentially difficult-to-pronounce names, or thinking through the emphasis of the message and learning the content of the talk.

Use these talks faithfully. Maybe we get tired of hearing it, but it is no less true: only God moves men and women to change their hearts. If these talks are, in fact, "skeletal," then we must be reminded that it will take the breath of God to make the "dry bones" come alive. Humor can't bring about spiritual change. Great illustrations can't do it. Neither can profound insight. Only the Spirit of God can turn these talks into pivotal decision points for the kids in our youth groups.

That means that the most important part of any youth message is the prayer that takes place before it is delivered. One homiletics professor once told his class, "Before you talk to the folks about God, you had better talk to God about the folks." Corny— but true. If you try to deliver these messages without adequate advance time in prayer, you will find yourself driving a first-class vehicle, with all the right extras, but with no motor to make it move. This may be the single greatest weakness in our communication with kids.

A Final Word

Have fun with this book. Use it with a sense of adventure and expectancy. Don't be afraid of the talk that bombs. We've all had our nights when we finished the talk convinced that God's will was calling us *out* of youth ministry! Be willing to risk some new forms of expressing old ideas. Our gospel is unchanging, but the means of expressing that gospel should always keep us on the progressive edge.

Finally, this is a book by youth ministers, for youth ministers. This book is only worthwhile if it's used. It is not a book to be read through and placed on the shelf. Even if some of these talks are a little different from the normal diet of your group, try them out! Variety is the spice of life!

Speaking of variety . . . why not send in one of your "great youth talks" for Volume Two? One clear lesson from this book is that there are some very creative and effective youth speakers out there, and they are not all the well-known names and faces that usually come to mind. Our sincere thanks to the well-known and not so well-known souls who were gracious enough to "give away" some of their great youth talks for this book. Why not look through your files and open up your "war chest" so that next time, in Volume Two, you can return the favor?

How to Give a Great Youth Talk

Larry Richards tells a story of the Prince of Granada, next in line for the Spanish throne, who was condemned to spend his life in the solitary confinement of a Madrid prison cell, a grim and fearsome place. As he lived out his life behind these ancient walls, in this prison called the Place of Skulls, he was given one book to read—the Bible.

For thirty-three years, this would-be king languished in his jail cell. Over the years, apparently, the Prince of Granada read through his Bible hundreds of times. And as he read through its pages day after day, year after year, he used a nail to scratch out notations on the soft stone walls of his cell.

His notations were intriguing:

The eighth verse of the ninety-seventh psalm is the middle verse of the Bible.
Ezra 7:21 contains all the letters of the alphabet except the letter J.
The ninth verse of the eighth chapter of Esther is the longest verse in the Bible.
No word or name of more than six syllables can be found in the Bible.

What is most profound about this picture of princely graffiti is, as Richards observes, that it shows us a man who spent the greater part of his life and the vast majority of his time reading his Bible. There were no interruptions, no distractions. And yet, if we are to trust the scratchings on his cell wall, the Prince of Granada "could cull only trivia from 'the greatest book known to Western man'" (from Richards' chapter, "Cognitive Development of Adolescents," in *Youth Education in the Church*, Zuck and Benson. Chicago: Moody Press, 1978).

Amazing—here was an educated man who could read, write, and count with at least average ability. He was clear enough in his thought processes to ask intelligent questions, make careful observations, and do precise investigation. And yet, from all his study in this Book of books, he gained only trivia.

It's a little scary to consider how much royalty from Granada we might have in our youth groups. Each week, year after year, they sit and listen to our Bible studies and youth talks—kids who are reasonably intelligent, who can count and even occasionally ask questions. But how many of them are walking away from our talks with changed lives, and how many walk away with just more Bible trivia?

We need to recognize that giving a talk is not the same as being given a hearing. Content is critical. We can be certain that our kids will walk away with Bible trivia if that is what we feed them! But the best message with the most profound content in the world will be of no value if you can't get your youth to hear it and act upon it. We can't afford to ignore such elements of the youth talk as style and technique.

Unfortunately, there isn't any quickie, handy-dandy formula for giving "great" youth talks. But there are some general principles that we can apply to make our communication more effective than it presently is. Here are some basic rules of thumb:

1. *Know what you are talking about.* We dare not allow ourselves to be sloppy in the area of study. Begin with a thorough study of the subject, and follow that up by preparing some visual aids to accompany your talk. If you're speaking about a Bible passage, make sure you study that passage. Check out a commentary or two. But do your homework!

I remember as a teenager hearing a youth speaker doing an "anti-rock and roll" seminar in which he warned us about songs that allude to drugs. Then he gave as an example a song by the Byrds called "Nine Miles High." Now, anyone of my age at the time who listened to as much rock and roll as I did knew that the name of the song was "*Eight* Miles High," and might also have known that the writer of the song said in a number of interviews that it was a song about piloting his own Lear jet.

Yes, it was only a minor error—but it was enough to convince this seventeen year old (who was looking for a reason to ignore the speaker anyway!) that this guy up front didn't know what he was talking about. And that gave me an excuse to discredit his twenty other examples that, for all I know, may have been accurate.

That doesn't mean we must be infallible. It does mean that we must be conscientious in our study. One of the best ways to lose credibility is to speak authoritatively in areas where we don't have the facts. Let's be sure to know what we're talking about.

2. *Practice good eye contact.* This isn't new counsel, of course. We've all heard speakers speak who were so dependent on notes, or so shy, that we never saw more than the top of their heads. In normal conversation, we know people are talking to us when they make eye contact with us. If we want kids to know we're talking to them, we need to practice that same eye contact.

That, of course, raises the whole issue of using notes or not using notes. Some speakers are violently opposed to using notes, others (some of the best preachers I personally know) preach every week from a prepared manuscript.

There are a few questions to consider with regard to this issue: (a) Can we speak without notes and still provide solid content? What's the use of speaking effectively if we don't say anything? (b) Can we speak without notes and still be comfortable enough in our speaking to put our listeners at ease? Sometimes we work hard at remembering our talk so that we can enjoy the "freedom" of not being tied to notes, but then the whole talk comes across as strained. (c) If we use notes, can we discipline ourselves to adequately prepare so that our face isn't constantly hidden in a notecard? Sometimes the security of knowing we'll have our notes causes us to get lazy in our preparation and less diligent in our study.

The bottom line is that notes or no notes is not really a big deal. Sure, if you can give a good talk with some depth in content, and you can do it without notes, that's great. But if you must use notes, and those notes *don't* distract you from good eye contact with your audience, then that's okay too.

3. *Give careful attention to body language.* This includes facial expression, gesturing with arms, and making use of your whole body to communicate. In this age of MTV, kids are simply not going to listen to a "talking head." They can go to concerts where musicians accompany themselves with laser lighting, smoke pots exploding, and strobes flashing all over the auditorium. What makes us think that those same kids will sit and listen to us when we talk quietly, without animation, and occasionally point to a map of the Holy Land?

The human body is a remarkably flexible tool for communication. We should try to incorporate all of our body in our message. Think of the incredible range of signals one can communicate just through the eyes alone. Add in hands, arms, legs, facial features, and shoulders, and you begin to get a sense of the limitless range of animation available to us.

In Marlene LeFever's excellent book, *Creative Teaching Methods*, (Elgin, Illinois: David C. Cook 1985) her chapter on pantomime discusses some of the range of emotions that can be expressed through different parts of the body: "Each part can be used to express a primary action or emotion. The head is the intellectual part of the body. Cock your head slightly and tap the top. You're saying, 'I'm smart.' The arms and legs are used to express physical actions. You clench your fist and wave it at someone. You are saying, 'Watch it. I'm upset.' The torso expresses emotions. Your shoulders droop and your back sways, 'I'm so discouraged,' you seem to say." The same range of body movements and messages are available to us as we communicate with youth.

4. *Be wise in your use of humor.* Everybody likes to laugh, and we all like to make people laugh. But too many youth speakers forget that humor is a tool. It can be used to keep the listeners' attention. It can be used to show acceptance of your audience. (You don't laugh and joke with people you don't like.) It can be used to make a sharp rebuke a little less offensive. (Tell me what a jerk I am and I'll ignore you. Help me to laugh at myself and I'll stay tuned.)

When we forget that humor is a tool to enhance our communication, we tend to fall into one or more of these three different traps. The first is that *we try to be "Mr./Ms. Comedian."* Humor is a fantastic tool when it is appropriately used. But sometimes we enjoy being funny more than we enjoy preaching the gospel, and that is when our humor becomes distracting. Like a good hammer, humor can be used to drive the point home. But if we keep pounding with the hammer after the nail is embedded, then we begin to damage the finished product.

Another trap we sometimes fall into with humor is *we force humor to happen even if nothing is funny.* Because we aspire to the image of the hilarious youth speaker who keeps everybody in stitches, some of us feel we must force humor into our talk. That's not a good idea for two reasons. Number one, we aren't all funny people. When we start to force humor with flat attempts and silly remarks, our audience can tell it's forced. Then we don't sound funny, we sound phony. Number two, some things just aren't funny. Let's have integrity enough to deal with some subjects with seriousness when seriousness is appropriate. If we are never serious, it shouldn't surprise us that kids never take us seriously.

A third trap is that *sometimes we sacrifice good taste for a good laugh,* and that's not the kind of modeling we want to do. Kids need to see that humor can be funny without being sarcastic or gross. If we can't demonstrate that, we are better off not trying to be funny. Sarcastic humor that gets a laugh at the expense of someone in the group is just the kind of humor that teaches our students that we can do anything for a laugh.

Two more considerations relative to humor:

1. Timing. It seems to be one of those intangibles—some people have it, and some people don't. But whether you have it or not, remember that even the world's funniest

joke still must be told carefully. An incredibly funny illustration can fall flat if your timing is all wrong.

2. Finally, whatever you do, don't laugh at your own jokes! For some reason there is nothing more annoying than a speaker providing the "laugh track" for his own monologue. In a slight paraphrase of Gamaliel's counsel to the Jewish elders (Acts 5:38–39), "If this joke is funny, people will laugh at it."

5. *Use your words carefully.* Words are the "stuff" of which great youth talks are made. The greatest sermon ever given, when reduced to its smallest component, turns out to be just words—but words well-chosen, words spoken "in season," words ignited and given life by the Spirit.

In giving a youth talk, a wise speaker chooses words carefully. Beware of theological jargon that is easily understood by theologians, pastors, and Bible scholars, but is Greek to most teenagers. There are kids in our youth groups who think "consecration" is a problem for which one uses Ex-Lax and that "supplication" must have something to do with the evening meal. Either do not use these words, or take time to define them.

Often we can help ourselves and our listeners by using "functional equivalents," words that mean the same thing, but sound a little less intimidating to our listeners. Jesus was a master of taking the lofty concepts of the faith and putting them into the everyday language of the people. Jesus, the most profound theologian ever to preach, sprinkled his teaching with illustrations of "salt," "light," "fishing," "mustard seeds," and "foxes."

Second, let's use decent grammar. Many speakers discredit themselves because they use such poor grammar that they sound illiterate. The excuse one sometimes hears for this abuse of the language is that poor grammar helps the speaker relate to the youth. What an insult! Having listened to some of the top youth speakers in the country, I am impressed that these people do not necessarily try to "talk like kids." They try to communicate with kids by talking like adults. There are few things more distasteful to most teenagers than some adult who tries to be very "hip" and "groovy" by trying to talk like a fifteen year old. It's just not cool.

6. *Be honest.* One of the mistakes we often make with youth is that we try to reduce all Christian truth down to some simple, trite answers. It communicates disrespect when we do not take seriously the tough questions with which many of our students honestly and legitimately struggle.

If a passage reads, "Now the Spirit of the Lord had departed from Saul, and an evil spirit from the Lord tormented him" (1 Sam. 16:14), we'd better be prepared to deal with questions like "Why did the Spirit of the Lord depart from Saul?" "What does that mean?" "Why is the Lord sending 'evil spirits' down on people?" Those are good questions, and to talk about the passage without dealing honestly with some of those questions is simply unfair.

7. *Know how you plan to end your talk.* One of the most common mistakes of youth speakers is that they will get a strong opening, followed by a pretty good message, but they really don't consider how they're going to close it. Those youth talks don't really end—they just stop.

The great preachers of the Bible were always careful to conclude their talk with some form of challenge that brought the point right down to the individual. Nathan concluded his conversation with David by saying, "You are the man!" (2 Sam. 12:7). Peter finished his sermon on Pentecost Sunday with this statement, "Therefore let all Israel be assured of this: God has made this Jesus, whom you crucified, both Lord and Christ" (Acts 2:36).

We need to be careful to finish up with that "therefore"-type challenge. That is what takes our youth talks beyond the realm of trivia. That is the difference between a great youth talk and a nice speech. Nice speeches don't affect the way people live. Consider what action or attitude you would want your students to adopt if they were going to completely buy into your talk. How would their lives be different if they actually took you seriously with this talk? Make sure that you make that kind of response statement clear to your hearers.

Knowing how you want to end will also prevent your wasting a lot of time at the conclusion. If we know where we want to go, it's much easier to get there. Put some punch in your conclusion with a good, crisp, clear closing challenge.

8. *Speak the truth in love.* One Christian worker was giving some instruction to his young disciple, and before he sent him out to preach, he gave him this reminder: "Remember that no one cares how much you know, until they know how much you care." There is a great deal of truth in that admonition.

So many times we speak to youth with all the care and sensitivity of Ehud, one of Israel's less delicate judges: "Ehud then approached [King Eglon] while he was sitting alone in the upper room of his summer palace and said, 'I have a message from God for you.' . . . Ehud reached with his left hand, drew the sword from his right thigh and plunged it into the king's belly" (Judg. 3:20–21).

I have always been impressed and challenged by Paul's description of his own ministry among the Thessalonians—a ministry that was marked on the one hand by firmness, "as a father deals with his own children," encouraging them, comforting them, and urging them "to lives worthy of God . . ." (1 Thess. 2:11–12). And yet, Paul's ministry was balanced on the other hand by the sort of gentleness characteristic of "a mother caring for her little children" (1 Thess. 2:7). We so need to cultivate that kind of balance in our communication with students.

Our youth will not have faith without hearing the Word, and hearing the Word comes by our being willing week in and week out to give our youth talks. Meanwhile, however, let's never forget the impact of pure, face-to-face, hand-to-hand love. That preaches a pretty powerful message too.

9. *Pray.* Youth ministry has become so professionalized, strategized, and over-resourced in recent years that we could very easily make the mistake of thinking that youth ministry can be done without God's direct intervention. Let's not kid ourselves.

It's God's Spirit that convicts and convinces youth. After you've been applying some of these suggestions for a while in your speaking, you will find that you are able to give, if not *great* youth talks, at least *better* youth talks. But no matter how accomplished we become, or how savvy we feel we are about communicating with kids, we will never move beyond the need for prayer. As you move through the pages of this book, and the talks unfold, remember that your personal prayer to the Father will be the match that sets these words ablaze with the kind of light that burns through the darkness.

Hot Talks

Freedom in Jesus

John 8:31–36

Brent Bromstrup

This talk takes a look at "freedom" and why it seems so hard to find. There are some good insights here for both non-Christians and Christians alike.

The opening will work best if you present to the kids a list of normal items of clothing, preferably written out on newsprint, a transparency, or a chalkboard. Then ask the youth to identify one article of clothing that best exemplifies their definition of freedom. Obviously, it will be important to follow up the students' answers with their explanation about why one article of clothing seems to them more fitting than another.

The idea behind this introduction is to highlight the fact that all of us have different ideas about or definitions for freedom, but almost everyone has in common the idea that freedom is something that is good.

For outline, see page 185.

Let me start off by giving you a list of items—and you tell me which comes the closest to symbolizing what freedom means to you. (*The articles: Hiking shoes, t-shirt, tuxedo, pajamas, bathing suit, sneakers, spiked bracelet, necktie, etc.*)

You can tell from the responses that we all have different ideas about freedom, but there's one idea we all have in common—the belief that freedom is good. We all, in one way or another, want to be free. The problem is that we can't seem to find freedom. There always seems to be one or more people placing requirements on us, whether it's parents, teachers, or friends. Someone always seems to have a hold on us that takes away that elusive freedom.

An article in *U.S. News and World Report* (December 14, 1981) made this comment:

> Most adolescents seem to share the idea that these are bad times in which to mature to adulthood—harder, they

29

believe, than their parents faced because of a pervasive drug culture and more broken families. Many teens suffer from stress and depression at being bounced from parent to parent after divorce. Youth from middle- and upper-income families often wilt under constant urgings to excel in sports or academics, to be popular, to win acceptance to good colleges or to aim for high-paying, professional careers.

People deal with their lack of freedom in a lot of ways. Some people, wanting personal control, just can't handle being under the authority of the home, so they run away. Statistics reveal that over one million teenagers run away from home every year. All of us have a bit of the running instinct, don't we? Bruce Springsteen, "The Boss," sings (with gravel in his throat) about being "Born to Run." And Jackson Browne wrote a song entitled "Runnin' on Empty".

Other people decide to run by staying put. They tune out to escape. They come home from school, disappear into their room, turn the stereo on, put on the headphones, and melt into their music. Or they daydream about a fantasy world where they can do anything they want because they're free. Or they turn to alcohol or drug abuse to forget the fact that they are not free.

One of the main reasons why we can never find complete freedom is that we are all copies. We need approval of other people to feel liked and to feel needed, and we'll work very hard to have those needs met. Don't get me wrong—we *are* born originals. But we soon become copies of the people and the culture around us.

We have a lot of the same characteristics as the chameleon. When I was a kid, we used to buy chameleons for pets. They were a lot smaller than horses, and even if they weren't housebroken, they were small enough that you couldn't tell (if you know what I mean). The chameleon is a fantastic animal because it has the capacity to blend into most kinds of backgrounds. If you place it in a green plant, for instance, it would soon turn green in order to protect itself. If you put it on your algebra book, it would soon blend in with that color. The only thing it can't do is plaid; plaid makes it puke. Because the chameleon *always* has to blend in with its background, it has no ultimate control.

Imagine being a chameleon. You'd get up in the morning out of your little chameleon bed (having taken on the color of your sheets). You might look into the mirror and decide you want to be red. The only problem is that some goofy kid puts you on a green plant. And what happens? That's right—you turn green! Because you are a chameleon, you have no control over your nature.

That's precisely the problem we have—we are not naturally able to control our basic humanity. Jesus talks about that problem in John 8:31–36:

> To the Jews who had believed him, Jesus said, "If you hold to my teaching, you are really my disciples. Then you will know the truth, and the truth will set you free."
>
> They answered him, "We are Abraham's descendants and have never been slaves of anyone. How can you say that we shall be set free?"
>
> Jesus replied, "I tell you the truth, everyone who sins is a slave to sin. Now a slave has no permanent place in the family, but a son belongs to it forever. So if the Son sets you free, you will be free indeed."

Jesus made a statement that must have shocked everybody. He said that basically, we're all slaves—we're totally under the control of something other than ourselves, not an external master, but one that is even tougher because it controls us from within. He says we're slaves to sin.

What does it mean to be a slave? A slave has absolutely no control over his personal life. All decisions are made for him or her. He is like a robot going through life, having only to obey the master. There's no real hope for the future—only despair. No joy in the present—only desperation. And that search for freedom just keeps driving us—some to change locations, some to change boyfriends or girlfriends, or some to change the color of their hair. But we won't find freedom by making those kinds of changes.

There are three basic ways in which we are made slaves. In 1 John 2:16 (KJV), these three masters are called Lust of the Flesh, Lust of the Eyes, and the Pride of Life. Let's look at each of these three masters for a few minutes.

We'll begin with everybody's favorite—the Lust of the Flesh—sensualism. Basically, it means being a slave to what we feel. We tend to live as if there is no tomorrow, so we grab for all the gusto we can get. This slavery to the senses can be living for food. Some people live to eat; they look forward to the next meal before they finish the last scraps on their plate. They are like the cartoon character, Shoe, who said, "Of all the meals of the day, breakfast is my favorite. It's more important than the other five."

Sexual desire can make us slaves. According to a recent survey, nearly six out of ten sixteen- to eighteen-year-olds have had sexual intercourse. I know some people who look only for the next sexual experience—for sexual gratification. They date for the sole purpose of seeing how far they can get sexually with their date and are friendly to the opposite sex only to open the door for sex to happen. All of their actions are geared for sex. Sex is the master of which they are the slaves.

It's been said that you become what you think about most. If that statement came true literally, I shudder to think what some people in this room might look like! This would be a very unusual group. Some of us are consumed and enslaved by desires to experience, to do, and to feel. That is the Lust of the Flesh.

The Lust of the Eyes is the desire to have. This is the slavery of being obsessed with owning material goods. When we absolutely must have a certain car, wear certain clothes, or live in a specific place, we are slaves to ownership.

My wife and I spent two weeks in Texas recently, and I was amazed at how fashion-minded (if that's what you call it) some Texans are. Some people there must wear the intricately-tooled cowboy boots with pointed toes for killing cockroaches in the corner. Then there's the straight-leg Levis with a button fly and a round can of snuff stuffed into the back pocket. Finally, the outfit is topped off by a cowboy hat with feathers in the headband.

Of course, preppy is one style of dress common to the area in which I live. People wouldn't be caught dead dressing like a Texas cowboy in the suburbs of Minneapolis. No matter where we live, there are certain types of clothes you have to wear in order to have the right image. Doing your shopping by a blinking K-Mart blue light usually doesn't make it with the kids in our area.

Cars are another aspect of the enslavement to materialism. I know some students who will work every day after school just so they can have the freedom of having a car which takes them to work every day after school so that they can continue to have the freedom of owning a car. It's a vicious cycle!

Conservative estimates place a teenager's spending on recreation and non-essential items at $1,800 per person per year. Money is spent on clothes, albums, junk food, cars, and all the rest of the items that work toward creating the image we so desperately want. Materialism can make us a slave. I wonder how many of us are money junkies with a spending habit that starts to control us. That's the Lust of the Eyes.

The Pride of Life is the self-centered need to build up our own reputation. Basically, it's the desire to be looked up to. We want to be highly thought of so badly that we'll do almost anything to achieve the limelight and the strokes that we need. We become more concerned with image than with reality. We become like the set on "Miami Vice"—filled with beautiful colors, but not really dealing with the truth of existence.

When I was a sophomore in high school, I was a slave to what other people thought of me. I wanted to be seen as the macho dating machine in order to get everybody's attention, and I figured that the best way to be seen as the macho dating machine would be to date the most prestigious girl in my class. I sat down with a list of eligible girls and tried to figure out which girl hanging on my arm would be the best for my image. Some girls were rejected because they didn't live in the right part of town. Other girls were rejected because they weren't beautiful enough. Other girls were rejected because they thought I was a jerk. Finally, I hit on the right girl. Her father was the coach of the local pro team. She was bright, she was beautiful, and she didn't know me so she couldn't possibly think I was a jerk! Better yet, when I asked her out, she said, "Yes!"

I was filled with anticipation for the big night. I even washed the side of the car she could see. I mean, I went all out! I bought a corsage and appeared on her doorstep about five minutes late to show that I wasn't too anxious. However, when I saw her father—the football coach—I forgot everything. Here was my hero and I couldn't think of anything to say! Finally, after he helped me remember why I was there, his daughter came into the room, and she looked great. She looked so great, I made a fundamental mistake—I decided that I would pin on the corsage. It was all downhill from there! The pin stuck in the flower, and as I pushed harder, it suddenly pushed through and pricked her in the shoulder. I thought I was going to die.

The rest of the evening was a disaster as well, from getting lost on the way to the restaurant, to spilling gravy on my tuxedo shirt. I was devastated! She not only wouldn't talk to me after that, she wouldn't even look at me.

All of that pain because I was slave to the desire to create an image of myself that was not true. Slavery to the Pride of Life will lead us into all manner of ridiculous attitudes and actions.

The slavery that so many of us are struggling with is very real. It may be the desire to do, or the desire to have, or the desire to be. But whatever it is, we need to know that we can make a Declaration of Independence. Ironically, that kind of freedom only comes by making a *commitment* to make Jesus Lord of our lives. Jesus stated that he came to set us free, and as we're told in John 8:36, "If the Son sets you free, you will be free indeed." Jesus must become the significant factor in determining our actions. He came to set us free to love purely and without ulterior motives. He came to show us that we must find significance in him—not in our image, dress, or sexual relationships. The freedom Jesus brings is based on obedience to him rather than to ourselves or to the people or things around us.

In England, there is a peculiar form of government in which the country's most visible leader is the Queen. We all know of the special ceremonial occasions, like the launching of a ship, or the opening of a theater, or the wedding of one of her sons, when the Queen is highly visible, and usually a lot of pomp and circumstance (whatever that is) surrounds her.

However, there is also a Prime Minister in England, Margaret Thatcher. If laws need to be changed or decisions need to be made, the Prime Minister has the real power in the country, while the Queen has the image. Elizabeth may be the Queen, but the power of the government rests in the hands of the Prime Minister.

We tend to set up our lives like the government of England. We sing "Jesus is Lord," but under our breath we add, ". . . but I'm the Prime Minister." We give the image that Jesus is king of our lives, but inside we continue to be slaves to ourselves. Only when Jesus is Lord and Prime Minister of our lives will we find true freedom. Only when Jesus sets us free will we be "free indeed."

Encouragement

Hebrews 10:24–25

David Bruno

Here's a good talk with some practical ideas about how kids can "spur one another on toward love and good works." There are several ways to end this talk. Obviously, it would be very appropriate to ask the youth to take a minute to jot down (with paper and pen provided by you) a quick note of encouragement to someone else in the room, or to their parents, or to someone else who needs encouraging. Or you can close with a time of prayer in which the kids encourage one another by giving thanks to God for the way _____ adds to the group by the way he/she _____. Or you might want to close by reading Claude Steiner's familiar children's story, "A Warm Fuzzy Tale," a powerful little story in which the people in a town discover the power of affirmation and encouragement.

For outline, see page 187.

Murphy's Law says, "If anything can go wrong, it will." If Murphy was going to high school today, his law would probably read as follows:

- The shortest distance between two classes never takes you near your locker.
- Not even the most absent-minded professor will forget a test.
- Planned dates cause zits.
- If your folks plan to go out just one night a month, it will most likely be on the night you want the car.
- If you watch a television series only twice a year, the chances are better than 50-50 you'll catch the same episode both times.

Because our lives are full of Murphy's Laws, we really need encouragement. But this world in which we live can be a place of put-downs. "Try, but only if you succeed" is the philosophy today among so many of our peers. The problem with this philosophy is that it leaves no time or room for those of us who have failures along the way.

When we were little we'd taunt each other by saying, "Sticks and stones may break my bones, but names will never hurt me." But we know that's not true; some of the most painful wounds we have to bear are those inflicted by name-calling and sarcastic words. And sometimes those are the wounds slowest to heal.

This youth group should be more than a place for us to meet together. It should be a place for us to come and feel support from others, a place where we can share our feelings, our struggles, our problems, and even our failures. Because we are more than just a youth group—because we are a body of believers in Christ—God in his Word gives us some guidelines to help keep us afloat as we flounder in a sea of put-downs. Hebrews 10:24–25 says, "And let us consider how we may spur one another on toward love and good deeds. Let us not give up meeting together, as some are in the habit of doing, but let us encourage one another—and all the more as you see the Day approaching."

We know that God wants us to encourage one another, so why is it so hard for us to reach out to others? One main reason could be that we live in a society that forces us into isolation, making us avoid involvement with others. Banks have automatic tellers. Stores have voice-activated computer-checker machines. You can actually drive through a fast-food restaurant and not have to talk to a human being. (Jack-In-The-Box at least used to have a clown that looked like a person.) There are cars that will talk to you, and when you fill up the car with gas, you don't have to talk to the gas station attendant anymore—all you have to do is punch in your secret code number and fill it up.

This world is slowly gearing us to become so isolated from each other that we will soon believe that we are beyond the need to interact with others. But we're not fooling anybody. We all know down deep that *God created us as social creatures.* We have a built-in desire within us to be involved with others. So with the world on one side telling us to isolate ourselves, and with God on the other side saying that we need to get involved with others, we sometimes are confused as to what we should do in this tug-of-war.

I honestly believe that most Christian young people sincerely want to please God. I feel that they honestly want to reach out to others with encouragement. They just don't know how to do it.

I would like to give you three different ways in which you can encourage one another:

First, there is *verbal encouragement.* Words can be very powerful. Everyone has a nickname that haunts them, and they feel a pain every time they hear that nickname mentioned. If words can be powerful enough to hurt our feelings, they can also be powerful enough to heal our feelings, to uplift us, to even bring us pleasure.

Guys? How many of you love it when a girl comes up to you and says, "Hey, you really look good today!" On the outside you might look somewhat apathetic about the remark, but on the inside, you are doing cartwheels!

Girls? What about when a guy comes up to you and says, "You really look foxy today!" You say to yourself, "Oh, come off it!" but you feel good inside because someone gave you some words that encouraged you.

I am not saying that you have to use words like "you're looking good" or "what a fox" to encourage someone. However, it is important that you express *something positive* about the person when you speak to them.

If you have trouble verbally expressing yourself, write that person a short note. Some church youth groups have little postcards provided at their meetings in which young people can write someone a short positive note of encouragement. Then one individual in the youth group makes sure that these cards are addressed and mailed each week.

Another method to encourage someone is through *material encouragement.* Sometimes words just don't do enough. James 2:15–16 says, "Suppose a brother or sister is without clothes and daily food. If one of you says to him, 'Go, I wish you well; keep warm and well fed,' but does nothing about his physical needs, what good is it?"

If I drove home today and found that my house had burned to the ground, I would need more than to have someone say, "I'll be praying for you." I would need someone to provide me with a room, clothes, and even some food.

There are times when words aren't enough. Sending someone a small gift to brighten up their spirit can be just the encouragement they need. There are those in this youth group who need money for camp. There are those who have never had anyone give them a special gift. You don't have to spend big bucks here; you can give cookies, a candy bar, a poster—anything to bring encouragement to their life.

A third way to encourage someone is to give them *emotional encouragement.* Sometimes words will mean nothing. Even a small gift won't satisfy the need for encouragement. When someone is hurting, deeply distressed, just being there with them can mean the world to them. This is what I call the "I'm with you" gift of encouragement.

Sometimes an encouraging hug can be an emotional encouragement. Recently, at the library of Los Angeles's Valley College, Barbara Toohey, head librarian, posted a sign at her desk proclaiming herself the campus "hug therapist." She found that both students and faculty members streamed through the turnstiles for her deluxe bear hug to help them make it through the day. It was a huge success; in fact, during exams the business got so heavy that Barbara had to call on help from other librarians.

If you don't believe in this emotional encouragement, the next time you are sitting in school, keep eye contact with your teacher. While he or she is lecturing, act like you are really agreeing with what he or she is saying. In fact, when your teacher says a point that you really agree with, nod your head. It's fun to watch them get fired up about improper fractions just because they think they're cooking up there! In fact, you'll probably have to call in the paramedics when your teacher has a heart attack from all the excitement.

Audiences can play the role of an "emotional encourager" to a speaker. When you look as though you are inter-ested in what they are saying, you encourage them to get excited about what they are saying.

Emotional encouragement can take the form of a back slap, a smile, a hug, or something as simple as a thumbs up. Sometimes, when you're having "one of those days," emotional encouragement can be like ice water to a parched mouth.

There are those in this youth group, this body of believers, that are hurting right now. The problem is you may not even know who they are. We have become professionals at hiding behind the mask of a smile, at acting like everything is going great. We can be smiling on the outside and crying on the inside. That is why it is so important to reach out with encouragement to those who are part of this youth group.

Within the next week, I want to ask you to encourage someone in this group, maybe someone whom you don't know that well or someone whom you see is being excluded by many of the others in our youth group. A note, a small gift, maybe just a friendly smile or handshake can make a world of difference to someone who is going through some rough times.

Reach out—you may be the only encouragement that person ever receives.

Forgiveness

Ephesians 4:26

David J. Bruno and Duffy Robbins

How to forgive—and why we must do it—is the topic of this talk. The closing story is a powerful one, and you should be careful to follow up on the impact that it will make. You may want to close this talk with a time of silent prayer. Or you may have the kids write down wrongs done to them on slips of paper that they can cut up or throw into a fire—some sort of act that symbolizes their willingness to put these offenses behind them so they can concentrate on forgiveness.

For outline, see page 188.

A group of high-school and junior-high students gave the following answers to the question: "What ticks you off?"

- People who cut in lines
- People who blow smoke in your face at restaurants
- People who leave all their ski passes on their ski jackets just to impress others
- People who serve peas or lima beans with their meals (don't lima beans taste like little pieces of green chalk?)
- People who use a foreign language near you and you hear your name mentioned
- People who leave the toilet paper roll empty
- A friend who starts liking the same person you want to date
- People who let their little kids go wild in stores
- Situations in which somebody gets us mad, and *we* have to offer forgiveness

Some of these situations don't demand many of our "forgiveness capabilities." But there are other situations that do: Some of you have been physically or verbally abused; others of you have had crimes committed against you or your family. Some of you have had your hearts broken by someone whom you looked up to—a teacher, youth leader, or even a pastor. Now that person is asking for your forgiveness and you are struggling with it. Others have been hurt deeply by the faceless crowds who have spread rumors and gossip about you.

It's hard enough for most of us to accept the fact that we have been forgiven (1 John 1:9). The only thing harder for most of us is forgiving others. Why do you suppose that is the case? Why is it so hard to forgive?

(Allow time for students to share answers.)

There are a number of possible reasons why we don't want to forgive others. Today we will focus briefly on three of these.

The first reason we may not want to forgive others is *we enjoy holding a grudge.* There is some pleasure in resentment. We think that we're driving the person crazy with frustration by giving them the silent treatment. You know the routine: You wait by the phone hoping the friend you've had an argument with calls you to apologize. You keep watching the phone, and when they finally call, you're so excited. But you pick up the phone and say coolly, "Oh, it's you. I'm sorry, we don't have anything to say to each other. I don't care to talk with you right now."

Or: You've had an argument with a friend, so you've decided that you're not speaking. Okay, but you need a homework assignment. So you go through elaborate means—asking somebody to ask your friend, writing notes, gesturing—in order to avoid talking with them.

Sometimes it gets very silly. I remember a friend in school who asked me to ask his girlfriend if she would go to the prom with him. He wanted me to go through all this business of making it a very classy invitation, with flowers, a poem, and the whole bit. I thought it seemed kind of weird so I finally said, "Hey, look, she's your girlfriend. Why don't you ask her yourself?" He said, "Oh, because I'm not speaking to her. We had a huge fight."

I have seen students go for weeks without talking to their friends. They walk around with their noses in the air, believing that the other doesn't deserve their forgiveness. Then they almost get mad when their friend finally apologizes—because they were having so much fun reveling in righteous anger!

The problem with the "silent treatment" is that the one holding the grudge usually ends up the loser in the end. They get frustrated because they have to put on a "you hurt me" front, and by doing so they often miss out on some special times with their friends.

Robert Louis Stevenson, in one of his books, talks about two Scottish sisters who were perfect examples of this. "The pair inhabited a single room. From the facts it must have been double-bedded; and it may have been of some size; but when all is said, it was a single room. Here our two spinsters fell out— on some point—but fell out so bitterly that there was never a word spoken between them from that day forward. You would have thought that they would separate; but no, whether from lack of means or the Scottish fear of scandal, they continued to keep house together where they were.

"A chalk line drawn upon the floor separated the two domains; it bisected the doorway and the fireplace, so that each could go out and in, and do her own cooking without violating the territory of the other. So, for years they coexisted in a hateful silence, their meals, their ambitions, their friendly visitors, exposed to an unfriendly scrutiny; and at night, in the dark watches, each could hear the breathing of her enemy. Never did four walls look down upon an uglier spectacle than these sisters rivaling in unsisterliness."

That's the problem with unforgiveness. It may start being kind of fun, in a weird sort of way. But if you're not careful, lines will start dividing up your world—pushing you into a little corner that gets smaller and smaller.

A second reason we don't like to forgive others is *we feel insecure*. When we are in the position to forgive another, we are in the "power" position. If we're insecure, we want to hang onto that power. We may feel that, if we forgive, we will lose the opportunity to be in control.

Watch parents of children at times when the child knows that he has done something wrong. "I spilled bird seed in the Kool-aid trying to give Peepsie a little snack, and now I'm dead meat." When Mom finally uncovers the crime she confronts the child, and the kid—with fear and trembling—always says, "Whatcha gonna do to me?"

Then Mom starts playing the game. She says, "Go to your room; I've got to think about it for a while." Then she has fun thinking up all the things she can ask that kid to do, which, of course, he'll do immediately. "Yes Ma'am, Mom. You bet, you wonderful woman! I'll be happy to wash the driveway and sweep the front lawn. Sure, Mom. Anything else?"

What incredible power! And, of course, she knows the scam is up once she forgives, so she holds the grudge as long as she can. We know how to do that too, don't we? We've played that game plenty of times. The only problem is that we start wondering when somebody's going to pull that trick on *us*. Wondering breeds—you guessed it!—more insecurity, which is what led us to be unforgiving in the first place.

The third reason why we don't like to forgive others is that *we are angry*. We become so angry that we want revenge. For example, have you ever gotten so mad at someone that at night in bed you begin to fabricate a conversation between yourself and the person who wronged you? You come up with some zingers, two or three lines that you know will devastate them. The next morning, you get up earlier than normal, your blood pumping fast. You run to school and can't wait to see them to deliver the great lines you rehearsed through the night. However, before you can get any words out, you hear them say, "Will you please forgive me?" What a letdown!

When you're angry, it's tough to forgive somebody. But unresolved anger held over a long period of time can eventually turn into bitterness. And bitterness, as it deepens, makes it increasingly impossible for you to forgive that person. Maybe that is why God says in Ephesians 4:26, "Do not let the sun go down while you are still angry." He follows that by saying, "and do not give the devil a foothold."

The Bible realistically states that today's unresolved anger becomes tomorrow's bitterness. And tomorrow's bitterness gives the devil a foot in the door to really foul up relationships. It's like the difference between trying to pull up a newly-planted sapling versus trying to pull up a fully grown oak tree. It's easy enough to get the sapling out of the way. But if you wait too long, it's not so easy to wrap your arms around an oak tree and jerk that baby out of the ground!

Before we close today, I want you to remember three things about forgiveness:

1. Forgiveness takes time. Some situations will require a much longer healing period than others.

2. Forgiving someone doesn't always mean that the other person is going to change. According to Scripture, when someone asks for forgiveness, they do so with the idea of changing their ways. Hopefully, they are not only saying, "I am sorry for what I've done," they are also saying, "I will try not to do it again." But even if they don't change their ways, we as the forgiver must remember that we are *commanded* to forgive.

3. After we've forgiven the wrongdoer, we won't forget the wrong deed done against us. However, we will learn, through time and with God's help, not to be *controlled* by the hurt or desire to get even.

Nancy Warnath, a blonde-haired, middle-aged woman, was not the sort of person you would expect to find speaking to prisoners at the Montana State Penitentiary. But the prisoners and volunteer workers were straining to hear her whisper-soft voice as she explained her reasons for being there.

Up until several months before, Nancy Warnath scarcely even knew about the Montana State Prison, and what she did know, no doubt, wasn't the sort of thing that would prompt her to spend long hours talking and counseling with the inmates in that facility. She started thinking about the institution the day a young man named Gary was sentenced to serve time for the brutal, pre-meditated murder of a soft-spoken, "gentle-giant" of a man named Jack.

She could have been bitter—as many people were—but she hurt for this scared young man. She somehow knew the guilt he was feeling, and the shame and the hurt that his crimes had brought upon him. Even more than that, Jesus Christ had changed Nancy Warnath's life and heart, and she knew that she had been called to offer the same love and forgiveness that God had offered to her through Jesus.

So, that day in the courtroom when Gary was convicted of murder and sentenced to prison, she began to feel drawn to this young man and to others like him who needed to know God's forgiveness. It wasn't easy though. Forgiveness never is, especially in this case. You see, Nancy Warnath was in the courtroom that day because the young man brutally and senselessly murdered by Gary was her own 23-year-old son, Jack.

It's amazing how her soft voice speaks so loudly, even in this room right now. She finished her talk by saying, "God forgives us our sins as we forgive others. If we don't forgive, we will be held accountable." (Story told was from the Prison Fellowship newsletter, *Jubilee*, July, 1986.)

Dare to Dream

John 5:2–11

Jim Burns

This could be used as an evangelistic talk, or as a motivational talk for kids who are already Christians. It's a talk with the broad theme of "being all that you can be," certainly a phrase that kids have heard but with which they have not closely identified. This is also the kind of talk that, with very few changes, you could use at a public high-school assembly or at a baccalaureate service.

For outline, see page 190.

Once upon a time in a land far, far away from here, there was a group of people called Laconians. The Laconians looked a lot like you and me and acted a lot like you and me. They went to school; they had friendships; they went on dates. They dealt with the same types of issues that we do. They were into break dancing a little bit, but not a whole lot.

These Laconians had all the same types of hassles with school and work and parents, but there was one thing different about them. Connected to their ankle, every Laconian had a metal brace. Connected to that metal brace was a thick metal chain. Connected to that thick metal chain was a ball—like the chain gangs you see in movies. Every Laconian wore that ball and chain. And what was fascinating about it was that they didn't even realize it was different. Everyone in Laconia had one, and they'd play softball and they'd run as if they didn't have anything attached to them. Of course, they couldn't run well, but they never noticed. Nor did they miss swimming or surfing; they just never did such things.

One day the hero of our story— we'll call him Tommy—went into the woods. As he walked around looking at the trees, the chain caught on a stone and broke. Tommy looked at his foot, stunned—he'd never been without the ball and chain before! He put out his newly-freed foot, shook it a little, watching it carefully to see what it would do, and took a step. Yike! He almost fell. His foot was too light—he just couldn't walk without that heavy metal ball to anchor him down; he was afraid he'd go flying off without it. But when nothing happened after the first step, he took another. Yes, this was . . . different . . . maybe even (dare he say it?) better! Then he heard a twig snap. His head shot up and he looked around nervously for several minutes. Not hearing or seeing anything, he hastily put the chain back on and returned to town, thinking all the way.

One day he returned to the woods and took the chain off again. This time he left it off for a while, learning to walk like no one else in Laconia had ever walked before. He was free of the useless weight, free of the burden everyone else carried without even knowing it. Still, he told no one. Every day after school he went to the woods and learned to do things that the Laconians had never been able to do, like hop and jump and run and swim and skip and climb trees. He was light; he was air; he was *free!* But no one else in Laconia knew.

Finally he decided to tell his friend, Aaron. Now Aaron wasn't the most adventurous boy in the world, so when Tommy took him to the woods to show off all his newly-acquired skills, all he could say was, "Put that thing back on. You're being weird."

Tommy was disappointed by Aaron's reaction, but he still resolved to share his discovery with all of Laconia. So one day, in the midst of a big town gathering, he walked down Main Street with the ball under his arm. The people stopped and stared, laughing and pointing at the strange sight. Mocking him, they told him to put it back on. "You're *weird*," they all said. Even his family was embarrassed. They told him to put that ball and chain back on and never to change it—to get it welded together and be one of them. They said, "The family that wears chains together is the family that remains together."

Tommy decided right then and there that he could never stay in the world of Laconia. So he packed all of his belongings except for the ball and the chain and moved to a distant land. And there, as the story goes, he lived happily ever after.

There's a story that has a lot to say to men and women like yourself. In fact, when it was written a few years ago, the writer was thinking about a group of high-school kids. The writer knew that often, like the Laconians, we go through life dragging around our own little ball and chain. It's not a real ball and chain, of course, but it can be just as restraining, just as confining. And what's so tragic is that we consider it normal—the way it's supposed to be.

If you asked the average Laconian whether he liked having that thing on his leg, he would try to con himself into thinking that it wasn't so bad. You'd say, "Don't you get tired of that thing?" and he'd answer, "Oh, no, it's a ball." The Laconians were settling for second best in their life when what they needed to do was break the chain and be set free.

It's interesting that Jesus said, "So if the Son sets you free, you will be free indeed" (John 8:36). As I hang around with high-school students and adults as well, I see men and women who have settled for second best, who are willing to live tied to some ball and chain. Whether that be peer pressure, sexual temptation, trying to make big bucks, pressure in school, pressure at work, pressure with their relationships, even pressure with their attempts to be religious—whatever it might be, I see people with this heavy burden dragging them down. They need more than anything to break that chain and be set free.

Graduation can be a strange experience because there you see friends you've known for a long time. As you watch these people walk up and receive their diplomas, you can't help but remember some episodes in their lives. Some of them have made good decisions; you can tell that some of them have matured and even grown as Christians. You feel proud to be their friends because you sense that they've accomplished something. They have found some measure of success—not "success" in the world's terms, but "success" in terms of fulfillment.

However, you may also feel some negative emotions. You see people who have made bad choices, choices with consequences that cannot be changed, and you're saddened because you know—those people settled for second best. And you wonder: What will their lives be like in ten years? What will they be like when they gather again for their tenth high-school reunion?

The sad fact is that most of the people who have settled for second best in high school are going to settle for second best ten years from now. And that most of those people who have not settled for second best in high school will be the ones who are going to be fulfilled ten years from now.

Some of us—like me—have been to our ten-year high-school reunion. There you see the reality of what you only suspected at graduation. Many of the "nerdish" kids in high school who had their lives together are now people who are fulfilled. And many of the people who settled for second best in high school have over ten years gone through unbelievable turmoil.

Because life is so short, you're going to want to choose to be the man or woman that God desires you to be—to break the chain, whatever that chain is. I can't tell you what your chain is. Only you know. With God's help, you can break the chain and be all that he created you to be.

A story very similar to the Laconian story is found in John 5. It reads, "Now there is in Jerusalem near the Sheep Gate a pool, which in Aramaic is called Bethesda and which is surrounded by five covered colonnades."

Let me stop a minute to make sure you get the whole picture. A large crowd of sick people, the blind, the lame, and the paralyzed, were all lying on the porches. They were waiting for the water to move, because every now and then an angel of the Lord went down into the pool and stirred up the water. Supposedly, the first sick person to enter the pool after the water was stirred was healed of whatever disease he had.

Hear this, "One who was there had been an invalid for thirty-eight years." That's a long time. "When Jesus saw him lying there and learned that he had been in this condition for a long time, he asked him, [and this is the big question] 'Do you want to get well?' 'Sir,' the invalid replied, 'I have no one to help me into the pool when the water is stirred. While I am trying to get in, someone else goes down ahead of me.' Then Jesus said to him, 'Get up! Pick up your mat and walk.' At once the man was cured; he picked up his mat and walked." The same thing happened to this man that happened to our friend, Tommy the Laconian—he broke free from his ball and chain.

Here we have a beautiful pool surrounded with fantastic marble-type porches covered with all types of sick people. Among them is a man who has been ill for thirty-eight years. Do you realize how long thirty-eight years is to be ill?—to be not whole?—to be not well? That's a long time!

But apparently, he had grown quite comfortable with all of his friends there. It was kind of like a summer camp—"Camp Sickandyin." They all got to know each other, played some cards, gossiped a little, and even developed some friendships. But all these people were living with, and trying to make the best of, second best.

Then Jesus came to this man who had been sick for so long, pointed to him, and said, "Do you want to get well?" What was his answer? It wasn't yes. It was, "But sir, when the angel stirs the water, someone always gets there before me and gets healed, so I never get healed." He didn't even answer Jesus; he just made an excuse. Jesus said, "I want you to pick up your mat right now and become whole." So, lo and behold, the man was made whole.

You and I may not have the same sickness, but we're a lot like that man because we've become comfortable in our lifestyle. We're comfortable with peer pressure. We're comfortable at wild parties. We're comfortable even in our sin. And Jesus comes up to you and me and says, "Do you want to be well, right now, in high school, or are you going to put it off for thirty-eight years?"

Strangely enough, we often answer Jesus the way the man did: We make an excuse. "As soon as I get out of high school, Lord, then I'm going to give you everything. But right now there's these things . . ." When we get in college, we say, "Well, Lord, I'm in college. I'm going through some things right now. As soon as I go through these things, or when I get married, then I'll be a better person." We get married, and then we say, "Once we have a child, that'll help my relationship with you." And we keep on making excuses until, before we know it, years and years and years have been wasted.

What Jesus is saying to you and me is, "Do you want to be whole? Are you willing to pick up your mat and walk *now?*" Christ is in the business of changing lives because he loves you unconditionally—not for what you do, but for *who you are.*

I'm afraid that too many people who are in high school today are settling for second best; they just want to be average. I can remember some classes where I was happy to get a "C." But a "C" is really a dud grade, an average, blasé, boring thing. If it's the best we can get,

okay. But why *aim* for average? Do you realize that with Christ you can break the chain, and you don't *have* to be average anymore?

I love the story of the prairie chicken who found an egg and sat on it until it hatched. Unbeknownst to the prairie chicken, the egg wasn't a prairie chicken egg; it was an eagle egg. For some reason this egg had been abandoned, so an eagle was born into a family of prairie chickens.

While the eagle is the greatest of all birds, soaring above the heights with grace and ease, the prairie chicken doesn't even know how to fly. In fact, prairie chickens are so lowly that they eat garbage.

Well, you know what happened: Being raised in a family of prairie chickens, this eagle began to think he was a prairie chicken and act like a prairie chicken. Then one day he looked up and saw a majestic bald-headed eagle soar through the air, dipping and turning. He asked what it was, and his family said, "It's an eagle. But you could never be like that because you're only a lowly prairie chicken." The eagle spent his life looking up at the eagles and longing to join them among the clouds. But it never once occurred to him to lift his wings and try to fly himself. Unfortunately, that eagle died thinking he was a prairie chicken.

You have the ability to be eagles, to

soar above the rest of the crowd, to get over the hang-ups and peer pressure that bring you down. God calls you to break free from the crowd, from the ball and chains that tie you down, and to soar with the eagles.

We make excuses. We say, "Lord, I don't live with prairie chickens, but I *am* being raised in a family of turkeys . . ." And too many times we settle for less than we were born to be.

I pray that you will be men and women who are willing to break your chains, who are willing to say "yes" to Christ, who are willing to soar above the heights. That's not going to happen by excuses, nor will it happen by daydreaming. The only way it will happen is when

we invite Jesus to be Lord of our lives and Lord of our ambitions.

An Old Testament prophet, Isaiah, put it this way: "Do you not know? Have you not heard? The LORD is the everlasting God, the Creator of the ends of the earth. He will not grow tired or weary, and his understanding no one can fathom. He gives strength to the weary and increases the power of the weak. Even youths grow tired and weary, and young men stumble and fall; but those who hope in the LORD will renew their strength. They will soar on wings like eagles; they will run and not grow weary, they will walk and not be faint" (Isa. 40:28–31).

How To Know You're In Love

1 Corinthians 13:4–7

Jim Burns

> Jim's practical talk will help Christian and non-Christian kids alike as they evaluate the depth of their relationships.
> *For outline, see page 191.*

Recently I watched a group of high-school girls on the beach "check out" a handsome lifeguard. (Who says guys are the only ones who look at the scenery on the beach?) As the lifeguard leisurely walked to the water to cool off, the girls went crazy with excitement. One of the girls making the most noise sighed and exclaimed, "I've never seen such a fox! I think I'm in love!"

I don't think her reaction was unusual. In fact, it was quite normal. I even remember saying very similar words when I was in high school and college (not about male lifeguards, of course). Let's think about the girl's remarks, though. The lifeguard may have been a fox, but I doubt that the girl was really "in love." Instead, she was "in infatuation." She was attracted to this young lifeguard on a physical level. Perhaps she even had a fantasy of walking hand in hand with him down the beach at sunset, but was she "in love"? Not at all.

I remember my first crush on a girl named Geri. She was absolutely beautiful. I was totally convinced that someday we would walk down the aisle together. I think I liked her most because she was a better baseball player than I was, and she was also the only girl in elementary school who would play sports with us guys. I liked her for years. In fact, once in junior high school, I wrote a note to her and signed it with, "I love you." From that day on she hardly ever talked to me. I think I scared her away. Was that love? No, it was infatuation. It was what is sometimes called, "puppy love."

Infatuation is a normal part of life. Infatuation involves many of the same emotions and feelings that real love does. The major difference between love and infatuation is that real love stands the test of time.

From the moment I met Cathy (the woman who is now my wife), I was attracted to her. In fact, I was infatuated with her. I knew that I *loved* her, however, when I was still attracted to her after two and a half years of dating. Furthermore, I was *committed* to her. When I first met her, I never imagined that she had the normal human faults everyone else has—I thought that she and our relationship were perfect. As time went on, I saw otherwise. Neither of us was (or is) perfect. The relationship wasn't perfect, and it wasn't always easy. But when I saw that even after an argument I still cared deeply for Cathy, I knew that this was becoming more than infatuation. Real love stands the test of disagreements and of time.

There is no easy way to determine whether you are in love for keeps or not. If you are a teenager, it is quite possible that you will "fall in love" about five different times between the ninth grade and your second year of college. As a teenager, you will experience different degrees of love, but the odds are against you marrying your high-school sweetheart and living happily ever after. I'm not saying that it doesn't happen. I am saying that the statistical odds are against it happening.

As I said before, there are no simple answers to the important question, "How do I know I'm in love?" I do, however, want to give you a few practical guidelines to help you decide if a particular person might be "the one"!

1. *Are you willing to give 100 percent of yourself to your mate?*

Do you believe your mate is willing to give 100 percent of himself or herself to you? True love is selfless love. Even when you are tired or have had a bad day, selfless love will enable you to meet the needs of your partner. A selfish love grows old quickly when its own needs are not being met.

2. *Do you like the other person?*

I'll never forget a scene in the movie *Shenandoah*. One young man approached another man to ask for his daughter's hand in marriage. The father asked, "Do you like my daughter?" The young man answered, "I *love* your daughter!" The wise old father said, "I didn't ask you if you loved her; I asked you, 'Do you *like* her?'"

Sometimes people get married even though they don't really like the personality or behavior of their partner. Often they think they'll change the other person. This plan is rarely successful. So ask yourself if you like your partner even with his or her faults. And consider, too, whether you could live with his or her faults. Finally, consider whether you could live with his or her faults *forever!*

3. *Are you transparent with each other?*

Is your relationship one in which you can be open and honest with each other? Open communication is one of the major tools in maintaining a positive relationship. I've never seen a good relationship that didn't have this element of transparency.

4. *Are you and your special friend too dependent on each other?*

There are two different types of relationships: "I love, therefore I need" and "I need, therefore I love." The second type can be a real loser in the long run. Many relationships, however, are based on this "I need, therefore I love" idea, and those usually fail. Either one person ceases to "need" and therefore ceases to "love," or the other person gets tired of this total dependency and eventually leaves.

5. *Is your love self-centered?*

When a person is infatuated with someone, that person is often asking, "What's in it for me?" This type of love involves *getting* rather than *giving*. A self-centered love is not a true love; it is counterfeit love. Our goal in love should be what the Greeks termed *agape* love. This is a love with no strings attached. It's the same type of self-giving, self-sacrificing love that God has for you.

6. *Do you have a mature love for Jesus Christ?*

I believe that a good test of true love is to ask if both people involved can honestly say, "I have a desire to be all that God wants me to be. I am willing to put the Lord Jesus Christ first in my own life and in my friend's life. Our relationship to each other is second to my relationship with Christ." The couples I know who are doing well are those who have a good relationship with God individually and together as a couple. A love that is tied together with the love of God is the strongest kind of love.

I would suggest that you take a good hard look at the type of love Paul talks about in 1 Corinthians 13. The qualities of love he describes in his "love chapter" can be a measuring stick to help you examine if you really are in love. When reading this chapter, look especially at the qualities of love in verses 4–7:

> Love is patient, love is kind. It does not envy, it does not boast, it is not proud. It is not rude, it is not self-seeking, it is not easily angered, it keeps no record of wrongs. Love does not delight in evil but rejoices with the truth. It always protects, always trusts, always hopes, always perseveres.

Love is a uniquely wonderful experience. Unfortunately, the genuine experience of love can be closely imitated by an experience of infatuation. As time passes and presents us with storms to weather and new perspectives on our lives, we can then better distinguish between infatuation and real love. Right now, however, you can ask yourself the questions that I presented here, study the ideals of love which Paul set forth, and trust God to show you his desire for your special relationship.

A Fresh Look at God's Love

Genesis 1, 2; John 8:2–11

Chap Clark

> Kids have a lot of misconceptions about the character and personality of God. In this talk, Chap Clark tries to help kids think about God and his love in some new ways.
>
> This talk has several personal illustrations, so it may be necessary to substitute some of your own personal experiences. Or you may be able to refer to this speaker's personal illustrations in a "third person" way. (Example: In the latter part of this talk, Chap talks about his experience in a football game. You can use the experience by introducing it with a phrase like, "Let me tell you a story about a guy named Chap. . . .")
>
> This talk may be longer than you can use. Break it down into a five-part series, using each of the five parts of this talk as a talk in and of itself. You might be able to have some good discussions on these talks if you use them in a shortened format.
>
> *For outline, see page 193.*

Why do we need a fresh look at God's love? I'll tell you why we're doing this. I met the Lord at a Young Life Ski Camp when I was in high school, then moved to San Jose, California two weeks later. There I got involved in a great church where I learned a lot and was excited about my faith. Then I went down to San Diego and helped start a youth group—that was great. Most of high school and college was like that, spending lots of time and energy trying to make my Christian life work. You see, I was a crummy Christian, and I thought that I had to do a lot of stuff to be a "good Christian person."

I wasn't doing well in my Christian life, and when I couldn't figure out why, I'd say something like, "I've got to pray more." So I'd really work hard at praying for about a day and a half. But nothing changed. Or I'd hear an inspiring talk, so I'd decide to read my Bible more or share my faith more. My impression of God was: He loved me, he made me, he came to earth, he died for me, he rose again, and now he's *done.* It was now *my* job to make the Christian life work. Because I thought that way, I experienced horrible guilt every time my Christian life didn't measure up to par.

For a while I thought that if I loved God more, I'd be a better Christian. I read verses like 2 Corinthians 5:14, where it says that "Christ's love compels us." Since loving Jesus was supposed to compel me to live a Christian life, every time my life wasn't going well, I figured I wasn't loving God enough. But I didn't realize that it's not *my* love for Jesus pushing me to live for him. No, it's *his* love for me that motivates me to live a Christian life.

All of you have heard of God's love, again and again. I'm going to give you five characteristics of God's love, and you can tell me if they match up with all your preconceived notions and teachings you've heard before. The topic may seem an old one, but I'm going to make it new and revolutionary, something that will change your relationship with God.

God's Love for Us Is Passionate

When you think of passionate, you probably think of General Hospital, Days of Our Lives, slow dancing, necking—that's passionate. But that's not what I mean. What I mean by passionate is that you are *into* it—you are psyched. That's what the real word passion means.

And you guys say, "You got it wrong." Many of you think God is like a cop, hiding around the bend in the road, waiting to pounce on the next person who steps out of line. He's one of those people who is easily offended and who is cold and calculating.

But the creation story doesn't give that picture of God. If God were rational and businesslike, he probably would have said in his best matter-of-fact voice, "Let's make earth, Son." "Okay, Dad." Fling—there it is, stuck out there. "All right now, we're going to be needing some animals." "Good, okay." Cow . . . mosquito . . . aardvark. And the Son says, "I still don't see why we need an aardvark." And the Father says, "How else are we going to start the dictionary? Now, come on. Get to work!" Then, the next thing you know: zap, boom, bang . . . we have all these animals.

But when I read the story of creation, there's no way I can see God as some cool, calculating cop. He's passionate! I think that the Father, Jesus, and the Holy Spirit started thinking about this project and getting excited. "Let's make the earth!" God said, and the Spirit and Jesus said, *"All right!!"*

I do not picture God saying, "Okay,

I guess we should make the earth." No, do you know what he was thinking? He was thinking of you and me, not just of making the earth for the earth's sake. God had in his mind from before time that he was going to make you. But just because he had it in his mind to make you doesn't make him calculating. On the contrary, he was probably thinking, "All right!! Let's make Suzie!!" And then his conversation with himself went like this:

"How we going to make Suzie?"

"Well, before we make Suzie, guys, first we gotta make her mom and dad and grandmothers and grandfathers and . . . Where are we going to start? Okay, let's start with Adam and Eve."

"That's a good idea."

"What are we going to give them for a world?" And they sat around brainstorming.

"Horses."

"Yeah, horses. Let's give them horses!"

"Flowers."

"Yeah, flowers. Let's give them flowers."

"Hmm, okay."

"And an ocean!"

"Wow! For everybody?"

"Nah, you know, just for people on the coast."

"Yeah. Good idea. What's a coast?"

Can't you just hear the Father and the Spirit and Jesus getting more and more fired up? And the whole point is that creation was for you and me.

I know you're thinking, "No way. God wouldn't make all this for me." So listen to what he wrote to you in Genesis 2:8–9: "Now the LORD God had planted a garden in the east, in Eden; and there he put the man he had formed. And the LORD God made all kinds of trees grow out of the ground—trees that were pleasing to the eye and good for food." God could have made ugly trees, you know, but he chose to make *beautiful* trees. If he's the kind of God who's out to get you, he probably would have made ugly trees with fruit that always tasted like spinach. Spinach apples, spinach pears—ugh. But he didn't. He made variety and beauty.

Creation isn't the only thing that tells us God is passionate in his love. Look what happened when Adam and Eve walked away from God. God's response was not that of some businesslike boss: "You screwed up, so you're fired!" Nor did he say, "I'm going to Mars to start over again." What's his response? If you read through the Old Testament, you'll see his response is pain. God is hurt; his bride has left him; the people he loved so much and created so much stuff for have walked away from him.

God is not saying, "Boy, I'm really hacked at those turkeys," but "I *love* them." There's passion in God's love. Whatever you do, don't leave here thinking that God is a cold, calculating cop who's usually ticked at you. He's an active, passionate God who's alive in the universe—and in *you.*

God Is Also Very, Very Tender

Tender is a strange word that we don't use very often. Guys don't sit around the locker room going, "Hey, were you tender with Cheryl last night?" Yet tender is the most positive way to describe love. It's saying, "I will do whatever I can to meet your need in the most sensitive and penetrating way I can."

The best example of tender loving comes from God through Jesus. We can see that love in action in John 8, where he tangles with some religious leaders—and comes out on top.

The setting of the story is the temple, where all the Jews worshiped and where all the religious leaders did their teaching. The people would sit around listening to the religious leaders, who soon began to think they knew it all. Not only that, all the attention began to swell those leaders' heads.

One morning Jesus walked into the temple, sat down, and began to teach. People in other groups caught a few words and started drifting over to his corner, leaving the other religious leaders behind. Pretty soon the entire crowd in the temple, perhaps as many as two thousand people, was gathered around Jesus. The religious leaders, left out, were grumbling to each other. "We've got to get him. Jesus is misleading the people with all this 'love stuff.' God isn't loving; he's *righteous.* He's a *judge.*"

So they decided to trick Jesus. Dragging a woman into the temple who was caught in the act of adultery, they threw her at his feet. The crowd gasped and was silent; they knew that Jesus was being put on the spot. They remembered the Old Testament penalty for adultery—death. Not a quick and painless death, but a slow and painful death by stoning.

If Jesus said, "Let's stone her," the crowd would rebel. They wouldn't listen to Jesus talk about God's love if it meant killing this woman. But if he let her go, he would discount everything the Old Testament said. The leaders had Jesus trapped. And the woman lay at his feet, sobbing, all her sins laid bare to the crowd of watching people.

Here's what Jesus did: He bent over and began to write in the dirt. That surprised the crowd. They had all been staring at this woman, but now they started watching Jesus. Meanwhile, all the religious guys were getting antsy, shifting around, poking each other, and saying to him, "Come on, Jesus, come on. Tell us what you're going to do."

Jesus straightened up, calmly scanned the crowd, then looked the religious leaders in the eye. "Yes, she's guilty and should be stoned," he stated. Expressions changed; a look of triumph stole into the leaders' faces. But he continued to speak: "The one among you who has never sinned before can go ahead and throw that first stone."

One by one, the crowd left, because they realized they were in the same boat as that woman. They realized they'd screwed up, perhaps as badly as the woman. It wasn't long before they had all left, and Jesus was left alone with the woman. He said, "Go ahead, go home. But don't sin again."

Do you see what Jesus did by writing in the dirt? He took all the attention away from the woman and put it on himself. He loved her tenderly, giving her exactly what she needed—to get out of the spotlight, to be released from the feeling of failure.

If you are like me, there are many times when you need a tender God, a God who loves you as you are and forgives you for what you do. Sin is serious to God, of course, and his righteousness demands perfection. But thanks to Jesus, we *are* perfect, and we are loved—tenderly!

God Is the Greatest Fan You've Got in Your Life

When I was a five foot sophomore in high school, I was defensive back for our junior varsity football team. We played on Saturday afternoons at one, and the varsity team would play at three. So at half-time everybody would show up to wait for the varsity game and cheer for us.

The year I played we had a great team; we were undefeated going into the last ball game. With one minute to go, we were ahead one point—we were about to win the JV Championship against Stanford High, our rival. The stands were packed and rocking with cheers. It was fourth down, and they had two yards to go. All we had to do to win the ballgame was stop them.

To me, this was an extra-special game—my dad was there. Somewhere, packed among the screaming crowds, he was there, cheering for me!

We were in a defensive huddle when one of our guys said, "They got a tight end in there that's huge. Remember that play coach warned us about." He was talking about a play where the six-eight end takes two steps out, turns around, catches a pass from the quarterback, then runs over all the little defensive backs until he scores with about six of them hanging onto his shoulders. Now, our coach had called a defensive play in which all of the backs were spread out in case they called a dive play. But we all knew that this same formation made it easy for them to execute this short pass play.

They said, "Chap, if they do this,

the only thing stopping the guy from a touchdown is you." I thought, *Wonderful*. So we lined up, and I looked up to see this big old tight end looking me right in the eye.

I won't tell you exactly what I thought—it probably wasn't very nice. Sure enough, the ball was snapped. The big guy took two steps; the quarterback tossed him the ball. He caught it easily and tucked it under his arm about five yards away from me. I decided, "I don't care about life. I gotta do this." I ran as fast as I could toward that guy. And "bam!" we crashed into each other. The ball popped up, our linebacker grabbed it, and we scored a touchdown.

Meanwhile, I was lying there in a daze beside this guy, and everybody in the stands was going crazy. Amidst all the noise from the stands, I heard one lone voice yell, "Way to go, Chappy!" It was my dad. Everybody else was running up to this guy who scored the touchdown, but I heard my dad shouting, "Way to go, Chap!" It was an incredible feeling—better than crashing into the big guy lying next to me!

I want you to realize this: God is our greatest fan. When you have a big test, and you study hard or maybe you don't study at all, and in the morning you're brushing your teeth, worrying, and you're thinking, "God is going to be ticked if I blow this test, I just know it," remember that—God is cheering you

on. If your colors are blue and gold, he's up before you've even stirred and put blue and gold balloons all over the house. He wakes you up with cheers, "Come on, Billy, go for your grade on the test." And as you ride on the bus, Jesus is right next to you saying, "You're going to do great, Billy."

God is on our side. He's always by our side, encouraging us, cheering us on. As Romans 8:31 puts it, "If God is for us, who can be against us?" God's love, after all, is powerful enough to knock down *any* opposition!

God's Love Is Unconditional

You've probably heard this before, but I'm not sure you know what it means. Unconditional means absolutely, without exception. No matter what you do, no matter how you think, Jesus is still going to love you.

How do we know that? Look at the Gospels, where you read about Jesus and his friend Peter. The night before Jesus was killed, he told Peter, "You're going to disown me. Even though I'm your best friend, you're going to tell people you don't know me."

Peter replied, "No way! I would never do that." But you know what happened—Peter denied his best friend. He not only went back on his word; he also abandoned his friend when Jesus needed him most. Let me tell you, nobody would want Peter as a friend after that. But Jesus, when he rose from the dead and came back in John 21, gave Peter the charge to lead the church! Jesus never said, "Peter, for three days I was so angry at you that I don't even want to think about you anymore." No, Jesus completely and totally loved Peter, even though he messed up.

Let me tell you about Tom, a friend of mine with a three year old named Brandon. One day, Brandon sees Tom eating chocolate chip cookies and says to himself, "Daddy loves chocolate chip cookies with milk. So I'm going to give Daddy a glass of milk." Tom, sitting in the family room, watches him drag a chair from the dining room into the kitchen, leaving a trail of scratch marks on the floor.

Brandon climbs up on the chair and hitches himself onto the counter. He pulls at the cabinet door. Wham! He opened it all right. Then he grabs a glass, and in the process of grabbing a glass, two glasses fall. Crash! Tinkle, tinkle. But Brandon doesn't care; he's thinking, "I'm going to get Dad some milk."

Meanwhile, Tom's watching all this, wondering when he should step in and say something. But he stays in his seat and watches as Brandon scrambles off the chair, carefully dodges the pieces of glass, and heads for the refrigerator. He pulls violently on the refrigerator door and it smashes open—and stays open, of course. Brandon puts the glass on the floor—out of harm's way, supposedly—and grabs, not the little half gallon of milk . . . no way! Brandon grabs the big gallon container of milk. Full. Grabs it, rips open the top, pours it. Some milk does get in the glass, yes, but there's milk many other places too.

Finally done, Brandon puts the milk carton on the floor and picks up the full glass yelling, "Daddy, I got something for you." He runs into the family room, trips—and covers Tom with milk from his face down. Brandon stops short and looks around. He sees broken glasses, milk everywhere, cabinets open, his dad with milk from his eyebrows to his toes. All of a sudden Brandon realizes, "I think I messed up!" And he looks at his dad like, "What are you going to do to me?" But Tom, looking at his three year old, doesn't see a kid that messed up. He sees a beautiful little boy who loves him, and it doesn't matter what he's done. Tom thinks, "This is my son!"

Even though like Brandon we often make a mess of things, God loves us like a father—unconditionally, no matter what.

God Enjoys Us

Did you know that God enjoys you? You think, "Okay, God, I know you love me because you're supposed to. But do you *really* enjoy being around me?"

I have a friend named Tessa who is a friend of our family. Once she and I were at a family camp. She sat next to me after playing volleyball, and looking at me she asked, "Chap, do you like me?"

I said, "What are you talking about? I *love* you. Of *course* I like you."

"I know you love me," she said, "but do you really *like* me? Do you like to be around me? Are you proud of who I am? Do you want to hear the things that are inside of me?"

It hurt me badly that somebody I cared so much about didn't know how much I enjoyed her. So I said, "Of course I like you. I tell everybody how much I like you. I am so excited about you, Tess, that I can't stop talking about you when your name comes up."

I bet that most of us know that God loves us. But I bet that very few of us are aware that God *likes* us. If Jesus had a wallet, he would be carrying around a picture of every single one of us. And when the angels came up and said, "Oh, Jesus, I gotta talk to you about Bill," Jesus would say, "Bill? Ah, Bill!" He would take out his wallet. "Have you seen this one?"

"Yes, I've seen it, Lord, about ten times!"

"No, let me show you this picture. This is Bill in his little league uniform. And this is Bill in his sophomore year in high school."

"Okay, Lord. Never mind Bill. I gotta talk to you about Sarah. The things Sarah's done . . ."

"Sarah! Have you ever heard Sarah play piano? She hates practicing, but man, is it beautiful. I love sitting next to Sarah when she plays the piano."

God is so excited about who we are! In Psalm 139:13 it says, "[God] knit me together in my mother's womb." You weren't just a fluke of nature. God didn't just create this big world of people and shove you out there. He decided, "I'm going to make a person. And I'm going to knit this person together in her mother's womb." Before you were born, God was thinking about you, and even now he thinks about you constantly.

Then you wonder, "How do I *really* know that God loves me?" The best way I know of to illustrate this is to tell you about a guy named Brennan Manning. I've heard Brennan talk about how he got his name, and about something that happened to him back in the Korean War in the fifties, when he was fighting beside his best friend, Ray Brennan.

Ray and he were in a foxhole together with a couple of other guys when somebody tossed a grenade into the foxhole. Ray barely hesitated before flinging his body down on top of the grenade. It exploded, killing Ray instantly, but leaving everyone else untouched.

Brennan was so amazed by this that he began looking for God. Four years later, he became a Catholic priest. Now, in this particular division of the Catholic church, you had to pick a saint's name to take as your own. So he picked Ray Brennan's name and became Father Brennan Manning.

Father Manning began to speak in city after city about the love of Christ, telling people how much God loved them and how excited God was to know them. But somewhere deep inside he didn't feel this for himself. Brennan Manning needed to know, "Did somebody love me? Has anybody ever really loved me?"

While passing through Chicago a short time later, he decided to get off the plane and go see Ray Brennan's mom. He had visited with her often before, but this time when he went up to see her, he decided to ask her a question: "Did Ray love me?"

She looked down and chuckled a little bit, "Oh, sonny, sonny, you're such a kidder."

And he said, "I gotta know. Did Ray really love *me?*"

Her face turned dark and she said, "Don't you ever say that about my Raymond again."

He took his hands and put them on her shoulders and said, "I need to know. Did Ray really, really, love me?"

Shaken, she tried to push him out the door. She just couldn't handle it anymore. Finally, she looked at him with tears in her eyes and said, "Love you? He died for you. What more could he have done? He died for you. What more could he have done to prove that he loved you, Brennan Manning?"

Jesus Christ came to earth to die. And not only did he die, but he was crucified. And not only was he crucified, but before that he was whipped. And not only was he whipped, he was spat upon. And not only was he spat upon, but he was mocked as the King of kings.

God has gone to extravagant lengths to prove to you and me that we are truly loved. Passionately, unconditionally, God cares about us. And that's so important for us to remember. It's not our love for Christ that gives us the motivation to live the Christian life. It is what God has done for us—his love for us. That's where we get the strength to hang tough. We are not loved by a cold, calculating cop of a Lord, but by a passionate, extravagant, encouraging Lover!

Fit for a King

Luke 2:1–7

Chap Clark

> Christmas is always a tough time for speakers. It's not that the story isn't incredible. It is. It's just that kids tend to feel they've heard it all before. Chap's creative challenge based on the irony of the God/man being born in a manger will provide a thought-provoking talk during the Christmas season.
> *For outline, see page 195.*

I love Christmas!

Yes, of course, I love the presents, Santa, singing, and tinsel. But I also love the real Christmas story—the day that God became a baby. You know the story . . . God chose a young girl named Mary to be Jesus' mom. She and her fiancé, Joseph, had to go to Bethlehem for a Roman census just when she was about to give birth to Jesus. Let me read it to you:

> In those days Caesar Augustus issued a decree that a census should be taken of the entire Roman world. (This was the first census that took place while Quirinius was governor of Syria.) And everyone went to his own town to register. So Joseph also went up from the town of Nazareth in Galilee to Judea, to Bethlehem the town of David, because he belonged to the house and line of David. He went there to register with Mary, who was pledged to be married to him and was expecting a child. While they were there, the time came for the baby to be born, and she gave birth to her firstborn, a son. She wrapped him in cloths and placed him in a manger, because there was no room for them in the inn (Luke 2:1–7).

What a story! The great God of the universe, the King of all kings, came to earth by way of a small stable—surrounded by hay, animals, and the stench of a well-used barn. God could not have chosen a more humble beginning for his entry into human history. That lowly manger was fit for a King!

Looking at this story, I wonder how often we forget that Jesus loves to come to the most humble of places. We see him, later in life, acting most comfortable with the outcasts, the hurting, the "bad" people. He's right at home where most of us don't think God fits, ready to be in the midst of everyday life. And most of his ministry he spent looking for humble "manger-type" places and people to touch.

Are there any mangers in your life? Places or relationships where you don't want Jesus to enter because he doesn't quite fit? Maybe you have a circle of friends where you wouldn't want Jesus included. Maybe some of the things you do or talk about with them is not right for Jesus to be a part of. You really want Jesus with you, but you are afraid that your friends don't want him around.

Or maybe, for a few, it's really hard to let Jesus into your family. There's too much garbage and fighting, or too much talking about him and not enough walking with him. You might think that Jesus wouldn't even want to be around your family.

Or maybe you find it hard to make Jesus part of your dating life—or lack of it! "After all," you say, "Jesus has more to worry about than my struggles. He never dated. And besides, he wouldn't like to be around me anyway. He'd see all that guilt I carry with me constantly. How could Jesus understand what it's like growing up today? He just doesn't fit!"

But don't you see? Those are exactly the "mangers" he wants to enter—those tough, awkward, uncomfortable places where we think God wouldn't or couldn't penetrate with any help or compassion. Jesus Christ has proven over and over that he wants to walk with us in the midst of life's most trying and humbling situations.

How can he understand how we feel today? He was born in a manger, he died on a cross as a common criminal, and he is alive today to identify with us in the pain and struggles of life. In both his birth and his death, God has let us know there is:

> no place he won't go
> nothing he won't do
> and no person he won't actively
>   pursue.

This Christmas, don't hold onto those areas where you need the most from our great God; don't hold back your mangers from Jesus. Every area of my life, every area of your life, is fit for the King!

Our Deepest Need

Mark 2:1–12

Chap Clark

This short talk is an excellent evangelistic message. It helps kids understand that, while many of them feel that their problems arise from family, friends, lack of ability, or some other problem, their deepest need is to deal with the problem of sin in their lives.

For outline, see page 196.

One of my best childhood memories is the sled races we used to have in our neighborhood. We had this driveway that was about a quarter-mile long with a banked curve to the right about halfway down the driveway. During the winter it would snow like crazy, and the plows would move the snow to the sides of the driveway. Soon after, the snow would melt and at night refreeze just enough to provide solid ice walls on the sides of our "track" and a half-inch sheet of ice on which to race our sleds.

One perfect New Year's morning we had the most unbelievable race of the year. Scotty and I were in the finals of the doubles competition. In doubles one guy would lie on the sled and steer, while the other guy would run for a few feet, push the sled, and then jump on top of the driver. As the race began, I was the driver, and it was Scotty's job to get us off to a great start.

Just before the curve, as the fans were screaming wildly, Scotty looked back and yelled, "All right!"

I turned back to see why he yelled. I saw that we were in great shape with a five foot lead going into the turn, so I yelled, "All right!"

I turned back to steer—remembering at that moment the only really important part of driving on this course: You had to make a very hard right turn at the bank or you would spin out or crash into the ice wall. I didn't spin out.

As I was yelling, my face (which was acting as a hood ornament for the sled) deeply implanted itself into the solid ice wall of the driveway. Wham!!!

Scotty went flying somewhere over the wall. Immediately I realized that we'd lost the race. So I pulled my face out of the ice, struggled to my feet, and began yelling, "My sled! My brand new Flexible Flyer! Oh, no!"

Kids started running toward me. But as they got closer, they stopped in their tracks and turned away. As Scotty ran up to me, I was complaining about wrecking my new sled. He covered his eyes and screamed. Then he pointed to my face, my clothes, and the ground. Blood was everywhere! I touched my face and looked at my new red jacket (which used to be white). Only then did I begin to see that I had a much bigger problem than my sled being broken. I had nearly lost an eye!

I thought that I knew my biggest need. I honestly thought that the greatest damage from the accident had been to my sled. It took someone else—someone who had more information and a clearer picture of reality—to help me see that I was in much worse shape than I thought.

Jesus once encountered a man that needed a clearer perspective of his biggest need, much like I needed Scotty's perspective. Let me read the story to you.

(Read Mark 2:1–12.)

Just like me in my accident, this guy knew his deepest need. It was obvious! He was paralyzed, and the thing he needed Jesus to do for him was to heal him and make him able to walk.

But, just like Scotty, Jesus had a clearer understanding of the situation. Yes, this guy was in need of physical healing. But that was minor compared to his need of forgiveness for his sin. This paralytic's deepest need was to be in a relationship with Jesus Christ, his Creator. Sin had prevented that from happening.

I know that most of you are probably saying, "The guy was paralyzed. What could he do? What sins could he have committed?" But the real power of sin is not the things we do—those are just symptoms of a deeper problem. Sin is rebellion to God's rightful authority in our lives. Sin is saying to God, in actions, if not words, "It is my life, God, and I will run it as I please!"

The result of this human condition is a self-inflicted separation from God. Because of sin, we have been cut off from any relationship with the God who loves us so much (Rom. 6:23). Our only hope of returning to him is his willingness to forgive us for this sin. But forgiveness won't come easy, because rebellion against God's love and guidance in our lives is a serious offense to his character.

God is not some gentle, senile old man who looks down on humanity, sees our sinfulness, and says with a chuckle and kind smile, "Look at those humans! I declare, aren't they cute? Just look at 'em sinning down there. Well, humans will be humans."

God takes our sin very seriously. A lot of us think committing sin is like tearing one of those tags off your mattress that says, "Do not remove under penalty of law." R-r-rip. Big deal. No problem. But it's not that way. Our holy God is offended deeply by our sin. He loves us very much, but he hates our sin.

Put yourself with Jesus in the room with that paralytic. You're next in line with your "need." Would you be surprised if Jesus looked at you and said, "John, I'd love to fix your bad temper problem, but first I have to forgive you for not trusting me with your life"?

Or, "Sally, I know you're not getting along with your parents, but how can I help you out unless I first make you right and clean before my Father?"

Many of us are as crippled as the paralytic because we don't seek Christ's forgiveness. So when Jesus examines us, he knows that what we need most of all is his forgiveness so that we can be brought under his continual healing care.

One of Hollywood's most popular leading men had a small brown blemish just below the right side of his chest. It was really more of a bump than a blemish, but it was a nuisance, for the camera eye would catch glimpses of this ugly brown blemish. He hated it—it just didn't fit his image. But he was one of those guys who always played the macho parts in the films, so he didn't want to go to the doctor or admit any hint of weakness. He put off his examination until this brown blemish had grown much larger and much more obvious, to the point that he would not appear on camera with his shirt off. That's when the studio insisted that he go to the doctor.

As the examination began, the actor was cool, cocky; he knew it wasn't "anything." But the doctor said to him, "Let's do a quick x-ray just to be sure." That was when they found it. A large tumor—a cancerous tumor about the size of an apple—just below the rib cage. The verdict was obvious: Operate or die.

The actor was stunned. "But Doc, I've never felt better. That's impossible. I just wanted you to remove this little blemish, and now you're telling me you've got to remove cancer. I can't believe it." At that point, the doctor interrupted with an icy stare and a stern warning: "Listen to me. You believe it, or you will die."

So often we're like that guy: There's a blemish or a bump in our lives, and we try like crazy to cover it up. We don't think we can afford to let our audience know that we've got a problem. It just doesn't fit our image. Until finally, it becomes obvious.

That's when we turn to the Lord. "Lord, my parents are breaking up—can you get us out of this mess?" "Lord, help me in my relationship with Bill." "Lord, I think I might be pregnant. Help me." "Lord, I've got a real problem with my grades. I need your help."

Just when we're feeling totally in control—strong except for a few blemishes—Jesus, the Great Physician, probes down inside to the point of our deepest need. We protest. We can't believe it. But the diagnosis is true. Our deepest need is to deal with the sin that grows like a cancer, slowly killing us.

It may not fit our image. It may be hard for us to accept. But Scripture teaches that all of our problems are a result of that deepest need. And if we don't allow Jesus Christ to come in and operate, the Scripture tells us that we will face a slow, eternal death.

Jesus Christ has come to let us know that we are valuable and that he wants to be involved in our lives. He has shown us throughout the Bible that our biggest, deepest, most urgent need is one only he can see and only he can handle. That need is forgiveness for our sin—nothing else comes close. Let Jesus forgive you. Give him your life as he deserves; then watch him take care of all those "little" needs—the bumps and blemishes that bother you. He made the paralytic walk; he can make you soar!

The Only Solution

John 14:6

Byron Emmert

Here Byron gives us a clear and concise statement of the gospel. This message, directed particularly to non-Christian kids, might well be part of a series of messages in which you talk about the problem of sin and the plan of God.

For outline, see page 197.

We have something to cheer about this morning; we definitely do. We've all heard the bad news that sin separates us from God. It keeps us from having a personal relationship with him—unless we have the solution. That solution is simply this: We can approach God and even have a personal relationship with him through Jesus Christ.

Why do we need to know that? Why do we need to understand that? Because it's the *only* solution, and if there is only one answer we had better know it, right?

Let's start with an obvious question: Why Jesus Christ? Why is he the only solution? Listen to what he said about himself in John 14:6: "I am the way and the truth and the life. No one comes to the Father except through me." Some of you are thinking, "Boy, who does he think he is?" Pretty presumptuous, isn't he? Here's a guy saying "I'm the answer. I'm the way you get to God."

How can he say that? Today we'll see how, for we're going to look at some of the evidence that points out that Jesus is the way.

First of all, how many of you were born with regular-type parents? Okay, just about everybody, although a few of you are still trying to figure that one out. Now think about this: Jesus Christ was born of a virgin. Wouldn't you say that makes him a little bit unusual? Just a little.

Imagine this—a couple thousand years ago there were these two teen-agers, Mary and Joseph. (We'll call them

Mary and Joe, for short.) They're out on a date, and they've been dating for about a year or so maybe, and it's a beautiful moonlight evening there in Israel. They're riding on the back of a donkey, having a nice romantic time, Mary in the front, Joe in the back. Then Mary turns her head and says softly, "Joe."

"Yeah, Mar."

"There's something I need to tell you."

"Go ahead, what is it?"

"Joe, this is going to be hard for you to believe, but I'm pregnant."

"Ha, that's good Mar! Come on now, quit the jokin'. Watch the road, will ya?"

"No, Joe. I'm serious. I'm really pregnant."

"You really are serious . . . But Mary, you . . . come on, because you and I . . . never. Mary, you know you and I have never even messed, I mean, we have not done any . . . Wait a minute! If you and I haven't . . . All right! Who's the guy? Tell me! What's his name? I'm going to get him. Turn this mule around!"

"Hang on, Joe. Hang on. No other guy . . . it's . . . the Holy Spirit made me pregnant."

Can you imagine a situation like that? No? But it really happened—the mother of Jesus never had intercourse. She was a virgin. God, through the power of his own Spirit, made Mary pregnant. And she bore his Son, who was God himself. God came down in the form of man—an unusual entrance. I guarantee no one has ever done this before and no one ever will again.

Jesus didn't just start off in an amazing way; his whole life was amazing. For one thing, he was sinless— absolutely, *totally* without sin. How many of you can claim to be sinless? If you're claiming that, you don't have a pulse and you're not breathing. Well, Jesus was sinless. Never blew it once. Never. Some of you are going, "Now come on, Byron, he lived here on this planet. He must have messed up just once." Nope. The Bible says he never did. Some of you are going, "I know, but can you believe everything you read?" Yeah, because you know who wrote that about him? The people he lived with, the people he hung around with.

If you don't believe that, let's go back to your hometown. We'll put up a big 24 by 32-foot video screen there and interview your friends. "Tell us about so and so here. Has he ever messed up?" Ha, we'd have to sit through the reruns all afternoon, probably.

Our friends know us, and they know when we've messed up. Yet the family and friends that Jesus lived with for over thirty years say he never sinned once. He never had a bad attitude; he never even lipped off to Mom and Dad.

Some of you are going, "Maybe so,

but I've seen those Jewish foxes. He must have seen one of those babes and had at least one lustful thought." No, he never did. He was perfect. Now, is that unique? You'd better believe it.

Just because Jesus was sinless doesn't mean he led a boring life. He didn't hide himself in a corner, pull a bag over his head, and say to himself all day, "I'm not going to sin, I'm *not* going to sin." No, Jesus was action-packed! When's the last time any of you has walked on water? Or when's the last time any of you raised a dead person or made blind people see? Jesus did all of this stuff and more—incredible, unbelievable, supernatural miracles.

Here's an example, just one. Some of you may have heard the story about how he raised his friend Lazarus from the dead. Let me take that story and put it into modern-day terms so you can picture it and relate to it:

Let's pick one of your hometowns— say, Lansing, Michigan—and imagine for a minute. You go to school at Lansing High and are about to graduate when one of your good buddies, Harry, is killed in a car accident. Everybody knew and loved Harry, and they're totally freaked out by his death. It's a bad scene. It's a tragedy. And every single kid from Lansing High turns out for Harry's funeral.

About three days after Harry's funeral, some of you go over to the local cemetery to put a few more flowers on his grave, pay your respects, and talk about good times you had with him. You're standing there, some of you breaking up a little, when all of a sudden a little red VW pulls up and a guy gets out. You recognize him because he used to go to your school, but he's been away for several months.

He gets out of the car and comes over to you. Seeing your solemn faces, he says, "Hey, what's wrong with you guys? What are you so sad about?"

"Hey come on, man. It's good to see you, but haven't you heard about Harry?"

"Well, to be honest with you, I have. That's why I came. Hey, I don't want you to be so sad anymore about old Harry. We're going to take care of him."

"What are you talking about?"

"We're going to raise Harry from the dead."

Some of you snicker and say, "Yeah, well, what if he don't want to come back?" But you are grief-stricken. You try to humor the guy.

"Okay, what are you planning to do?"

"I got some shovels along in my VW here. Why don't you guys get the shovels out, come back here, and start uncovering the grave."

Of course, most of you are scared to death (so to speak), but there's always one looney in the crowd up for anything. You say, "Come on, let's go."

You go over to the VW, get the shovels, come back, and start digging. The dirt flies, surrounding you in a little brown cloud, and some of you are getting just a little bit nervous about this, especially when the shovel clangs against the coffin. A few of you back off and watch. "I don't believe we're doing this." You shake your heads. "We could get in *big* trouble for this."

Then your old friend puts his shovel aside, wiping his hands briskly, and says, "Okay, gang. Hang tight. We're going to bring Harry back." He bends over the grave and calls: "Harry! Harry, you've been dead three days now; come on now, that's enough. I want you to get out of that coffin and come on up."

You and your friends are rolling your eyes and making loco signs with your fingers. "Oh, man, this guy is gone. He's *gone*."

Your friend calls again, "Come *on*, Harry!"

Just when you're about to keel over laughing hysterically, the latch on his coffin flips open. The coffin lid slowly rises. You see the tips of his fingers at the lid, then the whole hand. Sure enough, it's Harry. You'd recognize those warts anywhere. The hands grab the lid of the coffin, lift, and push it off to the side where it thumps dully onto the grass. You're still looking at the coffin lid, trying to absorb it all, when out jumps Harry! He goes, "Hey, guys, it's good to see you! Man, it's been lonely these last three days. What are you all looking so grave about? What's the big deal?"

If that happened to you, do you think you'd listen to what that friend was going to say next? Do you think you'd watch him to see where he was going to go and what he was going to do? You'd better believe it!

The most incredible thing about Jesus is yet to come: He not only raised someone else from the dead; he also raised himself! And before any of this happened, he predicted it. He said, "I'm going to get killed, then three days later I'll raise myself up from the dead." There may be some real looney birds out there who have made some claims like that, but how many do you know who have ever pulled it off? Well, Jesus did.

But why should Jesus have to do this—why did he have to die? Listen to what it says in God's Word. "For Christ died for sins once for all, the righteous for the unrighteous, to bring you to God" (1 Peter 3:18). Jesus died in order to bring us to God, and it was no easy trip. He suffered—for us.

(At this point in the talk, Byron makes use of a book entitled, Hey, Who is That Man?, *written by Barry St. Clair. This book, published by Sonpower Books, has an excellent description of the crucifixion.)*

The prisoner stood without speaking as the soldiers stripped him to the waist, tied his hands together, and bent his body across a rail. One of the soldiers picked up a whip made of leather strands onto which bits of metal had been tied at the ends. Then began the ordeal commonly called the "half-way death"—so called because it was intended to bring the victim just short of dying. It was a form of torture peculiar to the Romans. The Jews did it differently. Their laws limited flogging to a maximum of thirty-nine strikes of the whip, but the Romans had no such rule. They flogged till the man doing the whipping got so tired, he couldn't go on. After the flogging his back lay open like a newly ploughed field.

The prisoner was led to the palace of the Roman governor. A company of soldiers, perhaps as many as 600, had gathered. They draped a purple robe, symbol of royalty, around the prisoner's shredded back so that the blood, as it coagulated, stuck to the fabric.

Someone had broken a branch from a thorn bush and fashioned the ends together to form a crown. The soldiers placed it on the victim's head, jabbing the long thorns into his scalp. And to complete the mockery, the soldiers struck his head with a rod, spit on him, and bowed down to him shouting "Hail! King of the Jews!" The prisoner reeled half-conscious before the jeering soldiers, and a day of unimaginable punishment had just begun for the prisoner they called "Jesus of Nazareth."

That same morning a hideous procession wound its way through the crowded streets of Jerusalem. A heavy wooden beam had been lifted on Jesus' bruised and bleeding shoulders. Weak from blood loss, pain, hunger, and lack of sleep, he stumbled forward, carrying on his back what was to form the horizontal beam of that cross. Somewhere along the way, Jesus stumbled and fell. A man called Simon happened to be passing by and the soldiers forced him to carry the cross for Jesus.

When the procession reached Golgotha, a place known as "hill of the skull," the soldiers nailed Jesus to a cross. They hammered a spike through each wrist between the two long bones of the forearms. Next they nailed his feet to the cross. Jesus' flesh ripped as the soldiers stood the cross upright and dropped its base into a hole in the ground. By three o'clock that afternoon, the crucifixion which the Roman historian, Cicero, called the most horrible torture ever devised by man, had finally ended.

The man who claimed to be the Son of God was dead, and the question screaming in the minds of his followers was "Why? Why had it happened?" It happened so that the penalty for sin—death—could be paid.

Let's imagine for a moment that you had committed a crime. You're appearing before a judge in a courtroom, and the judge gives you three months in jail and a fine of $1,000. You're standing there saying, "Man, have I ever messed up. I don't even want to go on living."

All of a sudden, somebody in the courtroom walks forward and says, "Hey, judge. Hang on. If you don't mind, I'd like to pay the penalty for this person." Then he looks at you and says, "Is that okay? Would you be willing to let me sit in jail and pay your $1,000 fine so you can go on living?"

Of course, you're astounded that anyone would do that for you, but the offer is too good to pass up. You say, "Yes, thank you!"

What this person did for you is exactly what Jesus Christ did on the cross. That's why he had to die. God had set up a plan: In order for the human race to be forgiven, the penalty of death had to be paid, and in this situation, to pay the penalty for the entire human race would require the death of his Son, Jesus. Then anybody who put his trust in Jesus could be forgiven.

You just heard described one of the most gruesome types of torture that man has ever devised, but I am convinced that the physical pain Jesus experienced on the cross was not as traumatic as the emotional and spiritual pain he experienced. Do you know what happened to him while he was hanging on the cross? Literally, every sin that you and I have ever done and ever will do as long as we're alive passed through him and hung on him. For the billions of people who will ever live in the history of the universe, every one of their sins hung on

him at the same time. If that isn't bad enough, at that moment—because his own Father cannot look at sin—Jesus was abandoned. All this, to pay our penalty.

There's one final reason Jesus is the only solution, and it's very important. In fact, if it wasn't for this, I guarantee you that I wouldn't be wasting my time talking up here. I would be out partying, and I certainly wouldn't bother trying to be a moral person. But the last thing changes everything: Jesus rose from the dead.

Listen to Paul's testimony in 1 Corinthians 15:3–6: "For what I received I passed on to you as of first importance: That Christ died for our sins according to the Scriptures, that he was buried, that he was raised on the third day according to the Scriptures, and that he appeared to . . . more than five hundred of the brothers at the same time . . ."

Many religious figures throughout history, from Buddha to Jim Jones, claimed to be the answer. But they're all lying in a grave somewhere. Only Jesus raised himself from the dead.

Why is that so crucial? Think about it. Actions speak louder than words, don't they? If somebody tells you that they love you, but there are no actions to back them up, do you believe them? No way! But because Jesus rose from the dead and no one else has ever done that, we can believe what he said. It's the proof. It's the evidence. No one else compares with Jesus Christ.

(To close this talk, Byron quotes Peter Marshall's classic description of the "One Solitary Life.")

More than 1900 years ago there was a man born contrary to the laws of life. This man lived in poverty and lived in obscurity. He did not travel extensively. Only once did he cross the boundary of the country in which he had lived and that was during his exile in childhood. He possessed neither wealth nor influence. His relatives were inconspicuous and had neither training nor even formal education.

In infancy he startled a king! In childhood he puzzled doctors! In manhood he ruled the course of nature, walked upon the billows as if pavements and hushed the sea to sleep. He healed the multitudes without medicine. He didn't even make any charge for his services.

He never wrote a book and yet perhaps all of the libraries in the world could not hold all of the books that have been written about him. He never wrote a song and yet he has furnished the theme for more songs than all other songwriters combined. He never founded a college, but all of the schools together could not boast of having as many students.

He never marshalled an army nor drafted a soldier nor fired a gun, and yet no leader has ever had more volunteers who have, under his orders, made more rebels stack arms and surrender without firing a shot. He never practiced psychiatry and yet he has healed more broken hearts than all the doctors far and near.

Once each week the wheels of business cease their turning and multitudes make their way to worshiping assemblies to pay homage and respect to him.

The names of the past, proud statesmen of Greece and Rome have come and gone. The names of the past scientists, philosophers, and theologians have come and gone, but the name of this man abounds more and more. And though time has spread 1900 years between the people of this generation (right here in 1987) and the scene of his crucifixion, yet now he lives. His enemies could not destroy him and the grave could not hold him, he stands forth upon the highest pinnacle of heavenly glory, proclaimed of God, acknowledged by angels, adored by saints, and feared by devils as the risen, personal, Jesus Christ, Lord and Savior.

Jesus is the answer to life; he is the solution. Only through him can we have that personal relationship with God. Think about it today. Do you have that relationship with him? It's the most phenomenal relationship you can have, and Jesus is the *only* way to get it.

The Legend of Eric the Hairball

John King

This talk makes use of a parable to communicate an important spiritual truth about sin. While some people may be uncomfortable with any message that doesn't "preach the Word," we ought to remember that those who use parables to teach profound spiritual truth are teaching in the tradition of the Lord himself.

Sin is one of the toughest topics to talk about with a group of teenagers. Growing up in today's culture, sin simply isn't a part of their world view. It's with topics like this that a wise speaker may choose to employ parables. John King's modern parable about sin will allow you to introduce some truths about sin, while doing an "end run" around some of the normal defenses that kids might have.

Remember that in using the parable, it is not necessarily important that you explain every grain of truth. Sometimes it is more wise to just let the kids think about and work out the lesson themselves. John originally used this parable to talk with high-school kids, but it would probably work well with junior-high kids as well.

For outline, see page 199.

Once upon a time there was a young man, a teenager, named Eric Hairball. Lying in bed one winter morning, he awoke to find the house dark and cold. It was nice and toasty under those covers, and he kept thinking of how nice it would be to make a day of staying right in that bed. He wondered, "Why should I get out of this bed and go out into that cold rain?" So Eric just lay there.

That's what Eric was thinking when suddenly someone said, "Eric! Hey, Eric! How ya' doin' there, buddy? Let's get out of bed. Heeeyyy!" Eric looked around the room. He figured it must be a dream, so he hit himself on the side of the head until he was certain that he was very much awake.

"C'mon, Eric. Hey, up here!" Eric tried to look up over his head, straining to find where the voice was coming from.

He jumped out of bed, forgetting now all about the cold, ran into the bathroom, and looked into the mirror. Holy cow! There was a little head sticking out of his head! And it was still talking to him. "Hey. Hey, Eric. How ya' doin' there, buddy. Let's get this face shining."

Needless to say, Eric was horrified. He ran back into his room, shaking his head around, but he could still feel that little lump up there. He ran back into the bathroom. There it was—still there, just smiling at him.

Eric went to school that day, terribly embarrassed, but kind of glad it wasn't the day for senior pictures. His head was hurting though, and the little guy on his head just wouldn't shut up. At lunch, his friends noticed his growth—and he noticed that they were all wearing hats. He had never noticed that before. As they talked, it turned out that they had little growths on their heads too.

They all said, "Listen, Eric, there's a psychiatrist down in the village. All you have to do is call this guy and he'll take care of your problems. Only fifteen bucks for an appointment." So Eric ran out to the pay phone outside the cafeteria and called the psychiatrist to make an appointment for that afternoon.

He ran down after school, and the doctor smiled understandingly as he walked into the office. Meanwhile, the growth had become very silent. That little person was ticked. He didn't want to go to any psychiatrist. The doctor nodded his head and said, "Ah, you've got your hair growth, huh?" Eric explained, "Yes, I woke up this morning and this guy starting talking to me and he won't shut up and it's starting to hurt a little bit."

The psychiatrist said, "Well, we have several procedures for taking care of problems like this. The first one is really the one that can nip it in the bud. Here's what you do. Just pretend that the growth's not there. If you can really discipline yourself and just make up your mind that there is no growth on your head, then you won't have any problems."

Eric thought, "Good grief, it cost me fifteen bucks to come up with that solution. I could have thought of that myself, but I guess it's worth fifteen bucks." He walked back home saying to himself, "I have no growth on my head. I have no growth on my head. . . ." Upstairs, on top of his head, the growth was saying, "Eric, you'll never do it, baby. Hey, who cares anyway? We can have some great times together." But Eric drowned out the little voice by repeating, "That growth is not on my head. That growth is not on my head. . . ."

Day after day went by, and Eric just couldn't ignore the thing. The growth kept talking to him, getting bigger and bigger all the time. Its head began to open up a little, and almost unnoticeably, the growth began to spread down Eric's neck and back. Not only that, but the pain was getting much more severe.

Eric went to the doctor again to find out about some new kind of therapy—some new kind of cure. He shelled out another fifteen bucks, and the doctor was quick to calm his fears. "A lot of my patients cannot handle that first chore. They just don't have the discipline or fortitude to persistently tell themselves that the growth is not there. So, here's step two: Blame it on your mother or father. After all, you've inherited the growth from them. It's their fault. It's not your fault—you didn't decide to have this growth."

Eric thought to himself, "Why didn't I think of this? Another fifteen dollars for such simple advice."

When he got home, he headed for the kitchen where he unloaded on his mother. He really let her have it. And it felt good. And when his father got home, he nailed him too. The release was wonderful! Just for good measure, he decided to take it out on a few neighbors as well. Every place he went where he met people he knew—he even went back to his elementary school—he pointed to the growth and started screeching at them, blaming them for his growth. Every time he yelled at someone, the growth joined in too.

Meanwhile, the growth got bigger. It began to move down into his chest cavity. The growth not only moved up out of his head a little bit more; it began to develop a body as well. And the body began to grow bigger and bigger.

As a result, Eric had to lean over a bit as he walked. When he swung his weight forward to take a step, the growth pulled his head back and pointed his nose up high in the air.

The growth was getting more and more difficult to live with. The pain was excruciating, and Eric began to take aspirin after aspirin, thinking that maybe the answer was in even stronger pain relievers. After Eric vented his initial rage, he realized that it didn't matter how much he yelled at anyone else. No matter how much he blamed his mom or dad or friends, it didn't do any good. The growth got bigger and the pain got worse.

He decided to go to his doctor again. He couldn't think of any cure that made sense, but the doctor always seemed to have some ideas. The doctor smiled (a fifteen dollar smile) when Eric entered his office. He spoke with authority, "I have one more cure you can try and here it is: Cover up the growth! As long as no one knows it's there, it will seem like it's in your imagination."

Eric thought to himself, "That's pretty obvious, why didn't I think of that?" And fifteen bucks poorer, Eric headed home, stopping at Woolworth's to buy as many different hats as he could find. He was pleased with the choices— stocking hats for every occasion. As he stepped out of the store and pulled the hat over his growth, he felt like a new man. Even though the pain was still there, he at least looked okay on the outside. An added benefit of the hat was that it even muffled the sound of the voice a little bit. Every time the growth tried to talk, out came this muffled voice *(muffle your voice with your hands here)* "Hey, Eric, let me out of here."

But before long, the stocking caps became too small. As Eric tried to pull them on and over, they split open. This called for drastic measures. Eric headed (no pun intended) for the costume shop. He found some tall top hats. There, that seemed to do the job nicely, except that each day, he had to extend the hat higher and higher. And the top hat, unlike the stocking cap, not only didn't muffle the little voice, it seemed to amplify it and allow it to echo in a most embarrassing way. "Eeerrriiiccc, let me out of heeerrree."

As each day passed, the spectacle became more humiliating. Instead of hiding the growth, the new hat began to accentuate it, making it even more noticeable. By now the growth grew out of the top of his head and arms were protruding from its little body. The pain became unbearable and the growth began to make its way down inside Eric's internal organs. It wasn't yet affecting his life support functions, but it definitely made a difference in his overall health. The growth was so big now that he couldn't lift his head forward at all. He had to walk with his shoulders bent over. He looked like a four-armed, two-headed man.

Meanwhile, the growth never stopped talking to him. Sometimes it spoke quietly. Sometimes loudly—but this little voice was always raring to go. Even when Eric tried to sleep at night, the noise on the outside and the pain on the inside made it impossible. Finally he went to the psychiatrist for one last shot at relief. Eric told him everything. "Doc, I've tried to pretend it's not there. I've blamed it on everybody I could think of. I've tried to cover it up with hats and blankets and everything else. None of that stuff worked. It kept growing and growing, getting louder and louder, and the pain is getting more and more intense. What can I do?"

The doc shook his head, knowing there was only one thing left to do. "Here's what you do: Dress it up, enjoy it—don't deny it. Stop pretending it's not there. Try to become friendly with it." Fifteen dollars later, Eric dragged himself home, not too optimistic about this new idea but willing to try it out. He stopped at a tailor and ordered a couple of special suits sized just to fit the growth. Even Eric had to admit that the little growth looked pretty dapper in its new clothes.

Eric had always had a good sense of humor, so it only made sense that he would take his little dressed-up growth and enter show business, beginning of course with the Senior Talent Show. But he was surprised when he and his growth were a huge hit in the show.

But that was only the beginning. After topping the school talent show, Eric and the growth began to do local clubs. Being full of school spirit, they even decided to contribute their abilities to the school cheerleading squad, where the two of them, again, were everybody's favorite.

On the outside, everybody thought Eric was just super because he laughed and cracked jokes and was so well-dressed. It wasn't long before Eric and the growth made an appearance on the Carson show, and again, he was a smash. The invitations came from all over. He did Vegas and Atlantic City. He was even asked to star in a movie, "Eric and His Growth," a box-office hit that made him as popular as the Muppets. Kids loved him. Adults loved him. Ev-

erybody identified with him, and he was making money hand-over-fist.

Then one night during a performance in a Vegas nightclub he saw in the audience an old friend from high school—one of the guys seated around the lunch table that first day that he went to school conscious of the growth. Eric could scarcely believe this guy's growth. It had shrunk to almost nothing at all.

After the show, Eric invited his old friend backstage, and they began to talk. Eric was asking about old friends and talking about old times, when his friend interrupted, looking him squarely in the eye. He said, "You don't fool me, old pal. You're funny up there on stage, just as you were in high school, but I know that on the inside you're racked with pain—not just physically, but emotionally. I know what growths can do, and I know what you're really feeling. But Eric, I've found a doctor who can cure the growth."

Eric leaned forward in his chair, eyes riveted on his friend. "Where is he? What can I do?" The hope in Eric's eyes was so obvious that it almost made his friend feel like crying. The friend warned Eric, "This guy doesn't operate like other doctors. It's going to be a little different from what you're expecting. But listen carefully. Do what he says. Trust him, and you'll begin to see that growth shrinking. But mark my words: He's the only one in the world that can cure these kinds of growths."

An excited Eric Hairball walked into the office of this new doctor. He had traveled almost halfway around the globe to a little village to talk with this man, and he couldn't wait to hear his secrets. "Hey, Doc, I hear you can cure these growths. Please tell me; I'll pay anything."

The doctor smiled warmly. "Yes, I can," he said. "I'm the only one in the world who can. But, I warn you, the cure is costly. Most doctors charge around $15 for their cures, but mine is much more expensive—so expensive, no one in the world can afford it."

Eric looked at him with disbelieving eyes—eyes once filled with hope, now turned to anger. With all the energy he had left, he cried out, "Why did you let me come here then? First you told me there was a cure. Then you told me I couldn't afford it. What kind of deal is this?"

It was all the doctor could do to calm Eric. In a soft voice, the doctor began to explain. "Many years ago, the wealthiest person who ever lived left a foundation to cover the cost of this cure. The stipulation is that anyone who wanted to be cured of this disease could get all the funding necessary through this foundation. The only catch is that you must admit your need, and ask for the money, and take it—no strings attached."

Eric couldn't believe what he was hearing. "Hey, wait a minute. I make bundles of money. There's no way that with my income I should let some foundation pay my bills. I don't need anybody's charity. I'm not some kind of beggar asking for a handout." The insult to Eric was so real and so deep that he ended the conversation right there. He left the doctor's office resolved to make so much money that he could afford anything he wanted—even this very unusual cure for the growth.

So, Eric, determined to triple his already unbelievable income, talked to the people in Vegas about adding extra shows each day. He contracted with MGM to do another movie, a sequel to his last film that had already grossed millions of dollars. Eric was really raking it in.

About one year and several million dollars later, Eric went back to face the doctor and buy the needed cure. The office looked exactly the same. Once again, the doctor greeted him with a firm handshake and a warm smile. This time, Eric began the appointment by putting down a cool three million in cash on the examining table. "Think maybe I can buy that cure now, Doc?"

Very sadly and quietly, the doctor shook his head. "I'm sorry. That is not enough money. There isn't enough money in the world to pay for the cure. You cannot buy the cure. It is only yours if you accept it as a free gift from the foundation." Eric, disappointed and insulted, resolved even stronger to buy the remedy. He turned his back on the only doctor with the cure and drove away in a cloud of dust.

Eric, now hard-driven by his determination to make even more money, stepped up his schedule another gear. He invested what money he had into high-return yields and high-rolling investments. Six months later, in the doctor's office again, Eric was met with the same disappointing answer. "It's not enough money. You'll never make enough money. Why won't you just allow yourself to be healed through the gift of the foundation?" But Eric was stubborn.

He walked out of that office and returned home to be completely absorbed in his touring, performing, and constant work. One evening, after doing his second nightly show at a major Vegas show spot, he was seated in his dressing room in a special overstuffed chair, designed to make him comfortable with his growth. As he sat there, tired, out of breath and out of hope, his eyes slowly closed. He slumped down in the chair wondering how long he could keep the show going. Within a few minutes, he stopped breathing—and died.

What started as a funny, cute story has become, in fact, a tragedy. And what makes it even more than just a cute story is the fact that all of us have that same growth inside of us. At first, it seems like a toy—very pleasant, very adventurous, and very funny. The Bible's name for this growth is sin.

At the heart, here's what it really is: It's the fact that, although we were created to have God at the very center of our lives, running our lives, we have, all of us, without any exceptions, rebelled against him and decided to run our own lives instead. That's the basic disease. It has all kinds of symptoms—many of which are quite approved of by the culture around us. We may try to deal with it in different ways, some by denying it's there, some by trying to psych themselves into believing it's not real, or others by just bringing it out in the open and trying to enjoy it. None of these strategies really works. All the while we waste our lives, our time, and our money, and the disease just continues to spread until the final result is death. And this is more than just a physical death. It's a spiritual death that will lead eventually to total separation from God, his love, his power, and his joy.

Picture the loneliest moment of your life and multiply it times infinity and you have an idea of spiritual death. Think of the time you broke up with your boyfriend or girlfriend. Do you remember how that felt? Multiply it times infinity and you've got death.

That's the bad news. And John, one of Jesus' best friends on earth, spoke very clearly about this problem that we've described as sin. He says that if we refuse to admit that we are sinners, if we refuse to admit that we have this disease within us, then we are living in a world of illusion and truth is a stranger to us (1 John 1:8).

But, he writes, if we freely admit that we have sin, that we have this growth in us, then we will find God utterly reliable and straightforward. He will forgive our sins. And not only that, he will make us thoroughly clean from all that is destroying us (1 John 1:9). We must admit our need, however. If we refuse to admit that sin is a problem that we can't handle, then we flatly deny God's diagnosis of our condition and cut ourselves off from what he has to say to us.

Eric Hairball tried a lot of methods. He had very authoritative information on how to deal with the problem. But he died a very unhealthy man.

It might be wise for us to think twice about whose diagnosis of our problems is most accurate: Is it the world's, or is it God's? Do you have a growth inside of you? The Bible says that you do. And until you are willing to accept that diagnosis, and God's free gift of the cure for that problem by faith in Jesus Christ, God cannot begin to do his healing work in you.

Taking on Temptation

James 1:2

Craig Knudsen

This talk on dealing with temptation will give students some practical ideas about how to confront temptation without being victimized.

The talk begins with two brief role plays. Be sure that you give adequate attention to good small group dynamics before you launch into this exercise. Kids should be divided into groups of no more than four, seated closely together, and told that the most important part of the role play is not someone's acting ability, but the role and response that they assume.

Marlene LeFever's book *Creative Teaching Methods* (Elgin, Illinois: David C. Cook 1985) can give you some more insights on how to effectively use role plays.

For outline, see page 201.

I'd like you to divide into groups. One person in each group is going to be the "tempter," the person who's going to tempt you. The rest of you are the temptees. Here's the situation: In an hour you have a big biology test that you haven't studied for, and the tempter has just finished the test. You're sitting in the quad area frantically cramming for the test. The tempter has the answers and is going to tempt you to take them.

(Give the groups about one to two minutes to carry out this role play.)

Some of you are pretty sly tempters!

Did anyone accept their arguments and take the answers? Be honest!

Pick a different tempter. Here's the situation: You're partying on a Friday night with all your friends. Your brand-new girlfriend or boyfriend, around whom you are trying to be very cool, is with you. Alcohol is being served all around. *Everyone* is drinking and *everyone* is getting a little toasty. The tempter comes up to you with a couple of brew-skis. The temptation is unbelievable. Tempter, do your thing.

(Again, allow about one or two minutes for role play.)

There's a great tempter over here. Don't run into him at parties! He'll have you out barfing on the sidewalk.

Exercises like this are interesting, aren't they? Of course, it's a lot tougher in the heat of a real situation. Then it's easy to say, "I didn't get a chance to study last night—let me have them," without even thinking twice. And it's easy to take that drink at a party where all your friends are watching.

Here are a couple of other situations. You're going out the door. Your parents have already told you that you cannot see your boyfriend or girlfriend tonight, but they're letting you leave the house anyway. You intend to see your boyfriend or girlfriend, but what do you tell them? You lie, saying something like, "I'm going to the library to study" or "I'm going to Johnny's house."

Here's another one. It's two in the morning, and you're with your boyfriend or girlfriend that you've been going with for several months, even years. Things get going. One thing leads to another, and he or she asks you, "What's wrong with going all the way? After all, we love each other."

Four tough situations, four tempting circumstances—we usually think of temptation in those four areas: cheating, getting drunk, lying, and going all the way. But let me tell you something:

There is more to temptation than just those four. In the next couple of minutes I will expand your view of temptation and help you recognize some that you've never noticed before. Some of them will hit even closer to home than the first four we mentioned because, frankly, some of us haven't had to deal with the "big four." Besides, there are other temptations we all face which may be more socially acceptable, but cause just as many problems.

What about the temptation to be impatient? I know three high-school girls who had a little spat in their relationship as friends. Now whenever they talk to each other, they don't listen to one another. They simply react by assuming the worst, saying things like, "Well that's Mary, she's all messed up." I know another guy who doesn't exactly flow with the social stream, and sometimes it's very hard to be patient with this guy. Then it's tempting for me to ask, "Why be patient with him? Why talk with him?"

How about the temptation to be uncaring—to be unmoved, unwilling to show feelings. Will you take the time to care for those who need your help, or will you just walk on by? It's easier for us to be a Pharisee than a Good Samaritan.

Another one is the temptation to be physically beautiful. As I look out on this crowd, I see a lot of physically beautiful people. There is nothing wrong with being physically beautiful. However, I know someone who is obsessed with the idea of having the perfect body. All there is to him is what is on the outside; all that matters is how he appears to others. He invests everything in that area of his life, always thinking about clothes, looks, hair, and appearance. But all those investments aren't going to pay off in anything *lasting*.

How about the temptation to gossip? Do you know what gossip is? Passing on news which isn't helpful. I know a wonderful girl who had a rumor started about her that she was pregant. Imagine! One day, when the news had gone full circle and come back to her, she said to me, "Craig, someone started a rumor that I'm pregnant. Everyone is looking at me like I'm some sort of slut." This girl was wounded by something as simple as words.

Then there's the temptation to be respected—for example, the temptation to earn respect by how much money you have. Once I was at a football game where the crowd was doing the cheer, "We've got spirit, yes we do. We've got spirit, how about you?" Some guys sitting in front of me yelled, "We've got money, yes we do. We've got money, how about you?" They weren't joking. They were saying, "Hey, we've got money, so you're nothing." There is a real temptation to think that our affluence should buy us influence.

Our culture is a *wealth*-pusher. We listen to songs like Madonna's "Material Girl"—"The one with the cold, hard cash is always Mr. Right." We watch Dallas and Dynasty, and we admire kids with the latest clothes and nicest cars. So we start to believe that wealth is the answer to life, that respect equals wealth.

How about the temptation to judge? You may not be sleeping with your boyfriend or girlfriend, but are you far too proud of that? Do you think, "Those scum who do that—what blatant sinners they are. They're going to hell on a skateboard"? Or do you avoid parties? That's fine, but do you label those who do go to parties? Every campus has group labels: the partyers, the head cases, the jocks, the sleezes, the nerds. Even those labels are a form of judging.

How about the temptation of power, to have control over other people? I had been working with a girl who had planned on going to a camp in Canada, a beautiful place where our youth group always has a great time. Then she got hooked up with a boyfriend, and I didn't see her for about a month. She disappeared. (That happens a lot when you get a boyfriend or girlfriend; you disappear from all your other relationships.) Finally, the week before the camp began, I called her. "Hi, Debbie," I said. "All set to go to camp?"

"I'm not going," she replied.

"Why not?"

"My boyfriend said I can't go."

I couldn't speak. Her boyfriend had so much power over her that he could say, "You can't go there because I don't want you to." He was manipulating her to gratify his need for power.

Let me mention one more temptation—the temptation to be cool. Do you know what coolness is? Don't risk. Don't reveal. Be bad. Keep up that image. Go right along with the clique. When your friends laugh at an unattractive girl that walks by, laugh with them. Dress like your friends, talk like your friends, act like your friends, and above all—hide the real you. After all, you don't want to earn your friends' disapproval.

What can we see about temptation after looking at all these examples? Temptation is, above all, a choice. And since life is composed of a series of choices, you won't escape temptation until you die.

Yet the Bible says we shouldn't dread temptation. On the contrary! Listen to what James 1:2 says: "Consider it pure joy, my brothers, whenever you face trials of many kinds." Now, I don't know about you, but when temptations come my way, I don't consider it pure joy. I just don't want to deal with them. But the third verse tells me *why* I should be happy: "because you know that the testing of your faith develops perseverance."

We need to see two things right away: Number one, we will never get away from temptation. The Scripture doesn't say "*if* you face trials" but "*whenever* you face trials." Number two: We must realize that temptation is not the same thing as sinning. That's very important to know!

You're at the beach and you see this girl clad in barely nothing. Your mind immediately goes to you-know-what. Now, the temptation to let your mind fantasize about this girl is not the sin. Saying "yes" to that temptation and *allowing* your mind to play with those thoughts is the sin.

How can you avoid those mind games? You see this great looking body—what are you going to do? Honk if you love Jesus? Put on blinders? Pray for strength, but pray with your eyes open? The temptation is not the sin, but how do we keep it from becoming sin? Let me give you a couple of examples.

Sex was created by God, and like everything else he made, he pronounced it "good." When he sees a husband and wife enjoying sexual intercourse, he says, "That's beautiful—I made that, and that's how it's supposed to be." Now, when the opportunity comes to abuse that pleasure, it doesn't mean that *sex* is bad, because God called it *good*. It means we are now faced with a choice. We can choose to save intercourse for marriage (as God intended). Or we can go for it and possibly face some real problems as a consequence.

Let me give you a more subtle example. Love was created by God, too. He's the one who invented the strange feelings you have when you see that special person. But I know of a situation where a high-school girl fell in love with a man who was married and had three children. Because they fell in love, does that make love bad? No, love's great, but they now have a choice. The girl can say, "Look, regardless of what's happening, you need to go back to your wife and your kids." And he needs to say, "I have to go back to my wife and kids." Just falling in love isn't sinful, but it does present us with opportunities to choose between that which is sinful and that which isn't. Temptation is not sin; it's the choice between whether *to* sin or *not* to sin.

We all have basic desires that can either bring us closer to God or make us stumble. One basic desire is the desire for a man or a woman. I remember dreaming in high school about marriage: "Won't it be great—I'll be the greatest husband. I'll meet someone wonderful, we'll get married, have kids. And I'll always love her." What was going on there? The desire in me was saying, "I want to be loved." I could take that desire and use it to build a healthy friendship with a girl that could become marriage. Or I could channel that desire into building relationships with friends and family. *Or* I could have treated girls like pieces of furniture—there for my comfort and pleasure. In short, I had the opportunity to channel that desire positively or negatively.

The desire to drink . . . who hasn't been at a party or been out with the guys and had a desire to "head for the mountains?" Do you know what's behind that? The desire to be accepted. Remember that role play we began with? If your friends were at the party and your girlfriend was standing right there saying, "Take it," you'd be thinking, "I don't want to look like a fool. I want to be accepted by my friends." There's nothing wrong with that, but that normal desire can lead you to make some bad choices, and there's *plenty* wrong with that.

So how can we deal with temptation? How do we keep from making wrong choices? The worst way to deal with temptation is to try to fight it alone—temptation has victimized many a "Lone Ranger." When you talk to someone about your temptation, or confess bad decisions you've made in the face of temptation, you can overcome temptation more easily.

All of us need friendships where we can safely express ourselves and thereby help each other with our struggles. I know of a marriage that was saved by friends. One guy was tempted to sneak out on his wife and have an affair, but instead of saying "yes" to that temptation and then covering up his sin, he shared his struggle with a group of guys he was meeting with, and they talked him out of it.

One of my friends used to be the biggest drug pusher on campus when he was a freshman in high school. Then he became a Christian, and everyone wondered what had happened. All the guys were saying, "Hey, where's the stuff, man?" He told me and some other Christian friends that he was really being tempted to get back into drug pushing. In that group, Scott—and I too—found strength in mutual accountability and sharing. He's been free from his old life about five years, and now he works with high-school kids to help them get a glimpse of who Jesus Christ is.

There are some other strategies in dealing with temptation. 2 Timothy 2:22 gives a very basic strategy: Flee. Don't get into situations that you know will put you under undue pressure. Don't climb into the back seat of a car with your girlfriend praying, "Lead us not into temptation. . . ." Be realistic enough to admit your weaknesses, and avoid situations in which you will become vulnerable.

Here's another suggestion: Build for yourself a group of friends that put you under positive peer pressure. Find Christians who challenge you and en-

courage you to make good choices. Most of us spend a lot of time around people with different values who often lead us into situations where we are confronted with temptations and tough choices. Christian friendships can help us handle those situations.

Let me give you another suggestion: Make some decisions ahead of time. In the sexual area, before you get into the back seat of the car at two in the morning—not a good time or place to make a decision about whether you're going to go all the way or not!—decide what your standards are and determine to stick by them. If you've already decided that you are going to diet, it won't be nearly as tough for you to choose between all those luscious items on the dessert menu. Some decisions are better made before you are faced with the options.

For example, remember the temptation to be uncaring? How about if you decide in advance, "I will not just walk on by. I'm going to stop and I'm going to say 'hi' and I'm going to ask her name." Or, with the temptation to judge, decide ahead of time, "I'm not going to judge this person by what I see. I'm going to take the time to get closer, to understand what makes her tick."

Another suggestion: Jesus battled temptation by knowing the Scriptures and by prayer. Those are two big factors. That doesn't mean that if confronted by someone who offers you a beer you should say, "Halt! I'm a Christian. First Corinthians, chapter five, verse fourteen, 'don't drink.'" (I doubt if it says that there, but you get the point.) Rather than being obnoxious about it, you can know in the back of your mind that the tone of the Scriptures seems to indicate that this could lead to a lot of trouble. Jesus met temptation by studying Scriptures to know what was right, and then by praying to God for strength to follow through on that. You can do the same.

One final suggestion—and this may be the most practical of them all so far—know how to refuse temptation with grace, courtesy, and firmness. Let me give you a couple of ideas.

Remember that first little role play we did on cheating? The tempter says, "Hey, come on. Here's the notes. Take them—get an 'A.' Who doesn't want an 'A'?" How could you respond to that besides coming across as a mightier-than-thou, holier-than-thou person saying, "I'm a Christian. I just don't *do* that." That answer may be true, but if that's our only answer, and we sense that it's going to cost us friendships, we tend to buckle under to temptation.

But what if you said something like this: "Hey, I really appreciate you. Thanks for taking the time to do those cheat sheets. But tell me something, why do you want to do that for me?" Coming back with a question will catch the tempter off guard. "Because you're my friend, that's why," they may say. Then you have a great chance to say, "Because you're *my* friend, and because I appreciate you doing that, I want you to know I don't need them. I didn't study, but I have to work on being honest. I want to graduate knowing that I did everything myself." That's integrity. That's a way of bowing out with class.

You can use the question strategy in other situations too. Like drinking: "Why do you want me to have a drink?"

"Um, well, because everybody's doing it."

"I like being with you, but that's not my idea of having a good time. So I'll just pass, okay?"

Or you can use it when someone is stringing you a line: "Why do you want me to go all the way?"

"I love you. Don't you love me?"

"If you really love me, we won't do this. I'd rather save that part of me until we get married."

How about gossip? When a rumor comes your way, what if you were the one to say, "Hey, we have no idea what's going on in that girl's life. We're probably being pretty harsh. We don't even know what she's like. One thing I do know: Her parents are splitting up. Rather than spreading all these rumors that she's being obnoxious, why don't we take the time to try to understand her?" Or you could say, "This might sound strange to you, but I see that girl the way Jesus sees her. I want to love her the way Jesus does."

Temptations will always come our way, some that we may not even see as temptation. But if we stay close to Jesus, he will reveal the temptation and give us the power to overcome it. Temptation can be positive, forcing us to grow, and even making us "mature and complete, not lacking anything" (James 1:4). Because of Christ, we don't have to dread temptation—because he gives us the means to deal with it.

Resisting Sexual Temptation

Genesis 39

Bill MacPhee

This talk, based on an episode from the life of Joseph, will help students in their struggle with sexual temptation. Both Christian and non-Christian teen-agers will benefit from this kind of honest, open discussion.

You might find it helpful to follow up on this talk by using the Youth Specialties "Talk Box" curriculum, "Yes, No, or Maybe So!" (available by writing Youth Specialties, 1224 Greenfield Dr., El Cajon, CA 92021). This will stimulate further discussion and give the youth a chance to apply some of the principles given in this talk.

For outline, see page 204.

I love to go to the movies, but these days it's hard to find a good one where the girl and guy don't jump into the sack together on their first date. That's only the movies—imagine what a visitor from Mars would think if he thumbed through our magazines, flipped on the TV, or made an in-depth study of our bill-boards. He probably would go home with the impression that sex is the only thing on our minds.

As a teenager I attended a Christian camp in which the speaker's message about sex could be summed up in three words: dirty, wrong, and sinful. Society seems to say sex is paramount; the church sometimes says sex is perverse. If you're like me, it's easy for you to ignore the negative message of the church and pursue the positive message of society.

I have since learned that sex is neither paramount nor is it dirty, wrong, and sinful. God created sex to be *good*—if we follow his divine design. That design demands that a sexual relation-ship be enjoyed by a man and woman within the context of a committed mar-riage relationship. When we take sex out of this proper design, we destroy its ability to bring long-term fulfillment to either partner.

A high schooler in my youth group came home from school one day and decided to set his sister's goldfish free. Pouring them out of the aquarium, he invited them to come outside and play with him. He soon discovered that fish have fun only in the context of water. The same principle is true of sex: Sex is designed to bring true fulfillment in the context of marriage.

We can find a good example for our actions in a young man named Joseph, who resisted the tempting sexual advances of another man's wife. The story is found in Genesis 39. From Joseph's experience we can discover four practical principles for resisting sexual temptation in the midst of a very sexual world.

First, let me give you a little background information to set the stage. Joseph was his father's favorite son. This wouldn't have been a problem if he were an only child, but Joseph had ten older— and jealous—brothers. As older brothers like to do, they decided to make life difficult for Joseph, kidnapping him and selling him as a slave to traders on their way to Egypt. The traders then sold him to a wealthy and important man named Potiphar who was on the personal staff of the Pharaoh.

The Lord was with Joseph in Egypt and blessed everything he did in Potiphar's house. It wasn't long before Potiphar put Joseph in charge of everything he owned, both in the house and out in the field. Although he was a slave, Joseph had great responsibility and freedom to manage all of Potiphar's household and business affairs. This is where we pick up the story in Genesis 39.

The text tells us that "Joseph was well-built and handsome" (v. 6). This is a polite way of saying that Joseph was a real looker. Because of his looks, Potiphar's wife took notice of Joseph and said, "Come to bed with me" (v. 7). I don't know about you, but I've never had a girl (except my wife) come up to me and flat out beg me to go to bed with her. Some guys would love for that to happen, but not me. At any rate, Mrs. Potiphar was available, horny, and very attracted to Joseph.

Principle #1: *Everybody is handsome in form and appearance to somebody.*

It is not just the so-called "beautiful people" that have to deal with sexual temptation. The movies would have us believe that the "Plain Janes" and "Average Als" of our world will never be faced with the opportunity for a sexual relationship. The truth is that all of us will face sexual temptation in one form or another. It may not be as blatant as Joseph's experience. It may not happen this year or the next, but sooner or later the opportunity will be ours. We need to realize that we are vulnerable. It is inevitable that someone is going to find us quite attractive and make themselves available for a friendship that can lead to sex. Don't be naive and think it won't happen to you.

Principle #2: *Set your standards ahead of time.*

The second principle is found in verses 8 and 9. Notice Joseph's response to Mrs. Potiphar's offer: He immediately refused her and reminded her that Potiphar had put him in charge of everything in the house except her because "you are his wife. How then could I do such a wicked thing and sin against God?"

Because Joseph had already made up his mind concerning his own sexual standards, he had the ability and strength to say "no" immediately. I really doubt that Joseph would have been able to resist this temptation if he hadn't set his standards ahead of time. Have you ever thought about the fact that if *you* don't set personal sexual standards for yourself, someone else will? I've talked with many students who confessed they had had no intention of "going all the way" and didn't really know how they got themselves in the back seat of the car anyway. We need to set our standards ahead of time, for it's usually too late once we get in a sexually tempting situation.

Joseph had adopted what the Bible says about sex as a standard for his life because his relationship with God was his highest priority. This is why he said to Mrs. Potiphar, "How then could I do such a wicked thing and sin against God?" (v. 9). He knew that the real issue at stake was his relationship with God. Sex outside of God's design not only affects our relationship with our date, but it also affects our relationship with God.

Principle #3: *Avoid contact with the temptation.*

Look at verse ten: "And though she spoke to Joseph day after day, he refused to go to bed with her or even be with her." This lady was persistent! Each day as Joseph worked she approached him with the same tempting opportunity. She probably used different approaches—all with the same goal in mind. "Come on, Joseph, just lie down beside me for a few minutes . . ." Or "Joseph, you're such a prude. I just want to be with you. Honest, no hanky-panky." Joseph knew her tricks and his vulnerability, so he made up his mind not to even listen to her. He avoided her like the plague.

The point of the principle is this: It's not wise for an alcoholic to hang around in bars if he wants to stop drinking. It's foolish for someone on a diet to sip coffee in a bakery. Do you get the point? Sexual temptation is powerful. It's like a magnet—the closer you get to it, the more it attracts you. The Pope would find it difficult to resist once the windows were fogged up at the drive-in. Before you go on a date, think about:

- where you are going to go
- what you are going to do
- whether you will "park and check out the view" or
- whether you will pursue a good night kiss and
- how long it should be

Joseph knew he needed to stay as far away from sexual temptation as possible. In our world where all forms of the media have become sexually explicit, we can't avoid the temptation completely. But we need to exercise discipline, knowing ourselves well enough to avoid situations that make it difficult for us to maintain our standards.

Principle #4: *Flee!*

One day while Joseph was working inside the house and none of the other men were present, Potiphar's wife grew impatient with his resistance to her advances. She grabbed him by the coat, pulled him close to herself, and said, "Come to bed with me!" (v. 12). The text goes on to say that Joseph "left his cloak in her hand and ran out of the house."

Joseph was smart. He knew that there comes a point when arguments won't work, and then it is time to run! Prayer is a powerful tool to fight sexual temptation, but once in a while we need

to put feet on our prayers and immediately get ourselves out of the situation. 2 Timothy 2:22 tells us to "Flee the evil desires of youth, and pursue righteousness . . ." It may be embarrassing to ask our date to take us home immediately, or it may be tough to get up and walk out of a movie that is polluting our minds, but there is a time when our relationship with God and our desire to stay pure becomes more important than what our friends think of us.

When Joseph ran, Potiphar's wife screamed. Joseph was thrown in jail for an attempted rape he never attempted. The consequences of commitment to God and sexual purity are not always easy to take, and our friends may not understand or like our principles.

While I was in college, my teammates and I were taking showers after a baseball game. The other players were talking about their sexual exploits and then asked me about mine. They shouted with laughter when I told them I was still a virgin. I never felt more naked than when I tried to explain my commitment to Christ and that I planned to save sexual intercourse for my marriage. It was a difficult afternoon. My friends thought I was weird. But when I got married a couple years ago, I discovered that all the waiting was worth it.

Just as God was with Joseph, he'll be with you as you struggle to set godly sexual standards and fight to keep them.

Understanding the Opposite Sex

Philippians 2:1–5

Bill MacPhee

This is not just another "sex and dating" talk. Originally delivered at one of Youth Specialties' "Grow for it" seminars, it is more of a general overview of the ways guys and girls relate to each other.

This talk will help both the Christian and the non-Christian audience. Notice that Bill carefully avoids stereotypes by basing his comments on data drawn from research. Even when making generalizations, he tries not to discredit his message by making statements that are broad and unsubstantiated. Any person using this talk will do well to also avoid that trap.

Bill's use of small group discussion is effective—a good way to introduce the kinds of stereotypes and misunderstandings that exist between the sexes. You might follow up this talk with more discussion about implications for specific areas of male-female relationships, such as dating, marriage, and friendship.

For outline, see page 206.

Guys, how would you feel if there were nothing but guys here? And girls, can you imagine what life would be like if earth were just packed with a bunch of girls?

Do you know something? There is something electric about a guy sitting next to a girl. And vice versa. When we're packed in so tight, we feel the electricity. I don't think we go through a day without hundreds and hundreds of times coming into contact with members of the opposite sex. That's one of the things that makes life so exciting.

If you're like me, some of the most frustrating experiences come when we don't understand the opposite sex. Now, I'm a guy, so from a guy's perspective, I think about girls. To me, there are few things as confusing to me as a girl. I know that girls feel the same way. Girls can get so frustrated with the thick-headedness of the guys they know.

I want you to picture in your mind, girls, the guys that you relate to. You have hundreds of them, I'm sure. And guys, think about the girls who are in your life. As we go through this talk today, I want you to think specifically of the relationships you're in right now. I know we have problems relating to the opposite sex, and I need your help to solve them. We'll start with the girls first. I would like you girls to begin to think about the characteristics that you see in the guys that you know. What are guys like? What are some of their key characteristics? Just shout them out.

(Allow girls to give their responses.)

Okay, girls, you had your chance. Now, I want to hear from the guys. Guys, what are some of the key characteristics that you've seen in the girls in your world?

(Allow the guys a chance to respond.)

I can tell that we definitely need this seminar today. You are not relating to one another very well–you make each other sound terrible! That list is full of stereotypes, too, and we'll be dealing with a lot of stereotypes today. But before we do that, I want to give you four quick ground rules that will help you through this seminar.

The first one is exploring what makes us male or female. There are some people who say that the differences between girls and guys are biological. In other words, we're born different. God made us different, and that's *why* we're different. Obviously.

Some people say, no, the differences are not so much biological, what we've been born with, as they are *cultural*. We learned how to be male or female as we grew up. The environment around us has told us what our differences are. Well, friends, I'm not going to try to prove whether our differences are primarily due to biology or primarily due to culture. The fact of the matter is, we *are* different. Genesis 1:27 says that God created us male and God created us female for a *purpose*. And praise God, I'm glad he did, aren't you?

So today we're going to try to understand those differences. The second ground rule is that to understand the differences between girls and guys, you have to *want* to understand. This is not an easy task, because it's so easy for girls to look at guys and roll their eyes and say, "I can't understand guys. They're so stupid." Or for guys to say, "I've given up on girls. They're just impossible to understand."

I think when we say, "I can't understand the opposite sex," what we're really saying is, "I don't want to understand." I think you're in this seminar today because you really do want to understand how to relate to the opposite sex. It's so fun and it's so important. But we have to *want* to do it. We have to really try hard.

The third ground rule is the fact that all of our differences are not necessarily due to our sex. Some of you are morning people. You got up at five this morning to meet the day, to watch the sunrise. You just love to get up early. Some of you, no way. You wait until ten P.M. comes along and all of a sudden you get fired up and you wake up and you skate right through midnight, one, two in the morning, flying high. You may be a morning person or a night person. That doesn't necessarily have anything to do with your sex.

Some of you are incredibly neat people. A place for everything and everything in its place. Some of you are walking pig pens. You're messy people. That's not necessarily due to our sex. There are some differences between us as individuals that may not necessarily be because you're a guy or because you're a girl. I think we have a problem in our world today. That is, that our definition of masculine—of what it takes to be a manly man—is all wrong. We say for a man to be masculine is to be everything that is *un*feminine. For guys, if they happen to slip over just a little bit into an area where girls traditionally operate, well, we question their manhood. Our model for masculinity is Ram-

bo. If we don't fit that, somehow, people question our masculinity. There are some guys who like to cook. And that's great. There are some girls who like to ride motorcycles, and that's great.

The fourth ground rule is that we're here to learn and we're here to have fun. So let's jump into our study. I'm going to move through these just about as fast as I can, so stay with me.

The first area we need to look at is how we relate physically. Researchers have been studying this for years. They have discovered that guys are ten times as likely to be color blind as girls, and girls are five times as likely as guys to cry in a situation. They've also discovered that guys have thicker skin than girls. Obviously, these are life changing characteristics that you need to write down because they're going to make a big difference in your life.

Seriously, did you know that generally speaking, girls can never really get as strong as guys? I would imagine that in this setting right here at your age, there are probably a lot of girls who could trounce all the guys in here . . . they've got a lot of muscles. But guys primarily have their strength in their upper body. That's where guys really make it. Now girls, generally speaking, develop their strength in their lower body. Many girls can equal and even surpass guys in their lower body strength. So, if you want to arm wrestle, guys, you know you'll win. But if you want to leg wrestle—watch out!

Girls can do great in the long distance activities like long-distance running and swimming. The women's best time in the English Channel swim, which is a long-distance swim, is three hours better than the best men's time. Way to go, girls!

Let's move on to the mental characteristics and look at some of the ways we relate mentally. If you ever want to start a fight, all you have to do is ask, "Who are smarter, girls or guys?" Do you know what scientists have discovered? Men are not necessarily smarter than women and women are not necessarily smarter than men. So, we can give up the fight. We don't have to worry about that anymore.

But they have discovered some differences—strengths that both men and women have. And they've discovered them through studying little tiny kids. They've discovered that guys tend to be more curious about objects than girls. Guys have a tendency as little toddlers to be more exploratory than girls. They also have a desire to solve puzzles a little bit more, and they tend to excel in math and mechanical skills.

Girls have some strengths as well. Girls usually end up talking a bit earlier than guys do. Guys are over in the corner drooling with puzzles and exploring while girls are beginning to verbalize. Girls tend to excel in foreign languages and in verbal skills and in talking. They've also discovered with tests on these little tiny kids that girls usually have better memories.

Our tendency is to want to point out these differences and to say that one group, girls or guys, are better than the other. Well, they're not necessarily better than the other. They are just different groups with different strengths. Now, let's move on to the emotional differences because this is where it really gets fun.

We really are emotionally different, and we relate to one another emotionally in different ways. All of us in this room, both girls and guys, need to know that other people like us. We all need to know that we're important, that other people care about us. Some researchers suggest that our self-image, how we feel about ourselves, is largely determined by how we think other people feel about us. If we think that other people like us and respect us, that builds our self-image.

This is my personal opinion, but I think girls and guys develop their self-worth differently. I think, to a great extent, guys tend to develop their self-worth by building a positive reputation through their own personal accomplishments. Guys build their self-worth through the things they do.

I think girls are a little bit different. Girls primarily develop that self-worth and feel good about themselves if they have relationships where they know that people love and understand them . . . relationships with people who really know who they are on the inside.

I think that's why in Ephesians 5 the Apostle Paul says, "Husbands, love your wives. Wives, respect your husbands." Because there really are differences in the way that we develop our self-worth.

Girls, here's a hint. If you really want to make a guy feel good, if you want to build a guy up, if you want to get on his good side, if you want to be kind to a guy that you know, then pay attention to the things he does well. And compliment him. We guys are insecure. Now, we don't want you to know that, girls. But we are. We are desperately afraid that you're not going to like us. One of the best ways you can build us up is to pay attention to the things we do well and compliment us. Help us develop a positive reputation and self-worth. You can really do that.

Guys, do you know what we need to do? We need to show that we really want to understand the girls who are in our lives. We need to understand, to really know and sympathize with the feelings that the girls in our world have, because they do have feelings.

Let me give you a personal example. My wife works with computers. One day she was working on a project which required her to feed paper into the printer so that printer would put out this put-together project she was working on. In the middle of all this, the printer went bazooey. As she was feeding papers, the printer was chewing them up and spitting them out. She'd feed more in and it would spit them out. She was getting so mad at this printer that she wanted to throw it out the window. The project never got completed, and it ruined her day. At dinner she began to recount for me the problems that she had had that day. She was still furious with that printer.

What did I do? I listened to her story, and I proceeded to try to figure out the printer's malfunction. Why wasn't it working right? I thought if I could figure out why the printer was screwing up, that somehow it would all go away, and she'd feel great and be excited. My wife, Cynthia, stared at me, looking as if she'd like to break my nose. She said, "Bill, I really don't care about the printer. I just want you to understand I had a lousy day."

Do you get the point? Many times girls just want to be understood. They want you to know that they have feelings and that they've had a lousy day. And we guys tend to be so task-oriented and problem-centered. We think if we can just solve all the world's problems everyone will be happy.

We need to understand each other and know that we have feelings. But girls, know too, for sure, that we guys have feelings. We may not want you to know it, but we really do, and you need to understand our feelings as well.

Not only do we have emotional, mental, and physical differences, we also differ socially. How do we relate to each other socially? It's amazing to me, but girls relate to girls one way and guys relate to guys a completely different way. When you leave here, pay attention to the way girls talk to girls and watch how guys talk to guys. It's just funny because we are *so* different from one another.

We guys get together—why? Primarily to do something. When we guys get together, we want to go surfing, or we work on a car, or we have some particular project—that's why guys get together—when they have something to do. We're problem solvers. We're task-oriented. We have to have an excuse for being together as guys.

Girls are different. Girls don't need any reason to get together. Girls get together, not necessarily to do something, but girls get together to talk. Girls love to talk! Most of you girls have been raised in an environment where you've been encouraged to talk. You're used to getting together with friends to sit around and chat.

We guys have not really been encouraged to do that. We've been encouraged not to talk together, but to go outside and play together . . . to do something . . . to work on a project. You girls have been working at talking for years and years and years. And you've become proficient at it!

Take, for example, a slumber party. Girls say, "Hey, want to come over to my house for a slumber party?" And what do you do? You talk all night long. Who needs to sleep? Just eat and talk and talk. It's great. You have such a fun time. You get up in the morning and you go home. You've had a great night.

Guys, when do you ever go over to another guy's house and spend the night? "Hey, friends, do you want to come over to my house? We're having a slumber party!" It just doesn't work that way, does it? Guys do not get together just to spend the night and chat together and catch up on one another. Why do we spend the night? So we can get up at 4:30 in the morning to check out the surf. We have to have a reason for getting together. We've got to have a place we're going—something that we're doing.

Hey, guys, we don't even know how to talk to other guys. We really don't. You're going to a party of adults. The wives in the party are all over in the corner talking together and finding out how they're doing. What are the men doing? What do they say to each other? "Well, uh, yeah, uh, so how's the business going?" We guys talk about the things we've been doing.

Guys stand next to each other, side by side facing out. Girls stand next to one another face to face. Watch for it. Pay attention to how it works, and you can learn something about communicating with each other.

Girls, the guys need your help, and here's how you can help us. When you talk to us, we need you to ask us questions—specific, helpful questions. And here's the kind of questions we really need from you girls. When you talk to us, ask us questions about how we feel. Don't ask us questions about what we've been doing. You do need to appreciate the things we've been doing because we need to be boosted up in our self-respect. Pay attention to what we're doing and compliment us, because we're insecure. But when you talk to us, ask us questions about how we *feel* about the things we're doing. Do you understand what I'm saying? It's a subtle difference, but asking us about our feelings can help us understand ourselves better.

Guys, when the girls ask you questions about how you feel, open up. Tell them how you feel. Don't just respond with the things you're doing. Guys, we need to learn how to share our feelings. We need to learn how to open up and share our feelings, not only with the girls that talk to us, but with one another. That way our relationships will grow deeper and stronger.

Girls, when you ask us those questions and we give you a lousy answer, and we grunt and we groan and we hem and we haw, be patient with us. Ask us another question about how we feel. It's going to take some time because we have a lot to learn.

Last but not least—how do we relate to each other sexually? I guess for you and for me, one of the areas that trips us up more than any other area, is our sexual relationships. You can hardly relate to a girl, if you're a guy, without it almost being a sexual encounter because our sexual feelings are so tied up with who we are.

I'm coming with a presupposition that God's design for sexual intercourse is for it to be kept in a committed marriage relationship. That is so hard to do. It's so hard to follow God in this area of our sexual desires and feelings. So, we need to talk about him as we help each other learn how to relate to the opposite sex.

Now, I don't want to sound stereotypical, but from my observations, I really believe that guys are turned on primarily through the "eye-gate," through what they see. The people in media have really picked up on that. Take a look at the movies and the magazines. They know that guys are stimulated by what they see, the things that come through the "eye-gate." The movies cater to that, the magazines cater to that, whether they be typical magazines that you and I read, or whether they be pornographic magazines.

Do you know something, girls? Guys are not discriminating. When they're walking down the street or when they're at the beach, they don't necessarily have to know the two girls in the bikinis who are walking by to say, "Oo-la-la, take a look at that!" It doesn't really matter. They don't have to have a personal relationship with the person who's turning them on.

Girls, on the other hand, are discriminating. I think girls need and want that relationship with a guy. For a guy, a sexual relationship can be primarily physical. If it feels good, you do it. For a girl, that sexual relationship is really an emotional experience. To a great extent, girls, as a general rule, are primarily stimulated and turned on through the touch of compassion and understanding.

Girls, do you know that the clothes you wear communicate very strongly with us guys who are visually oriented? Now, you may not intend that at all. You've heard of non-verbal communication. That's the communication that we give to one another without saying a word, through our facial expressions, our hands, our posture, and the clothes that we wear. These all say something about us. Girls, you need to know that the things that you wear can be very, very stimulating to a guy sexually. You may not intend to give that kind of a statement, but you need to know that many times that comes across. So think about what you're trying to say with your clothes.

Guys, we need to be careful about that casual touch, a pat here and there, or a squeeze or a back rub. We may not necessarily mean anything by it, but you need to take a look at what that communicates to the girls who are in your youth group or the girls who are in your school. What are you trying to say with that particular touch?

Now I want to hear from you, but you need to help me out and do this quickly. I want the girls to talk to girls and the guys to talk to guys. I want you to move into small groups—say about ____ people in each.

I want you guys to talk about some things that you'd like to say to the girls. Things you'd like the girls to know about you guys. And girls, I'd like you in your groups to think of some of the things that you'd like the guys to know about you girls. Someone in each group write all your ideas down, and later I'll ask a couple of you to read off your answers so we can learn from one another. You have three minutes, so go fast.

We'll start with the girls. Give me one or two of your best. Guys, these girls are speaking to you from their hearts. This is what they want you to know.

Sample responses:

- We want the guys to know that not all girls are airheads.
- Girls want you to know that you can trust them with your feelings.
- We girls want to be friends with guys without them thinking we're after them romantically.
- We want guys to know that girls don't always have to have some great physical shape.
- Girls get hurt really easily; please be sensitive to that.
- Girls want to be respected.
- Little things make us happy, like smiles.

I know you have a lot more, girls. I want to turn it over to the guys. Guys, what are some things you would like the girls to know about you?

Sample responses:

- We want girls to know that sex is not the only thing we think about. Fifty-nine seconds out of a minute we think about sex. One second of a minute we think about construction.
- Look on the inside, not just on the outside. Sometimes we have a lot of things to offer.
- We have feelings. Be patient with us.

I know you have a lot more that you want to say. Say those things to one another before this day is over. As we sum this up, Let me read you a helpful Scripture that we can apply to our relationships. It comes out of a familiar passage, but I want you to listen as I read, thinking about the relationships that you are in right now with your girlfriend or your boyfriend. Think about the friends that you have at school.

Philippians, chapter two, "If you have any encouragement from being united with Christ, if any comfort from his love, if any fellowship with the Spirit, if any tenderness and compassion, then make my joy complete by being like-minded, having the same love, being one in spirit and purpose. Do nothing out of selfish ambition or vain conceit. . . ." It is so easy for us to fight and to think that guys are better than girls or girls are better than guys. But listen to what the rest of the passage says: ". . . in humility consider others better than yourselves. Each of you should look not only to your own interests, but also to the interests of others. Your attitude should be the same as that of Christ Jesus."

Friends, we need to care for one another. Let's not use each other. And do you know what else we need to do? We need, as girls and guys, to learn how to talk to one another. We need to verbalize the things we've said to one another in the last few minutes, because we don't know how to talk!

We drive to a movie, watch the movie, then we park and we make out. Or we just grunt and groan. We have forgotten how to really talk to one another and communicate with each other. Work at listening to the things your friends say. Work even harder at listening to the things that they don't say, but they really want you to know.

Find new ways of saying some things. We have the habit of getting into ruts with our relationships. Maybe you want to give a note to a friend to express something, or write your friend a poem. Be creative in learning how to say something in new, different, and fun ways.

Friends, if you make a commitment to someone else, then follow through with what you've said. Don't make empty promises about calling someone or doing something with a friend. If you say you're going to do something, then follow through.

This is the last thing I want to leave with you. Girls and guys, we need to go easy on the sexual pressure. We need to listen to what these girls said, and just be friends sometimes. We need to rediscover what it is to have a friend who is a girl and not make it a girlfriend-type of relationship. We need to learn to relax with one another and have fun with each other without thinking about the sexual pressure to prove ourselves.

In Christ, let's learn how to be friends, how to have fun, and how to encourage one another in our relationships.

How to Live With Yourself and Like It

1 Corinthians 6:20

Greg McKinnon

This talk addresses the familiar problem of self-image. Greg offers some workable suggestions for kids as they deal with this issue.
For outline, see page 210.

In the years that I have worked with youth, I have discovered that a large number of young people don't like themselves. As I travel around and talk with teenagers everywhere, I hear them all saying the same things. "I don't like the way I look." "I wish I were like Robert, everybody likes him." Or, "I wish I were as talented as Kate." Today we are going to learn how to live with ourselves and like it. Now for a lot of us that is hard to do, because we wake up in the morning and we look in the mirror and we don't like what we see—we would like to trade in that old mug on a new one. Then in the afternoon we get the results back from an achievement test that we've taken and we don't like what it tells us about our abilities. That night we ask somebody out for a date and they turn us down. Every day things happen that make us not like—or even hate—ourselves.

So today we want to get some handles on how we can learn to live with ourselves and like it.

Let's begin by looking at four different people. Now, they all have one thing in common—they don't like themselves. But they respond to that dislike in totally different ways. They are all people whom I have met over the years, and as you hear their names and I describe them, I believe you will realize that you've met them too.

The first person is Peter Pride. Peter responds to his poor self image by puffing himself up. He comes across as thinking that he is better than other people. You can recognize him from 100 yards, just by his walk. You know, that prideful strut—his nose so far up in the air that it is a miracle he doesn't get nose-bleed from the high altitude. We all know people like that. They are in our school, our church, our family, or they might be sitting next to us right now. Or maybe we saw them this morning, when we looked in the mirror.

Peter comes across as being cool, confident, and cocky. A lot of us are intimidated by people like that, because they seem so sure of themselves. But do you know what's funny? People who come across like this usually don't like themselves. The outward confidence is just a front, a mask they wear to cover up for their real insecurity.

Peter Pride makes up for his insecurity by developing his ability to cut other people down. He becomes the Cut-down King. He's the one that just waits for somebody to say something dumb or embarrassing, so that he can make it worse by saying something like, "If your brains were dynamite, you wouldn't have enough to blow your nose." The reason he does that is to make himself feel better—to give himself a sense of power. If he really liked himself, he would be much more accepting and considerate of other people.

The second person that I have run into is Pitiful Pam. Pitiful Pam responds to not liking herself in just the opposite way of Peter Pride. Rather than puffing herself up, she puts herself down.

A lot of times, she says things just to fish for compliments. When she says, "Oh, I'm just so dumb. I can't do anything right," she doesn't want someone to agree with her and say, "Yes, Pam, you really are dumb. You are about the dumbest person that I've ever seen." No, that's not what she wants at all. What she wants somebody to say is, "Hey Pam, don't say that, you're not dumb at all."

Because people like Pitiful Pam have such a low opinion of themselves, they need the approval of other people in order to feel good about themselves. Thus they become slaves to other people's opinions. But this poses one major problem—how do you please everybody? You see, everybody has a different opinion of what a person ought to be like. So Pitiful Pams turn into chameleons (those lizards that change colors in order to blend in and not be noticed). They wear different masks around different groups of people.

People like this lose all their individuality. The crowds' morals and standards and actions become their morals and standards and actions. They are simply a clone of the crowd.

Girls who have this put-down syndrome and need other people's approval in order to feel good about themselves are in a dangerous situation, because oftentimes they will give in to a guy sexually, simply to be accepted by him. Unfortunately, once they have given in, they feel even worse about themselves. It is a vicious cycle that never ends. And if they are eventually rejected by someone that they have done everything to be accepted by, then they are completely crushed.

That's Pitiful Pam. Always putting herself down, always needing other people's approval in order to feel good about herself.

The third person that I've met is Persistent Priscilla. Priscilla responds to her insecurity by pushing herself. She sees her self-worth in what she accomplishes. People like Priscilla give 100%, trying to achieve at athletics, academics, drama, music, or anything else.

The positive results that come from pushing ourselves are obvious: better grades, a scholarship, or a good job. But there are also some negative results that are not always obvious.

Often a person like this withdraws completely from other people. They live in their own little world. All they live for is the one area in which they feel a sense of achievement. As they grow older, they can become workaholics and, because their self-worth is tied to how they perform at work, they put their job before their family, their friends, and even their own health. People like this tend to become perfectionists. They are never satisfied with anything they do, and usually not with anything anybody else does, either.

The frightening thing is that if they eventually fail at the one thing they've been striving for—they are cut from the team, they don't make straight A's, they then don't get the lead in the play, they aren't first chair in the band—then they can be totally devastated.

The fourth person that I've met is Painful Paul. Painful Paul punishes himself. He feels like it's his fault that he doesn't perform as well as other people. He feels like it is his fault that he doesn't look as good as other people. He feels like it's his fault that he isn't as important as other people. And since it is his fault, who does he punish? Himself!

There are a lot of different ways a person like Paul might consciously or unconsciously punish himself. He might do it through alcohol or drug abuse. He has so little self-regard, and he blames himself so much, that he destroys himself little by little. Others like Paul may punish themselves simply through neglect, by not eating right, sleeping right, or exercising. They may overeat or undereat—which in the extreme cases can develop into anorexia or bulimia. But then others go even further. They are so down on themselves that they resort to suicide. Of course, this is the most tragic form of self-punishment because of its finality.

I got a call one day that a girl in my youth group (we'll call her Sally) was in the hospital. When I got to the hospital, I found out that she had tried to commit suicide. And she had intended to succeed. Before she slit both wrists, she went to her mother's medicine cabinet and took a large overdose of some drugs. She was found eight hours later in a blood-soaked bed. But she was lucky. She didn't die. What saved her were the drugs that she took. They slowed down her body so much that it was able to survive the massive blood loss.

As I talked with Sally, she told me that the night before, her boyfriend had broken up with her, and she immediately went home and tried to commit suicide. She thought it was her fault he had rejected her. She thought she had failed, so she was punishing herself.

Another girl, we'll call her Fran, developed an advanced case of anorexia. Her family had known for some time that she had a problem, but they never paid too much attention to it until she was found lying beside the road one day, almost dead. Fran was punishing herself because she thought that it was her fault that she couldn't measure up to her overachieving family's high standards of perfection.

As you can see, all four of these people didn't like themselves, but they all responded in different ways.

Peter Pride puffed himself up. He came across as thinking that he was better than other people.

Pitiful Pam put herself down. She needed other people's approval in order to feel good about herself.

Persistent Priscilla pushed herself. The way she felt about herself was tied up with her achievements.

Painful Paul punished himself. He felt like it was his fault he didn't measure up to everyone else.

What if you realize that you are like one of these four, that you don't like yourself? What can you do to learn to live with yourself and like it?

Let's look at some things.

The first thing we need to do is realize that God created us unique. He didn't cut us out with a cookie cutter, run us off on a copy machine, or pick us off the shelf at a local department store.

A lot of times we look at ourselves as worthless because we are always comparing ourselves to other people. It's an American pastime. And the way we compare ourselves is by asking questions. We ask things like, "How do I look?"

I would like for everybody to stop right now and rate how you feel about your looks on a scale of one to ten. Without asking one person here to tell me what you rated yourself, I can tell you that the overall average this group gave itself was pretty low. Now that's not because I'm looking at you and think that you're a pretty ugly group. Not at all! The reason I can be so sure that the average would be low, is because I know that of all the students who were surveyed, 80% said they didn't like the way they looked.

I can relate to that. The thing that I didn't like about my looks was always my height. I was the shortest kid in my class every year from the first grade right through the tenth grade. My parents never had a hard time finding me when I was in the marching band. They just looked out across the football field for the saxophone player whose saxophone was dragging on the ground.

Then, when I was in the tenth grade, I grew five inches in one year. And guess what? As my height went up, so did the way I felt about myself.

I was born and reared in L.A. Contrary to popular opinion, that doesn't stand for Los Angeles. It stands for Lower Alabama. I lived in Enterprise, Alabama, where I wrote jingles for a station called, of all things, WIRB. Once a week, WIRB had what they called "The Swap Shop of the Air." People would call in with items that they wanted to sell, and others would call in with items that they were looking for.

I was wondering the other day what it would be like if we had a body parts swap shop on the air. I don't think you would be able to get a call through. The lines would be busier than they are on the last day of all those big radio contests when they are giving away the car, or the $10,000 cash prize, or the big trip,

because so many people would be trying to call in to get rid of their nose, feet, hair, or complexion. Other people would be trying to get three or four extra inches of height in exchange for ten or twelve extra pounds. And then others would be trying to make even swaps. They would be offering curly hair for straight hair, blonde for brunette, some athletic ability for a little academic ability.

But there is a major problem that we run into when we begin to compare the way we look with the way that other people look. Whom will we compare ourselves to? There *is* no such thing as an outwardly-perfect appearance that everyone should look like. Standards are always changing. Marilyn Monroe was, in past years, a sex symbol. But I was reading a *People* magazine that said if she were to show up in Hollywood today, looking just as she did then, she wouldn't get past the front gate.

Think about the last time you sat around watching the Miss America pageant with a group of people. If your friends are like my friends, everybody in the group always has a different opinion of who should win. One lady walks out on stage and somebody gasps for breath and says, "How did she get into the contest?" And then, when the winner is announced, you can hear all the comments: "Oh, I just can't believe it. It must have been a payoff." The lady who is judged by some to be the most beautiful in the country is not even attractive to others.

So, as we ask, "How do I look?" we won't get a straight answer, because the standard will always be changing.

A second question we ask as we compare ourselves to other people is, "How do I do?" In other words, we want to know how our performance measures up.

In the years that I have worked with young people, I have been to a lot of cheerleader tryouts. But every time I go, I hate it! I mean, I love to be there to support the girls I know who are trying out, but I hate it because of all the girls who don't make it.

To me, it is so cruel the way they announce the winners. All the contestants are sitting in the stands in neat little rows with their numbers on. The cheerleading sponsor begins to call out the numbers. Number 21. Then some girl jumps up and screams, "Oh, I just can't believe it," as she runs down to the front. Then number 39, number 3, and so on down the list. But the closer they get to the end of the list the sicker all the girls in the stands begin to feel, because they know that their chances are getting slimmer and slimmer. Then finally the last number is called and all the new cheerleaders rush to the center of the gym where they are showered with attention. Meanwhile, all the other girls

fight to hold in the tears until they can get home alone and let it all out.

Those girls feel bad because their performance didn't measure up. The same thing often happens when we get our report cards, because they remind us of how we perform in comparison to other people. We not only don't like our mom and dad to see them, but we also don't want to face our friends when they say, "Hey, what did you make in algebra, or history, or geometry, or chemistry?" Because we know that we probably didn't measure up in that area of performance.

A third question we ask as we compare ourselves to other people is, "How important am I?" We all have our own criteria for deciding whether or not someone is important. Like, how much money they have, what kind of car they drive, where they live in town, where their family goes on vacation, and what their parents do for a living. Whatever our criteria for determining importance, it is hard to feel good about ourselves if we don't feel we measure up.

But if, instead of comparing our looks, performance, and importance to other people, we can realize that God made us unique for a special purpose, then we will like who we are a whole lot more.

Listen to what the Bible tells us in Ephesians 2:10: "For we are God's workmanship, created in Christ Jesus to do good works, which God prepared in advance for us to do."

From this verse we can see two things. One—God made us, we are his handiwork. We are just like he wanted us to be. We are his original. We are special because, as one writer put it, "God don't make no junk."

Two, he made us for a special purpose. The reason that many of us feel bad about ourselves is because we are trying to find our place in the world's puzzle instead of in God's puzzle. I've got an almost-three-year-old son, Wesley. And when Wesley tries to put together a puzzle, especially a "big-people" puzzle, he isn't exactly the most patient person in the world. If he tries a piece and it doesn't fit, he tries to *make* it fit. The only problem is, if it wasn't made to go there, it gets bent and scratched in the process.

In the same way, when we try to find our place according to the world's standards rather than God's standards, we get bent and scratched and hurt. But when we realize that God made us for a special purpose, then we can give ourselves back to him and let him place us in the exact spot we were made to go. Then we will find purpose and meaning in life.

Once we realize that we are special we can begin to develop the strengths that we do have rather than concentrating on our weaknesses. Now I know

what some of you are saying—"But I don't have any strengths." I don't buy that. One of my youth groups developed some rules to promote fellowship in the group. One of the rules went like this: "If you can't say something good about someone, get to know them better." When we get to know people well enough, we will discover that they all have good characteristics.

In the same way, the reason you and I feel like we don't have any strengths is because we have gotten into the habit of looking at the bad rather than the good. If we can turn that around and begin to look for our strengths, we'll all discover that we have them. Then God will use those strengths—if we'll let him.

What can you do this week to begin to develop the strengths and talents that you have? Decide right now that you will begin working on your talents today!

The second step in learning to live with yourself and like it is to realize that you are very special to God. So many people see themselves as worthless, but if we can just realize that God not only created us but claimed us for his own, then we won't think of ourselves as worthless anymore. 1 Corinthians 6:19–20 say, "You are not your own; you were bought at a price. Therefore honor God with your body."

There once was a little boy who loved boats, and who was also very good with his hands. One day he decided that he was going to make a boat for himself. He began working on it every spare minute that he had. When he finished it, it was perfect in every detail. His favorite pastime was sailing his little boat. He would take it down to the large lake near his house and sail it along the shore.

One day while he was sailing the boat, the wind began to pick up. He ran to get the boat before the wind pushed it beyond him. He was too late. Even though he frantically pulled off his shoes and splashed out into the water, he still couldn't reach it. All this time the wind was getting stronger and stronger. He ran back to the house to get his father to help. But when his father returned with him, the boat was nowhere in sight. The little boy, heartbroken, went home with his father.

All the little boy seemed to do after that was mope around. One day he was slowly walking home from school when he glanced up into a pawn shop window. There was his boat! He went into the pawn shop shouting, "That's my boat, that's my boat!" The owner of the pawn shop looked at him and said, "No, that's my boat. If you want it you will have to buy it." The boy looked at the price tag. It was extremely high, because it was such a great little boat. He didn't know what to do. He went home and began to think of ways to raise money.

He went all around the neighborhood cutting grass, raking leaves, washing cars, and doing anything else anyone would hire him to do. Each week he would count his money. Finally, after several weeks, he had earned enough money to buy the little boat.

He grabbed the piggy bank with his money in it and ran to the pawn shop. He ran into the shop and put the piggy bank on the counter so hard that it broke open. Then he told the pawn shop owner that he had come to buy his boat. The owner counted the money to make sure it was all there. He went over to the shelf and got the boat and handed it to the little boy. Then he heard the little boy say as he walked out the door, "Little boat, you're mine twice. First I made you, now I bought you."

That's the way it is with God. First he made us just like he wanted us, and then when we went our own way, he bought us back.

If you and I can ever grasp the fact that we are worth so much to God that he was willing to pay the ultimate price, the death of his Son on the cross, in order to claim us as his own, then we will never again think of ourselves as worthless or unlovable.

Try this. In the morning when you wake up, tell yourself you are a person of great value, because God was willing to give his own Son in order to claim you as his own.

The third step in learning to live

with yourself and to like it is to realize that God can cleanse you. Not only did he create you and claim you, but if you'll let him, he can also cleanse you.

If you are alive, if you have blood flowing through your veins, if you are breathing, then you have felt guilt. It can come from wrong things you have done or because of things you've failed to do. It could be because you feel you have failed to live up to other people's expectations for your life. It could be deserved or undeserved. But wherever it comes from, it is difficult to feel good about yourself when you are carrying around a load of guilt.

But, luckily for each of us, God—through Jesus Christ—has a cure for guilt. When Jesus came to this earth, he paid the debt for our sins. The Bible tells us in Isaiah 1:18 that "though your sins are like scarlet, they shall be as white as snow; though they are red as crimson, they shall be like wool." In other words, no matter how guilty we feel, God offers us forgiveness. We have to believe that Christ paid the debt and respond in faith by letting God have control of our lives. Christ does the rest.

How do you feel about yourself today? Good? Or, not so good? If you don't like yourself, for whatever reason, there are three things that you need to do.

First of all, you need to stop trying to fit into the world's mold and realize that you were created in God's special mold. There is no one in the world who has the same strengths and abilities that you have. You're unique. But it is only when you let God use you for the purpose that you were created that you can use all your strengths and talents—and therefore, feel good about yourself.

Secondly, you need to believe that you are a person of great worth because God created you. He claimed you as his own. The cost he had to pay was the death of his own Son. But you were worth that much to him. If you are worth that much to God, you should never think of yourself as worthless again.

Thirdly, you need to let God cleanse you so you won't have to continue carrying around a heavy load of guilt. No matter how guilty you feel, God can cleanse you.

Won't you start today, at this very moment, to see yourself through God's eyes? Won't you let God cleanse you from your guilt and misgivings about yourself? Won't you accept yourself as a person of worth just because God made you and claimed you for his own? Won't you thank him for the strengths and abilities he has given uniquely to you? Let's take a few moments right now and offer ourselves, just the way we are, to God. Let's pray together.

Choose Your Own Adventure, Part One

Genesis 12:1–4; 13:8–16

Duffy Robbins

This is part one of a three-part series on making good decisions. It's a talk that works with both Christian and non-Christian kids, although it may be a bit heavy for non-church kids.

This talk begins by using a book entitled *The Dragons' Den* by Richard Brightfield (New York: Bantam Books, 1984). This book is volume thirty-three in a series of books called "Choose Your Own Adventure." The genius of these little books is that the reader actually *participates* in the plot by making decisions throughout the book, and then by turning to a previously selected page depending on which decision was made.

As the cover of the book states, "You're the star of the story! Choose from 22 possible endings." There are probably several books in the Choose Your Own Adventure series that will work for this talk. In using *The Dragons' Den*, or any of the others in the series, it's probably wise to begin near the end of the book so the audience is allowed to collectively make about four decisions.

Feel free to rewrite sentences to suit your purposes. For example, the hero of *The Dragons' Den* finally escapes by swimming downstream to the way out of the darkness. When I first gave this talk, I made the hero swim upstream to get out of the darkness because that more closely illustrates the challenge of the Christian life.

Begin your talk by introducing the book and the concept by which the plot develops. Have fun with this—ham it up! Tell the kids, "*You're* the star of the story! Choose your own adventure . . ." The more melodramatic you can be, the more fun it will be. Before you begin reading, tell them that you will pause at the "decision points" at the bottom of each page, where you will allow them to choose their own adventure. Encourage them to choose by their applause, their cheers, or shouts of "Go for it!" Be sure to read with lots of expression—your enthusiasm will make or break this.

> When you have read the story and determined whether your group has survived or been massacred by little dwarfs with arrows, you are ready to move on into your talk.
>
> *For outline, see page 213.*

One of the best things about reading a book like this one is that if you don't like the ending, you can just go back and make a decision that leads to a different ending. But that's not all I like about these little books. I also like them because while you read books like this your decisions *count*. You're going to live or you're going to die, and basically, since you're the star of the story, everything hinges on the decisions you make.

Real life hinges on decision-making too. But the problem with real life is that when you make bad decisions, you can't always go back and start the story over again. You have to live with your decisions, the good ones *and* the bad ones. As the stories of each our lives unfold, we will look back and see what we can't always see now: that the decisions we make now *do* count. Just like in the book, the choices you make now will have a key effect on the outcome of the story. That's why we need to know how to make good decisions.

It's amazing how many decisions and choices we're forced to deal with in today's culture. We are a culture barraged by options. You probably don't even realize how many small decisions you've made just since this day began. What time will I get up? Or, for some of you, will I decide to get up? What clothes will I wear? How will I fix my hair? Which cereal will I choose from my Kelloggs Snack Pack? Everytime you turn around, you're making a decision.

One supermarket chain did research that shows that when we are in a grocery store, we pass by six to ten items every second. Kind of makes you want to stop and pray before you walk into Kroger's. And that's not all—listen to this bit of trivia. In May of 1985—in that one month alone—there were 235 new items introduced in the market. Just when you thought you knew which flavor you liked, they add six more! That number—235 new items—is the highest number of new products introduced in any one month for twenty-one years! (By the way, you might be interested in knowing that among these 235 new products was a worm-shaped version of gummy-bears. I know that's important to a lot of you. Another hot item introduced that month was the all-new graffitti fingernail writer. Exciting, eh?)

It's just amazing how many choices face us each day. You go to buy ice cream, and Baskin-Robbins flaunts over 100 flavors. You go to buy lipstick and find that Revlon has expanded their line of lipstick to over sixty different shades. Someone has found that just the menu options in a Bo-Jangles Fried Chicken fast food restaurant offer something like 480 possible combinations. You may not believe this, but there are actually twenty-three different flavors of Nine Lives cat food.

Let's face it. Decisions are the stuff of everyday life. Some are simple, and some are not so simple. It's the *non-simple* decisions that get kind of scary. And it's those decisions—the *big* ones—that most of you will be making in the next five years. Those decisions will literally shape the rest of your life. You can almost count on it.

Most of you in this room will have to make at least three critical, life-shaping decisions. Number one, you're going to have to choose, or realize that you've already chosen, a MASTER. You are going to have to recognize who or what is the most important person in your life. You're going to have to come to grips with who or what you want to live for. That will be your MASTER.

Secondly, you will need to decide your MISSION in life. What are you going to do? Our society expects you to choose a course after high school. Will you go to college, go into the service, go

on welfare, go to Hollywood? What are you going to do with your life? What will be your MISSION in life?

Thirdly, most of you, in the next five years, are going to make some decisions about a MATE. You're going to choose a marriage partner. I know that's hard to believe now, but statistically, those are the facts.

Those are some pretty key decisions. A bad choice in any one of those areas is going to make your story very different from what it might have been— it will lead to a very different ending. That's a scary fact, but that's life. And you can't avoid those decisions. You will be responsible for making them, and you will be the one who has to live with the consequences. As the book says, "You're the star of the story. Choose your own adventure."

That's when you start to give serious thought to how you make your decisions. Some people use the standard "close your eyes and pick" method. It has its advantages, but I wouldn't recommend it for choosing a mate. Others use the more scientific and logical "eeny meeny miney mo" approach. But that approach has its flaws too.

We're going to look at two different models of decision-making: one demonstrated by a seventy-five-year-old man named Abram, a name later changed to Abraham; another demonstrated by his nephew, Lot. One man made his decisions by faith. Another made his decisions by sight. We will see in their lives two totally different styles of decision-making—and we will see that each man's choices gave him a completely different story, with very different endings. For part one of our study in decision-making, let's read two passages in the Old Testament, Genesis 12:1–4 and Genesis 13:8–16.

(Read the texts.)

In Genesis 12:1, Abraham was faced with an extremely difficult decision. "The LORD had said to Abram, 'Leave your country, your people and your father's household and go to the land I will show you. . . .'" It was pretty clear cut—God had given Abraham a call to move. He didn't say where or why; he just called him to go. And for Abraham, the decision boiled down to one of two options: a "Go" or a "No."

This is where we see the first step in making good choices: Abraham made a firm *decision of allegiance*. What does that mean? Well, remember in elementary school how you began each new day with the pledge of allegiance to the flag? I'll never forget those times when I was chosen to lead the entire second grade class in the pledge. I got to go up to the front and lead those guys, and I felt like a real stud.

However, I didn't know the pledge real well. I would say with a completely straight face and somber tone, "I pledge legions to the flag of the ninety states of America, and to the Republicans for which it stands. One nation on guard, invisible (you cannot see it) . . ." Even though I didn't understand that pledge, I was still pledging allegiance, loyalty, and faithfulness. I was saying that I would support that nation and stand ready to serve it if needed. With that pledge I was making a decision of allegiance. That is where decisions begin.

What so many of us don't realize is that throughout the day, we each live out our own conscious and unconscious pledges of allegiance. When you use a certain kind of language, you are making a sort of pledge of allegiance. When you dress a certain way, it betrays a certain pledge of allegiance. The music you listen to, the friends you choose, the homework you do, the calories you count—all of these say something about little conscious and unconscious pledges of allegiance that you've made. That's why it's so important for us to consider what ultimate decisions of allegiance we have made.

If you look at Abraham's life, you see right away that his choices were shaped by a firm decision of allegiance to God. In verse one, God said, "Go." In verse four, "Abraham went." Every page of Abraham's story is affected by that choice to align himself with God.

And that was no wishy-washy decision. It was a solid commitment, and basically, it meant two things. Number one, Abraham's decision of allegiance to God meant he was willing to chuck some former allegiances. Go back and look at verse one: "Leave your country, your people and your father's household . . ." What an awesome request— to leave behind the old habits, the old haunts, and the old hopes to step out by faith and follow God.

That's what it may come down to for some of us. This may not be easy for you to hear, but you need to realize that sometimes saying "yes" to new directions from God means saying "no" to some of the old directions we've been choosing for ourselves.

Marriage is like that. I'll never forget the day I married Maggie (my wife). When the music began, she looked beautiful walking down the aisle in her gorgeous purple and polka dot gown— not really. But as she walked the aisle in that gorgeous white gown, I have to admit—maybe I'm the mushy type—but tears just began to roll down my cheeks . . . as I began to think of all the women that were going to miss out. Because I knew: From that day on, my "yes" to Maggie, at least in some ways, meant a "no" to any person who was not Maggie. I was making a pledge of allegiance.

James talks about that kind of clear decision (James 1:7–8) when he writes that "a double-minded man, unstable in all his ways, will receive nothing from the Lord." Some time ago, I read a newspaper article published by United Press International in which you get a good picture of the problem of double-mindedness:

Responding to an ad for a talented snake to appear in a movie, a pet shop owner, Lou Russo, showed up at auditions with his two-headed Florida pine snake, Gertrude. The creature is two separate snakes down to the stomach, where they join. "The two heads get along fine until feeding time," he said. "Then I have to keep them separated because the one that is not being fed will attack the one that is." At times, the two heads fight over which way to slither, he said. The snake was immediately hired. Someone asked Russo whether he thought the snake wanted to become an actor. And Russo answered with a smile, "Well, yes . . . and no."

What James helps us to understand is that a real decision of allegiance is not one that says "yes . . . and no." That kind of indecision makes for an unhappy snake and some messed up choices. Ultimately, like Gertrude, we must decide: Whither shall we slither? We have to understand that, at times, our "yes" to God is going to lead us to some difficult "no's."

We also need to see that Abraham's decision of allegiance was a "go for broke" decision. Abraham was banking everything on God. Look back at verses 2 and 3: "Go to the land I will show you, [and] I will make you into a great nation and I will bless you; I will make your name great, and you will be a blessing. I will bless those who bless you, and whoever curses you I will curse. . . ." You can tell just by hearing that one passage that Abraham had absolutely no guarantees outside of God himself. "I will show you . . ." "I will make of you a great nation . . ." "I will bless you . . ." Over and over again, "I will," "I will," "I will . . ." Abraham had no Plan B. For Abraham, it was God or nothing.

It all hinged on God, and there was no backup strategy. That's a *real* decision of allegiance. That's the kind of decision of allegiance that you make when you jump out of an airplane at 18,000 feet and hang your body on a parachute. That's the kind of decision that John and James made in Matthew 4 when Jesus called them and they left their nets, their boat, and their father to follow Christ. That's the kind of decision you see in Matthew 9 when Matthew left his job at the tax collector's desk and followed Christ.

It's tough to make that kind of decision, isn't it? . . . when you have to say good-bye to all the old securities, and all the old certainties, and follow Christ? That means that you have to say no to some of your habits, part of an old life-style, or maybe even an important relationship. That one decision of allegiance affects every other decision you make.

Abraham's nephew, Lot, never made that kind of "go for broke" decision for God. He made a half-baked commitment, just tagging along after Abraham until something better came along. In verse 4, the Scripture reads, "So Abram left, as the Lord had told him; and Lot went with him." See what's happening? Abraham was following the Lord. But Lot was just following Abraham.

This is the kind of halfhearted decision of allegiance that a lot of us make. Our parents follow the Lord, and we're just following our parents. Or, our current group of friends is following the Lord, and we're just following our friends. It's not a decision to follow Christ. It's more of a decision to tag along. And that kind of decision just won't stand the test of time. As soon as something better comes along, we're history.

That lack of allegiance usually shows up sooner or later. For Lot, it happened in chapter 13 when both Lot and Abraham faced a problem. Both of these guys had moved their families to an area called the Negev, and things were going pretty well. God had prospered their families just as he had promised. But as time went on, their property had increased so much that there wasn't enough room for both of them on the same land. Abraham's herdsmen kept feuding with Lot's herdsmen because they were getting crowded in the grazing space. Abraham and Lot had a tough decision to make.

They agreed that the only reasonable thing to do would be for them to split up, Abe and all of his kinsmen and servants going one way, and Lot with all of his family and servants going the other. So in verse eight, Abraham made an incredibly generous offer. Standing high above the Jordan River Valley, he told Lot to take first choice of the land he wished to settle, and Abraham would take the land left over. Abraham says in verse nine, "If you go to the left, I'll go to the right; if you go to the right, I'll go to the left."

This is a perfect example of Abraham's evident decision of allegiance. After all, he had already decided to bank everything on God, and God had already promised to bless Abraham, so he knew he couldn't lose in the deal. Abraham chose not to choose. He made his decision by faith.

But watch Lot in action. In verse ten, "Lot looked up," and in verse eleven we read, "Lot chose for himself the whole plain of the Jordan." He saw what he thought was the best land, and he snapped it up for himself. No generosity. No faith. Just selfishness. As the Scripture puts it, "Lot chose for himself." Lot wasn't banking on anyone else, or looking out for anyone else. He was looking out for old "numero uno." Funny how our real decisions of allegiance show themselves, isn't it?

When the heat is on, you can tell who is really lord of our lives—God or ourselves. Lot had only one loyalty, one allegiance, and that was to himself. When the deal went down, what mattered was what looked good to him, what felt good to him, what seemed good to him. That's what the Bible calls sin. As Isaiah puts it in chapter fifty-three: "Each of us has turned to his own way."

Ironically, Lot's decision leads to all kinds of hassles and hurts and heartbreak later on. He couldn't have known it that day up on the mountaintop when he was riding high. Nobody would have guessed it then, but before Lot's story ended, he would lose all his property, he would be kidnapped by an enemy king, and his wife would lose her life.

Not a happy ending, was it? And to think it all started with a wrong decision of allegiance. But then, that's the way the story works, isn't it? The choices you make now determine what choices and options you face later on. Sometimes, when you don't even realize it, today's choices shape the way the whole story ends. That's why it's so important now to make good decisions. We can start doing that by making a clear and firm decision of allegiance to God. Maybe that is where some of you need to begin right now. It's up to you. You're the star of the story. Choose your own adventure.

Choose Your Own Adventure, Part Two

Genesis 13:8–16; 19:15–30

Duffy Robbins

> This talk is part two in a three-part series on how to make wise choices and sound decisions. It is a talk in which the two decision-making styles of Abraham and his nephew, Lot, are compared and contrasted. Again, this is a talk that will be of use to both Christian and non-Christian kids, but if it's used in a context where there are a lot of non-churched kids, the speaker should expect to give some additional background and explanation to the Bible stories.
>
> *For outline, see page 216.*

The newspapers in Albany, New York carried an interesting story some time back. The headline read: "Kissing Booth Volunteer Found to Have Hepatitis." The article, published by Associated Press, was fascinating:

> A volunteer at a M*A*S*H* Bash kissing booth has been found to have hepatitis, and anyone who bought $1 kisses from her should be injected against the disease, health officials say.
>
> The woman volunteered at a February 28 party honoring the last M*A*S*H* television episode. More than 700 people attended the party here, which also was a benefit for the March of Dimes. The bash raised about $10,000.

Albany County Health commissioner Dr. William Grattan said anyone who bought a kiss from the woman should visit a doctor or go to the health department clinic. The clinic charges $5 per injection. The kissing booth made $70, which means up to seventy people visited it. Grattan would not release the name of the woman.

You know, one of the toughest things about making good choices is that things are not always as they seem. You see something that looks like a great deal, fun, harmless, for a good cause, very appealing, and you walk away from the thing with a potentially fatal disease! I mean, who would have suspected it?

I can just imagine this great-looking woman, manning this kissing booth—well, womaning the kissing booth—and from all appearances, this is too good a deal to pass up. She looks great. The kisses only cost a dollar a shot. Who can resist "a buck-er for a pucker"? After all, what's the harm in a little kiss?

But the confusing thing is that something that looks so good can potentially be so deadly. Not only that, but you also find out that to get injected against the disease is going to cost you another five bucks. The advertisement on the booth said, "Kisses. Only $1.00." Now you find out that there is a hidden cost that nobody told you about. What a pain in the neck! Then there's the pain of having to get a shot. That's a real pain in the . . . well, let's just say this will be another kind of "kiss on the cheek."

But that's the problem with making decisions based strictly on appearances. As the sayings go: "Appearances *can* be deceiving" and "Things are not always as they seem." When we make bad decisions because we've been fooled by the way things seem, we often find that what appeared to be so safe, and so harmless, ends up causing a lot of pain, a lot of hassle—and it usually ends up costing a lot more than you would have ever guessed.

Unfortunately, that was a lesson that Lot, the nephew of Abraham, had to learn the hard way. Today, we're going to read his story.

(Read Genesis 13:8–18; 19:1–2, 12–14. This is a lengthy passage so be sure to read it through in advance, and be prepared to read it with expression. If your group is junior-high age, or mostly unchurched kids, you may be wise to paraphrase portions of chapter nineteen.)

Lot and Abraham were relatives. Abraham had been called by God to move to a new land in the wilderness, and in obedience to God, he went. His nephew, Lot, because Abraham was his "gravy train," decided to tag along with his Uncle Abe. Now in chapter thirteen, we find these two men living as neighbors in the land of the Negev. The years had not been easy since they had originally left their homeland, but God had promised Abraham that he and his family would prosper if Abraham were obedient to him, and prospered they had. In fact, both Abraham and Lot had increased their herds and their families and their servants so much that they simply didn't have enough land to live together any longer. The only logical move was to split up.

What we see in Genesis 13:8 is these two men dividing up the land between them. Abraham, in a gesture of remarkable generosity, made this proposal to Lot: "Let's not have any quarreling between you and me, or between your herdsmen and mine, for we are brothers.

Is not the whole land before you? Let's part company. If you go to the left, I'll go to the right; if you go to the right, I'll go to the left."

We said in our last study that Abraham had already made a decision of allegiance to God. He knew when he made this proposal that God was Lord of his life, and that God's promises to him were not going to be short-circuited by any choices that Lot made. So, trusting in God's care, he allowed Lot to have "first dibbies" on the choice of land.

Of course, Lot had made a decision of allegiance too. We all have, you know. And sooner or later, those decisions show themselves in the little and big choices that we make everyday. It shouldn't surprise us then when we read Lot's response to Abraham's gracious proposition (13:10). "Lot looked up and saw that the whole plain of the Jordan was well watered, like the garden of the LORD, like the land of Egypt, toward Zoar."

Lot had one allegiance, one priority—himself. When he saw that the land of the Jordan valley was well watered, fertile, prime farm land, he immediately—without any hint of concern for his uncle—said, "I'll take it."

Watch what's going on here, because Lot is demonstrating a second key to making good decisions: Don't be fooled by the *deceit of appearances*. Go back and look again at verse ten of chapter thirteen. "Lot saw that the whole plain of the Jordan was well watered, *like* the garden of the LORD, *like* the land of Egypt toward Zoar." Underline the word *like*. It's important. Because—remember—things are not always as they seem. Some things that look good can fool us into making decisions that are bad.

The word *like* is easy to miss. It's only a small word, but it packs a wallop, because it gives us a glimpse of the true picture. Look back in verse ten. No sooner are we told that "the land appeared everywhere like the garden of the LORD, like the land of Egypt" in the fertile section along the Nile, than we are told the whole truth: "This was before the LORD destroyed Sodom and Gomorrah." I don't know if those names ring a bell for you, but if we were to read a few chapters ahead in the story, you would see that Sodom and Gomorrah was to be the scene in a few years of a cosmic barbecue!

Lot had selfishly, but unknowingly, chosen to move his homestead into a land so evil and perverse, that in later years, God would totally destroy all its land, its buildings, and its people. No one could have guessed it that day looking from the mountaintop, but Sodom and Gomorrah were only short years away from becoming a massive pile of ashes and ruins. As Lot looked over the valley that day, the beauty of

Sodom and Gomorrah must have taken his breath away. I'm sure he never would have guessed then that the destruction of those two cities would almost take his *life* away. Lot made a serious mistake. He was fooled by the deceit of appearances. He couldn't see sin from the mountaintop, but it was there. As the Scripture puts it just a few verses later in verse thirteen: "Now the men of Sodom were wicked and were sinning greatly against the LORD."

I'm convinced that one of Satan's greatest strategies is disguise, clothing himself as an angel of light, a wolf in sheep's clothing. It catches many people off guard who now face all kinds of hurt and grief, because they chose what looked *like* the real thing, what seemed *like* the real thing—but what turned out to be the *wrong* thing.

It happens in so many ways. We choose what looks like love, and it turns out to be lust. We choose what looks like real Christianity, but it turns out to be just some kind of formal religious game. We choose to pursue a goal or a relationship that seems so worthwhile, and it turns out that when we get there, we just end up getting burned.

One of the reasons making decisions is such risky business is because there are a lot of people in our culture who will lie to you. They've made a decision of allegiance too. And they are out to make lots of money, regardless of what they have to say, what they have to promise, whom they have to exploit.

Do you know why people lie to you? Because our culture is unbelievably gullible. We'll buy anything! And, sad to say, one of the main targets of all this deceit is guys just like you. Teenagers. Why? Simple. Because today's teenagers have money—more discretionary spending money (on the average, almost $20 per week for American teenagers) than any other group of people in our culture. You're buying, and that means a lot of folks are eager to sell.

There's another reason why teenagers make such convenient targets. It's that kids make a lot of judgments based on appearance. Think about it. What do you look for in a date? What do you look for in clothes? What do you look for in cars? If it looks good, you're interested. It's like that line in the song that goes, "It can't be wrong, when it feels so right."

Think about this sometime when you're thumbing through a magazine. Ever wonder why *G.Q.* and *Sports Illustrated* always run these Smirnoff ads with hunky men in dinner jackets and gorgeous women in sequined gowns sipping from crystal glasses? Because they know that it won't sell much vodka if they show a guy with vomit on his shirt passed out on the floor! They know we shop for image, and they're eager to con us into thinking that Smirnoff is part of that image. And you know what's incredible? We believe them!

I saw an ad in the *Philadelphia Inquirer* not long ago. It showed this beautiful woman lying on a bed of satin sheets, wearing a slinky satin nightgown; and down in the corner, there was a picture of a carton of Satin cigarettes. The caption across the top of the picture read "Spoil yourself with Satin."

I couldn't help but marvel at how well these guys were lying to people. Maybe there *is* something glamorous about smoking in bed with a satin nightgown on. But I couldn't keep myself from thinking that a more truthful picture might have shown a woman lying in a hospital bed, wearing a hospital gown, and across the top of the picture would be this caption: "Spoil yourself with cancer."

What's so sad is that a lot of us never look behind the images. We never take time to look beyond the appearances. And that's the very same mistake Eve made in the Garden when God said don't eat of the tree of the knowledge of good and evil (Gen. 2:16–17), "for when you eat of it you will surely die."

Remember what happened? In Genesis three, "When the woman *saw* that the fruit of the tree was good for food and pleasing to the eye, and also desirable for gaining wisdom, she took some and ate it." From the beginning of time, people have been making dumb decisions because they were fooled by the deceit of appearances.

Of course, the question we must ask is, "How can we keep from being fooled?" To answer that, we need to look again at Abraham's style of decision-making. Because if you go back to that meeting on the mountain between Lot and Abraham, you'll see very clearly that Lot chose by sight, but Abraham chose by faith.

Instead of trusting his own judgment, Abraham chose to leave his choices in God's hands. In Genesis 13:14 God says to him, "Lift up your eyes from where you are and look north and south, east and west. All the land that you see I will give to you and your offspring forever." Again in verse sixteen, as if to confirm Abraham's faithfulness, God reminds him that he will bless his descendants and multiply his household.

Okay, but what does this all mean for my decisions? Essentially, it means that when you choose by sight, you are trusting in your own judgment. Sometimes that can be very risky, because things are not always as they seem. Instead of choosing by sight, we need to stake our decisions on the judgment of One who sees what we can't see, who knows what we don't know . . . the God who knows the end from the beginning. That means trusting God. If you want to make the right decision, you will make your decisions based on what God tells us in his Word. "Isn't that a risk too?" you ask. Yes, sort of. But that's what it means to choose by faith. It all goes back to the fact that we have to make a "go for broke" decision for God.

Before you back away from that kind of commitment, consider the risks of making decisions based on your own insight. Turn over a page to Genesis 19:15, where you get a pretty fair picture of the kinds of consequences that we face when we make decisions that *seem* good, but turn out to be *real* bad.

(Read Genesis 19:15–30.)

Any way you cut it, it takes faith. Either faith in yourself, or faith in your God. But be warned: Wise decisions only come when we avoid the deceit of appearances.

An ad in a 1971 California newspaper read: "For sale, $200, Satan, pet South American Boa Constrictor. Educational, interesting, reasonably safe, and [I love this line] loves children of all sizes. Call Al Sanders. . . ." By Friday night of that same week, Mr. Sanders had received nine calls. Strangely enough, most of them came from women.

It was a full nine years later on November 10, 1980, that an enterprising reporter drew the connection between Satan, the pet South American Boa Constrictor, and a front-page headline which read: "Family's pet snake squeezes seven-month-old infant to death." The child's father, it turns out, bought the snake after a business trip. He thought it would be an interesting pet for his family. And *nine* years after the sale, that snake squeezed the life out of his child.

Men and women, that's not such an uncommon story. So many times we are duped by something that looks educational, interesting, and reasonably safe. "Why not do it?" we ask. But somewhere along the line, the squeeze comes. It may be right away, or it may be nine years down the road, but a lot of us are making very costly, maybe even deadly, decisions because we've been fooled by the deceit of appearances.

Abraham had made a firm commitment to God and that *decision of allegiance* shaped all his choices. That decision of allegiance will help you shape good choices. But then we must *continue* to make choices based on God's judgment. We need to beware of the *deceit of appearances* because as the Scripture puts it, "There is a way that *seems* right to a man, but in the end it leads to death" (Prov. 14:12).

I want to close today with Proverbs 3:5–6 because it sums up some of these early lessons on the lives of Abraham and Lot. It was one of the first verses I memorized from the Bible. "Trust in the LORD with all your heart and lean not on your own understanding; in all your ways acknowledge him, and he will make your paths straight."

Choose Your Own Adventure, Part Three

Genesis 13:8–13; 14:1–23

Duffy Robbins

This is the third and final talk in this series on how to make good decisions. The talk will work with both Christian and non-Christian kids but, especially with this talk, you must be very careful about using names and places that will be familiar only to kids who have grown up hearing Bible stories in church. Take the added time to make sure that you "set the scene" fully. Reintroduce each of the main characters, describe the setting, and don't assume that everybody will have some kind of familiarity with these stories.

To really get a good picture of what is going on here, you will need to cover a fair amount of the narrative. Chapter fourteen is a menagerie of names and places enough to confuse any reader, let alone any teenage listener. For that reason, use the loose paraphrase included in the text of the talk. It will cover the essential material without getting bogged down in names and places.

The talk begins with a "horse trading" problem. (See the text of the talk.) When you pose the problem to the kids, bring about four kids to the front who think they have the right answer. Ask them to give you their answers, one at a time. Then, after each has had a chance to give his or her answer, give any of them a chance to change their answer and go along with one or more of the other "contestants." The idea here is to allow these kids to make right or wrong decisions based on who they listen to, who they choose to side with. Just for fun, after each has decided on his final answer, have the audience applaud what they think is the right answer.

For outline, see page 218.

We're going to start off today with a little exercise in "horse trading." I'm going to give you a problem, and you can write down the figures as we go along, or just work it in your head. Then I'll give you a chance to tell us what the answer is. Ready? Okay, here we go.

Let's suppose that I bought a horse from a man, and for that horse I had to pay in cold, hard cash a grand total of $6.00. When I get home with the horse, everyone's excited. My kids think I'm a hero. And my wife, who's a penny pincher, thinks I'm a big spender. But the horse is great.

After awhile, problems arise. The horse is too big for the house, even though I've told the kids no galloping in the living room. It's getting expensive to feed this animal too. Finally my wife puts her foot down. "That horse has got to go," she says. So I take the horse back to the man who originally sold him to me, and he's gracious enough to buy the horse back for $8.00.

But I miss that old horse. A lot of times at night, after the kids have gone to bed, I can be found staring up at the moon and playing my harmonica, singin' old cowboy songs. My wife, bless her heart, can't stand to see me mope over old Calico, so she finally gives in. She lets me go back and buy that horse, that very same horse from that very same man. This time I pay $10.00.

You know what happened, I'll bet. No sooner did we get the horse back to the house than we began to face all the old problems again. The kids were still horsing around, and the horse was still doing a major number on the carpet. I could see the handwriting on the stall. I was going to have to get rid of old Calico. So, you guessed it, I went back to that same man and sold him my horse for $12.00.

Now my question to you guys is this: Through all of my dealing with that horse, not counting feed, or gas back and forth to the farm, did I make money, lose money, or break even? And, if I made or lost money, how much of either did I make or lose?

When you have an answer, raise your hand. Don't tell anyone else. Just put up your hand.

(Give kids a few seconds to think, and then follow the instructions given in the description section. After giving the kids a chance to vote for the answer they feel is right, you can have all contestants sit down, and then give the correct answer—I gained $4.00 . . . $6.00 plus $10.00 = $16.00; $8.00 plus $12.00 = $20.00; and $20.00 minus $16.00 = $4.00.)

It's funny, isn't it? Some of the problems that seem so simple can end up being a lot tougher than we think. Believe it or not, I got this problem out of my daughter's second grade math book, and look at how many of us got it wrong. And what makes it even tougher is when your friends or some other people disagree with you, and you're not sure if they're right, or you're right, or if you're all wrong. It's tough to really know whom to listen to.

That's one of the hardest parts of making good decisions in your life. It's easy to be influenced by your friends, sometimes in a good way—and sometimes in a bad way. You have to choose very carefully whom you are going to listen to—whom you're going to choose to side with in the face of tough decisions. That's why the third factor in making good decisions—the one we're going to look at today—is *discernment of alliances*; making wise judgments about whom you choose as allies, whom you choose as friends.

Choosing good friends is an important step in decision-making, maybe more than a lot of us realize. Because sometimes we are misled, not always on purpose, by the people we hang around with. Sometimes you think people are your allies, and then you find out later they've been telling you all lies. The Apostle Paul warns us in 1 Corinthians 15:33, "Do not be misled, bad company corrupts good character." I've also heard it put another way: "Don't kid yourself. If you sleep with the dogs, you're going to get fleas!"

One example of a "flea-bitten" man is our old friend Lot, Abraham's selfish nephew. Again, he gives us a prime example of what *not* to do. Let's take a look at the story in the Bible.

(Read Genesis 13:8–13.)

As chapter thirteen ends we see Lot and Abraham going their separate ways. Lot, choosing by sight, has made the decision to move his family eastward in the direction of Sodom and Gomorrah. Abraham, following God's cue and choosing by faith, moves his tent, family, and herds to the land of Hebron to the west.

As chapter fourteen opens we find out that this land of Sodom and Gomorrah, which looked like a fertile, quiet, and peaceful place, turns out to be right on the verge of war. The war escalates, leaving the two kings, Bera, king of Sodom, and Birsha, king of Gomorrah, embroiled in a battle that backs them into the Valley of Siddim.

The Bible tells us (Gen. 14:10) that this valley was full of tar pits. These tar pits were everywhere. I mean, it was "wall-to-wall tar pits." And these kings were locked in vicious combat. One empire would strike. Then the other would strike back. It was "Tar Wars" all over again! As the battle raged, the kings of Sodom and Gomorrah got themselves backed to the wall. Some of their men had actually fallen into the tar pits, and the ones who could escape hid out in caves. It was a hopeless defeat for Lot's homeland, Sodom and Gomorrah.

We probably ought to stop here for a minute and notice what has happened over these last few passages, because it's subtle and tricky, but it's very, very important. It's the kind of thing you think about after a movie like "Butch Cassidy and the Sundance Kid" or "Rambo." You walk out of the theater and realize that during the entire movie you were cheering for "the bad guys." Let's face it, Butch Cassidy and the Sundance Kid and Rambo were crooks, mass murderers, thieves. Because you were with them for two hours, you started taking their side and pulling for them in the battle.

That's what happened to Lot. He wasn't blind; he knew the kind of evil and wickedness that was going on in Sodom, but he moved in there and tried not to think about it much. He just tried to mind his own business. Even though he lived among rampant sinfulness, he truly figured that he wouldn't get mixed up in it.

Finally the kings of Sodom and Gomorrah go to war, and what happens? Lot finds himself cheering for the bad guys. He starts fighting their fights and cheering their victories. It was as if Lot's whole value system had been turned upside down. His decision-making had become so screwed up that he had started seeing the bad guys as the good guys. We just finished reading in verse thirteen that ". . . the men of Sodom were wicked and were sinning greatly against the LORD." And now, those guys, the enemies of the Lord, are the people Lot's pulling for.

That's when we realize that Lot's whole sense of right and wrong has been completely squashed. He is able to call evil "good," and good "evil," and he is fighting on the side of wickedness. How did he get to this point? Remember, the breakdown started all the way back when Lot made a poor decision of allegiance. Then things got even more messed up when he was deceived by appearances.

What finally torpedoed Lot's thinking process was when he moved among the people of Sodom and Gomorrah, tried to make friends with evil, and made himself comfortable in the midst of all that wickedness. In plain language, he chose the wrong crowd to hang out with. He lacked *discernment in his alliances.*

That can happen, you know. You start hanging around a group of friends, sharing in their conversations and daily lives, and before you know it, you start sharing in their thinking—even if they are "sinning greatly against the LORD."

I know a lot of kids who were neutral when it came to God—not really for him and not really against him. But somewhere along the line, they started hanging with a crowd that was not all that neutral. They were big time into sin and everybody knew it. It wasn't long before some of these guys chucked what little faith and what little morality they had. I have talked to some of these folks two or three years later and found that their whole sense of right and wrong has been totally screwed up.

They're adding up the numbers and they're coming up with answers that are totally off the wall because they're listening to the wrong friends. That happens, folks. It happens a lot. If you haven't made a firm decision of allegiance to be God's friend, you're fair game for any other friendship that comes along. Some of those friendships will lead you into hassles that may not include tar pits, but may turn out to be equally sticky situations.

That's exactly what happened to Lot. With the defeat of the army of Bera, the enemy army moves in and captures Lot and all of Lot's loot (v. 12). Not a pretty picture. Here was this land that looked so promising, so beautiful, and it turns out to be a battlefield full of tar. Lot chose for himself, chose what looked like riches, the good life, and easy street. And now, after making some bad decisions, he finds himself a slave, a prisoner of a hostile army.

I wonder how many of us are making those same kinds of mistakes, those same kinds of decisions, and are going to end up living out the same kind of defeat—a slave to a habit, or a prisoner of an unhappy marriage? And the wild part about it is that now Lot is in a position where he is a prisoner. He can't even make his own decisions any more.

Then the plot takes a strange twist. In Genesis 14:13 we read that one of Lot's servants escaped from the captors. And where do you think he ran? Not to his "friends" in Sodom. No way. He headed right back to good old Uncle Abraham.

And as the Scripture puts it, never mind that Lot had ripped off Abraham, never mind that he had never done a thing except watch out for his own neck. Abraham came to Lot's rescue. In verses fifteen and sixteen we read, "During the night Abram divided his men to attack them and he routed them, pursuing them as far as Hobah, north of Damascus. He recovered all the goods and brought back his relative Lot and his possessions, together with the women and the other people." (That's always struck me as a strange phrase: "the women *and* the other people." It's like they're two separate groups!)

There is one more important episode that we need to see in this drama if we want to understand what it means to make wise decisions by being discerning in our alliances. It unfolds as Abraham is returning from his dramatic rescue of Lot. Whom should he meet on the road in the Valley of Shaveh, but two different kings: Bera, the King of Sodom, and a mysterious king named Melchizedek, the King of Salem. Let me read the Bible's description of this close encounter.

(From Gen. 14:18–23) "Then Melchizedek king of Salem brought out bread and wine. He was priest of God Most High, and he blessed Abram, saying, 'Blessed be Abram by God Most

High, Creator of heaven and earth. And blessed be God Most High, who delivered your enemies into your hand.' Then Abram gave him a tenth of everything. The king of Sodom said to Abram, 'Give me the people, but keep the goods for yourself.' But Abram said to the king of Sodom, 'I have raised my hand to the LORD, God Most High, Creator of heaven and earth, and have taken an oath that I will accept nothing belonging to you, not even a thread or the thong of a sandal, so that you will never be able to say, 'I made Abram rich.' '"

Once again Abraham has to make a decision; this time, it's a decision between two kings and two kingdoms. One of the kings is Bera, whose name literally means "evil" or "wicked one." (His parents must have really thought he was cute as a baby—after all, they named him "Evil.") It's no wonder that Bera ruled the kingdom of Sodom, a land well-known as a place of wickedness.

The other king is a mysterious figure named Melchizedek, whose name means "king of righteousness." He is the king of Salem. It's interesting to note that Salem is the Hebrew word *shalom*, which means "peace." Scripture notes that Melchizedek identifies himself as the priest of the Most High God. What is even more unusual about Melchizedek is that he is the same man who is identified in Hebrews seven as a forerunner to the one real king of peace and righteousness, Jesus Christ.

Abraham, standing face to face with these two kings and their two kingdoms, finds himself in the middle of a bizarre auction. Both kings give him an offer. Melchizedek offers to him a spiritual gift . . . what the Bible describes as "the blessing of the LORD." Basically, it was just a promise that God would continue to see that Abraham and his family would prosper. No hard cash. Just the promise of God.

Bera, on the other hand, was talking some serious turkey. He came and offered to Abraham a material gift. "Take the goods for yourself," he said. "But give me back my subjects, Lot and his family."

What a drama. What a proposition. It's a cosmic summit meeting, and it's all come down to Abraham to once again make a choice. Both kings have offered him alliances. Both have offered to make him partners. One has offered the riches of God. The other has offered the riches of men. And now it all comes down to Abraham and the bottom line.

And, once again, Abraham shows us how to make good decisions. He knew that things were not always as they seem. It wouldn't be as easy as a simple business relationship. He used discernment in his alliances; he chose his partners carefully. And he knew, wisely, that the best choices are the ones we make by faith—not by sight. When Bera said to him, "Take the goods for yourself," it must have clicked in. That was just the mistake Lot had made—he had chosen for himself.

Wisely and faithfully, Abraham made his choice. He chose to not even flirt with evil, to not even come close to letting the issues get blurred. He knew: Melchizedek was his priest; Bera was his enemy. And in a strong clear voice he answered, "I have raised my hand to the LORD, God Most High, Creator of heaven and earth, and have taken an oath that I will accept nothing belonging to you, not even a thread or the thong of a sandal, so that you will never be able to say, 'I made Abram rich.'" It was a tough choice, but it was the right one. Only three chapters later we read that Sodom and its king Bera were buried in a smoking, fiery earthquake of God's judgment.

The strangest part of this whole story is that its episodes are still being written, even in this room today. The stories aren't always as dramatic. But *all* of us are being confronted with opportunities to side with the king of Sodom or the king of Salem, to make ourselves prisoners of the Kingdom of Evil or freedom fighters of the Kingdom of God. Sometimes the stakes are higher than we think, so it's crucial that we choose our alliances carefully.

When it gets down to that point, the only way we're going to make the right decision is to make a clear decision of allegiance: "I have raised my hand to the LORD, God Most High." Then we must follow up that decision with choices based on faith and not on sight—I don't care how good the deal looks. As Abraham put it: "I will take nothing belonging to you, not even a thread or a thong of a sandal." To maintain that kind of clear thinking, we need to be discerning about the kind of alliances we make, the kind of friends we choose. Abraham wasn't about to make deals with an enemy like Bera. He said, "No way, José. I don't want you telling anybody that you made Abraham rich."

As you face the tough decisions of the next few years, or the next few days, or even the next few hours, it might be a good idea to go back and check yourself. Who are you most like in your patterns of decision-making? Abraham, who chose by faith, or Lot, who chose by sight? Ultimately, you're probably going to find that your choices have brought you into citizenship of one of two kingdoms—the kingdom of evil, or the kingdom of God. The choice is up to you. You're the star of the story. Choose your own adventure!

The Wall

Nehemiah

Susie Shellenberger

> This is a good challenge for kids in your group who are already Christians. The call here is for deeper commitment and perseverance despite the normal setbacks of daily living.
>
> Susie's message from Nehemiah gives a good overview of this book. For most teenagers, the Old Testament is a "closed book" with weird names and strange customs. Any talk that can take these Old Testament truths, dust them off, and bring them to the attention of a teenager can't be all bad!
>
> *For outline, see page 221.*

For outline, see page 221.

Nehemiah was an outstanding basketball player. In fact, he was on a full ride basketball scholarship at Galilean Community College. He was also a strong leader on campus and was enjoying his junior year as student body president.

One of his friends, a high school senior from his hometown of Jerusalem, came to visit him and look over the campus of G.C.C. during Jerusalem's spring break. Nehemiah was ecstatic to see his old pal, and over a Coke and large order of fries at the Golden Galilean Arches, he casually asked how things "back home" were.

Putting the Coke down, and straightening his chair, the friend replied, "Well, things are not good. The wall of Jerusalem is still torn down and the gates are burned" (Neh. 1:3 TLB).

The Bible tells us that Nehemiah was so disturbed by the shocking news that he sat down and cried. During the next several days, he refused to eat. Instead, he poured out his heart in prayer to God.

Some of you have probably been in a crisis situation similar to Nehemiah's. You know what it feels like to be so bothered about something that to even consider eating seems like an absurdity, because food is the last thing on your mind.

Nehemiah was worried about his hometown. Try to imagine yourself in his place. What if it were you who were away at college, and a friend relayed the news that a devastating tornado had ripped through your hometown? You'd probably be as upset as Nehemiah was! After all, your hometown represents your family, your friends, and your security.

Nehemiah's high-school buddy informed him that the walls surrounding the city were down. The city wall was important. As long as a strong, sturdy wall was intact, the people inside were safe from enemy attacks. When the wall stood high, it also meant that the spiritual condition of the people was sturdy as well. *The wall* symbolized not only a physical wall of strength and protection, but also a "wall of righteousness." That wall was important!

Nehemiah had a great off-campus job. He worked part-time for the king. He was the kind of worker most kings would kill for. He always punched in on time, never took more than fifteen minutes for coffee break, and gave terrific visitor tours around the palace.

The king took a special liking to Nehemiah. Noticing that the boy was feeling a little down, he asked if anything was wrong. Nehemiah replied, "My hometown is a wreck! The gates have been burned and the wall that surrounds the city is down. Sir, that's my city, my security, my family, my friends. Could I have an indefinite leave of absence to go home and help restore the city wall?"

The king must have had a bowl of Cheerios that morning because he responded cheerfully and quickly granted Nehemiah's request.

Nehemiah packed his bags, walking away from his basketball scholarship, his job, and his student council position to return home and rebuild the wall. The rebuilding of the wall became the most important thing in his life.

He immediately went on Jerusalem television network and announced that he was forming a volunteer construction company to rebuild the wall of righteousness. He hit the radio stations and even put flyers underneath windshield wipers of cars in crowded shopping mall parking lots. Nehemiah finally recruited a pretty good group of volunteer workers and set them to work.

Meanwhile, the neighboring governors, Sanballat and Tobiah, heard about what was going on and began making plans to thwart the construction work. With the wall down, Sanballat and Tobiah had free reign to walk in and out of the city, flaunting their wickedness and working to sway the citizens to their own political views. They knew if the wall was rebuilt, their influence over the people within the city would be stopped. So they tried to distract and discourage the workers by hurling verbal insults at them.

"Hey Nehemiah, where'd you get your construction license—out of a Cracker Jack Box?"

"You call *that* thing a wall? I've seen stronger stuff built from Tinker Toys!"

"Nehemiah, my grandmother could build stronger walls than *that!*"

Nehemiah warned his men not to stop. "Don't pay any attention to Sanballat and Tobiah. We are doing the most important thing in the world—rebuilding the wall of righteousness. We will *not* stop!"

When Sanballat and Tobiah realized the insults weren't going to distract them, they decided to use an all-out physical attack. They began firing arrows and hurling stones at the crew. Nehemiah, calmly downing a Twinkie, instructed half of the men to deck themselves in the armor of God while standing guard against the enemy's attacks, and the other half to continue building the wall.

It didn't take Sanballat and Tobiah long to realize that God's armor couldn't be penetrated, so they put their heads together and came up with the master plan of parts A, B, C, and D.

The next morning they implemented Plan A. As the men were arriving for work, Sanballat and Tobiah set up a Kool-Aid stand right across the street from the construction site. Glowing with all the fake charm they could gather, they tried to entice the men with cold drinks.

"Listen guys, I know we gave you a hard time the other day, but we realize now what a super job you're doing for your city, and to show our admiration we're offering you complimentary glasses of Kool-Aid anytime you want it during this hot, scorching, day."

Nehemiah quickly instructed his men not to stop for *anything*. So the men worked consistently, and the two neighboring governors got waterlogged from trying to drink twenty-five gallons of strawberry Kool-Aid.

Sanballat and Tobiah were forced to go to Plan B. The next morning after Acme Brick Company delivered a fresh supply of bricks for the wall, the two governors invited Nehemiah and his men to a "special dinner."

"Look Nehemiah . . . we admire the work you're doing; we really do. And to show our appreciation for a job well done, we want you and your entire crew to be our guests of honor at a barbecued rib party tonight right after you punch out for the day."

Well, that sounded good! The construction crew was always tired and hungry at the end of the day, and barbecued ribs tickled their taste buds. Nehemiah's instructions to his men, however, were firm. "Men, we will *not* be sidetracked! We will *not* stop!"

No problem. Sanballat and Tobiah pulled out Plan C. They did their homework. They sent some FBI agents to G.C.C. (Galilean Community College) and found out that Nehemiah had walked away from a full ride basketball scholarship to rebuild the wall. They knew athletics was important to him and could possibly be his "weak spot."

"Nehemiah, we realize we've given you a hard time about rebuilding the wall, but the past is over and we'd like to do our part to help bridge the gap between our cities."

So far they sounded pretty good. Nehemiah knew the tension between Jerusalem and the neighboring cities needed to be resolved.

"Nehemiah, we've decided to sponsor an inter-city basketball tournament. We'll coach the teams from our cities, and we want you to coach the Jerusalem team."

Nehemiah's interest was rising high. He knew he'd make a terrific coach.

"Of course, this means you'll need to take a little time off from the construction site to recruit your players, teach them strategy, and get them into shape. Tell you what . . . we'll give you six months to get your team in shape and then we'll begin the tournament."

That sounded great. If there was one thing Nehemiah loved, it was sports. He loved the thrill of competition and the sweat of victory. That night he talked to the Lord about it.

"Father, this would be a great way to bridge the gap between the neighboring cities, and I know that's important to you."

"Yes, Nehemiah, that *is* important. But at this particular time, what's *more* important?"

"I guess, rebuilding the wall."

"That's right. Rebuild the wall."

"But God, this is such a *good* thing."

"Yes, it is. But what's the *better* thing?"

"Rebuilding the wall."

"Right."

So the next morning, Nehemiah turned down the basketball challenge, forcing the two wicked governors to their final plan: Plan D.

This time Sanballat and Tobiah forged a letter to Nehemiah from the king. The letter expressed gratitude and admiration for the work Nehemiah had done on the wall. It also stated that the government felt Nehemiah's life-style was an excellent role model for the youth of the nation, and because of his excellent leadership ability, the king was honoring him with a special seat in congress. Of course, this also meant that Nehemiah would have to take some time off to accept the award and fulfill some publicity obligations.

Nehemiah was ecstatic! He realized

this would be a fantastic witness to the youth of the nation. Because of the publicity he would receive, people would certainly listen to him when he gave his testimony for the Lord.

That night, he talked with God about the situation.

"Lord, this is fantastic! Think of the witness I'll be."

"Yes, Nehemiah, a good witness is important. But at this particular time in your life, what's the *most* important?"

"Rebuilding the wall of righteousness that guards our land?"

"That's right."

"But Lord, this is such a *good* thing!"

"Yes, being a witness in the public eye is good, but at this particular time in your life, what's the *best* thing?"

"Doing your will for my life . . . rebuilding the wall of righteousness."

"You're quick, Nehemiah."

Through discussing the matter with God, Nehemiah began to realize that the letter was a forgery and the two governors were secretly planning to kill him.

The next day, Nehemiah sent a reply to Sanballat and Tobiah. Let's take a look at his response, found in Nehemiah 6:3 (TLB): "I am doing a great work! Why should I stop to come and visit with you?" In other words: "What I am doing is the most important thing in the world, because I'm doing the will of God. Why should *anything* sidetrack me from doing my Father's will?"

In just fifty-two days after they had started, the construction crew completed the rebuilding of the wall around the entire city of Jerusalem! Wow! Less than two months is incredible! How in the world did they do it?

They were consistent. Day after day, they placed brick upon brick. They didn't allow *anything* to sidetrack them from doing God's will.

Just as God commissioned Nehemiah to rebuild the wall of righteousness, he also commissions us to build the wall of righteousness. How do I build the wall of righteousness around *my* life? By reading the instruction manual. God has given us his holy Word, full of instructions for daily Christian living. When we discipline ourselves to following his instructions on a *daily* basis, we are able to build a strong righteous wall around our lives.

Nehemiah realized some pretty important things. First of all, he realized *the importance of each individual.* "I am doing a great work." What *I* do for God is important! What *you* do for God matters! You may think you don't have a lot to offer, but you have a very important part in building the kingdom and in building a strong wall of righteousness around your own personal life.

Secondly, Nehemiah realized *the importance of wearing the armor of God.* Ephesians chapter six instructs us to clothe ourselves in God's armor. We're kidding ourselves if we think we can fight Satan's battles in the "blackboard jungle" called school without first pausing to spend time with our Lord and gird ourselves with his protection. That *daily* time with him is a must! We need his armor to live victoriously.

Thirdly, Nehemiah realized *the importance of determination*. I *will* build the wall of righteousness. I *will* stick it out. I *won't* allow myself to be sidetracked. I *am* going to see this thing called "Christianity" through!

Day after day, the crew laid brick upon brick. It works the same way in our spiritual lives. Day after day, we must determine to lay spiritual bricks. We must be consistent. We must read God's Word. We must wear his armor. We must *not* give up! How do I lay spiritual bricks? Again, by reading the "instruction manual," God's holy Word.

God is calling *you* to build a strong, steady, righteous wall around your life. Nehemiah was so "into" doing God's will that he *refused* to be sidetracked. What about you? Are you so "into" doing God's will that you are refusing to be sidetracked even by the *good things?*

Ezekiel 22:30 says, "I looked in vain for *anyone* who would build again the wall of righteousness that guards the land, who could stand in the gap and defend you from my just attacks, but I found not one" (TLB).

God is looking for *anyone* who will discipline themselves on a daily basis to build a strong, steady, righteous wall around their lives by reading the Bible, being consistent, and doing his will. *Anyone!* Will you build the wall? There is no higher calling than doing God's will for your life. God is calling *you* to build the wall.

What Kind of Person Does God Choose?

1 Samuel 17:1–47; Exodus 4:2–17; John 6:3–14

Susie Shellenberger

This talk addresses the point that God can use anybody he chooses to accomplish his purposes. It is not just the obvious leader, natural athlete, or charismatic person who can do something for God. In this talk, Susie Shellenberger uses humor and creativity to give three instances of God's ability to use those who are willing to give him their all.

This is a talk that would probably work especially well with junior-high kids. The issue of self-image and the common junior higher's perception that they are incapable of serving God will be met head-on by this message.

Susie suggests that this message might close with each student being handed a small dowel rod, symbolizing Moses' rod and reminding them of what God can do with ordinary things. You can use the end of the message to challenge your youth to place the rod where they will see it often. They could also write on one end of the rod, "I'm available," and on the other end the date.

For outline, see page 223.

The Bible mentions a man named Goliath. Most of us know one thing about him—he was a *giant!* But I'd like to share some inside information with you about Goliath.

First of all, he stood fourteen feet tall in his stocking feet. He wore a seventy-six-inch belt, and his throat was so big . . . (How big was it?) His throat was so big that he could swallow a Big Mac, large fries, cherry pie, and large Coke all at once!

He never wore deodorant. It took an entire can of spray for each underarm, and he realized pretty quick how expensive it could be!

No one wanted to be his locker partner at school, because everytime he "tossed" his books onto the shelf, the entire locker collapsed. The school administration was afraid to give Goliath the repair bill, so his partner always got stuck with having to ace the cost of defacing school property.

Biology class was horrendous! When they dissected frogs, Goliath with knife in hand not only cut through the left and right aorta of his frog—but took his knife right through the table as well.

This guy was a mess! He was a nightmare of a man! So what in the world was a twelve-year-old boy thinking, when he thought he could handle this scarey-berry mess of a giant?

David had a talent. He was good with a slingshot, and at a very early age, David committed everything in his life to God. At this early age, he just had one skill. But he gave his skill to God and expected him to use it. You see, it really doesn't matter how much *ability* we have. What really matters is how much *availability* we have.

It was no accident that David killed Goliath with a slingshot. It was not fate, and it was certainly no coincidence. David had practiced day after day for years with his slingshot. He was *consistent* with his availability. He had given his talent to God, and on a daily basis made that talent consistently available. God had spent a lifetime preparing David for this giant. It wasn't luck that made David the winner; it was the fact that he was available for God to use.

What has God spent your lifetime thus far preparing you for? I don't know what giant you may be facing right now. I don't know what giants will cross your paths next week or two years from now. But I do know this: If you'll commit everything in your life to God and make yourself *available* to him, he'll equip you with everything you need to handle the giants that cross your path.

What kind of person does God choose to use? Not always the person with the *ability*; but always the person with the *availability*. Which teen in this group will God choose to bless and do dynamic things with? The one who's overflowing with ability? No. Simply the one who chooses to be one hundred percent available.

Daniel is another man who wasn't overflowing with talent. He thought, "Lord, I don't have a lot to offer you . . . but I'm available to be used. I don't have much to give, but I guess I could pray. Yeah, that's it! I can be a prayer warrior. And I'll be consistent in my prayer life. Use my prayers, God. I'm available."

What happened when a young man gave his prayer life to God? God changed the course of his people, turning an entire nation around, all because one man became available with all he had to give.

The real issue tonight isn't your ability. God couldn't care less about how much or how little ability you have. What God is really concerned about is how much *availability* you have. Your availability is the key issue.

All through the Bible, God uses people we would *never* choose for leaders. God has used ordinary people with little ability to accomplish fantastic tasks, all because they were available.

Take Moses, for example. We would not have chosen Moses! *No one* would have chosen Moses! In fact, right after he was born, his own parents put him in a basket and set him out to sea. From that point on, he was the supreme example of a basket case. He made so many mistakes, they're uncountable! When the nation voted on whether or not they wanted Moses to take on the superman role of being their leader, the whole nation voted "no," thumbs down! *No one* wanted Moses to be their leader. Only one person voted for him, and that was his mother. The only reason *she* voted for him was because she was tired of saying, "Where have I failed?"

Moses had a lisp; when he spoke it sounded like he had a mouth full of LifeSavers candy. It was hard to understand him. Sometimes he stuttered, and it took too much effort to try to decipher his unorganized thoughts. *This* was the man God chose to lead his people out of captivity?

Moses certainly wasn't chosen for his ability! He had *nothing* going for him. But he was *available*; and God uses those who are simply available.

Whenever Hollywood produces a movie about Moses, they always give the part to some he-man with fake whiskers glued onto his face. The truth of the matter is, Moses probably looked a lot more like Herman the vacuum cleaner salesman than a weight-lifting monster. But God chose Moses! And he blessed him, protected him, guided him, and showed him firsthand what could happen when one committed *everything* to the Lord.

Now Moses didn't have any real ability to speak of . . . but he did have *something*. Moses had a walking cane. He placed great importance on this rod; it was the only material possession he owned. During the forty years in the desert, God asked for control of even Moses' walking cane.

"But God! This walking cane is all that I have! It's my security. I need it to guide me through the wilderness. Don't forget, I'm doing your work here. I *need* a walking cane."

God continued to deal with Moses about complete availability. When Moses committed his material possessions to God, he watched in amazement as God took an ordinary piece of wood and transformed it into a dynamic instrument full of power! The rod of Moses became the rod of God, splitting entire rivers in two and commanding water from dry rocks.

In the same way, God wants to do

exciting things in all of our lives, if we'll simply be available to him. What about you? Does God have control of one hundred percent of your life? Does he have control of your material possessions? Does he have control of your skills and abilities? God wants one hundred percent. He can't use you if you're only committed fifty percent to him. He can't even use you if you're committed ninety-nine percent to him. But he can and *will* use you if you'll be totally available to him and commit one hundred percent.

One day Jesus was speaking to over five thousand people. It must have been Labor Day, because nothing was open. Long John Silver's, McDonald's, and even Taco Bell were all closed. He quickly called a board of disciples meeting up front. "How are we going to feed all these people?" Jesus asked his main men. (He knew exactly where the food would come from, but he wanted to see if the disciples had done their homework.)

The big twelve quickly began estimating the size of the crowd. "Let's see . . . two fat ladies in the front row; a hundred or so in the Jones family; then there's the Rodriguez triplets; and the Baptist Youth Choir . . . h'm, there must be around five thousand people here. Sorry, Jesus. Can't be done. It would take over a year's wages to feed this crowd. No can do."

Andrew, however, had made friends with a small boy in the crowd who had offered to share his sack lunch. "There's this boy in the crowd—doesn't have much, but he's willing to share the little that he *does* have." So Jesus motioned for the small boy to come forward. The child gave Jesus his mashed fish and crumpled pieces of bread, watching in wonder and amazement as Jesus placed His hands over the food and blessed it.

Wow! The little boy had never seen anything like it in his entire life! The bread just kept on coming! Where was it coming from? Jesus had no sleeves; it was simply coming from his hands. It was magical, mystical, and miraculous! The boy's eyes grew wild with excitement. "Wow!" he thought. "If he can do *that* with my *lunch*, imagine what he could do if I gave him my *life!*"

A fantastic miracle happened that day. The feeding of the five thousand will always be a miracle to remember. But an even more important miracle occurred as well, and that's the fact that a little boy gave Jesus *all that he had*. The little boy was available!

Again, the issue today is not how much ability you have! God doesn't care about how much or how little ability you're carrying around. What God is really concerned with right now is your availability.

What happened when a twelve-year-old boy gave all he had to God?

God took what little he had to offer and killed a giant! God changed the lives of David's people, all because he was available.

What happened when one young man gave his prayer life to God? God rescued an entire nation through one man's availability.

What happened when a small boy gave Jesus Christ everything? A fantastic miracle was recorded in the Gospels, spiritually feeding infinitely more than the original five thousand.

What happened when a young man with no ability and no support gave God everything he had? God took an ordinary piece of wood and transformed it into a stick of dynamic power! Through one man's availability, God took a small band of slaves and made them into a great nation.

What kind of person does God choose to use? Not necessarily the one with the ability—but *always* the one with the *availability*. Are you available? Does God have one hundred percent of your life? Does he have control of your skills and talents? Are you using them to bring glory to him? Does he have control of your material possessions?

Right now would be a terrific time to give God one hundred percent, committing your availability to Him. What could he do with you if he had your talents, your material possessions, your very *self*? The sky's the limit when you're totally available to God.

(Suggestion: At the close of the service, give each teen a small dowel rod as a reminder of what God can do with ordinary things. Challenge each teen to place the rod where they will see it often. On one end of the rod ask them to write, "I'm available," and at the other end ask them to write the date.)

How to Make and Keep Friends

Ecclesiastes 4:9–10; Proverbs 27:5–6, 17; and 1 Samuel 18

Barry St. Clair

This very practical, down-to-earth look at friendship will be especially appropriate for Christian teens who haven't explored genuine friendship in the biblical sense. Barry's guidelines are specific enough that kids can use this talk as an inventory of their own friendships.

A quick reading of this talk is going to show that Barry makes frequent references to his personal friendship with "Rod." That personal illustration is one of the dynamics that makes this talk so effective.

When you use this talk, lace it with frequent references to your own friendships and how these various principles play out in real life relationships. While in some cases it might work for one speaker to "borrow" from the experience of another, this talk is one in which your honest sharing about *your own relationships* will be the most effective. Your illustrations may not be as funny, but they will be yours. In a talk about friendship, that kind of integrity is important.

For outline, see page 225.

The most important relationships that you'll have in your life, apart from your relationship with Jesus and your relationship with your family, will be the relationships you have with other Christian friends. Establishing friendships with people within the body of Christ is very, very important.

A lot of you have friends at school who don't even know Jesus Christ, and those friendships are important too. But your most important friendships, the deepest friendships, should be your friendships with people who love Jesus Christ and are trying to grow in him, just like you are. When that's taking place in your life, when you are growing in him, when your friends are growing in him, you can create the best kind of friendship.

We're going to talk this morning about friendship. I'll tell you how I got interested in friendship. I began to study it when my third son was born, whom we named Jonathan. Jonathan. I started doing a Bible study just to find out about his namesake.

I read about Jonathan's friendship with a young man named David, about how they respected each other, sacrificed for each other, and cared for each other. And I began to realize that there were things about friendship that I needed to know and to share with folks like you—ideas about how we can develop the kinds of friendships that are deep and exciting.

Then I asked myself this question, "Do I have any friendships like the one Jonathan and David shared?" I thought back to high-school days, when I won honors, athletic awards, and all kinds of senior superlatives. But at that time I didn't have a close friend. I knew a lot of people; a lot of people knew me, but I didn't have one single close friend.

I think that's probably the way it is with some of you. You really want close friendships, but they're not easy to build. To show you how I deepened a friendship, I want to tell you about my friend Rod.

One time Rod and I were in Oklahoma City and were planning a flight to Albuquerque, New Mexico, the next morning. We were standing in the hall, discussing our plane tickets and flight, when a man walked by and overheard our conversation. He knew who we were because he was attending the same meeting as we were. He said, "Hey, I've got my private plane. I'll take you to Albuquerque."

I looked at Rod. Rod looked at me. Neither one of us had flown on one of those little jobs. I said, "Tell you what—I'll go if you'll go." He said, "I'll go if you'll go." I said, "I tell you what—I'll go if you'll go, how's that?" He said, "Well, I'll go if you'll go." I said, "You big chicken; I'll go if you'll go." Finally, we decided we'd go.

We got up early the next morning, a little nervous, and went out to the airport where this plane was tied up. It was kind of windy, and when they untied the plane it rocked back and forth. I thought, "This thing's going to blow away. We'll blow off into the distance somewhere and no one will ever hear from us again."

But then they started loading the luggage, which weighed the plane down and stabilized it. So much so, in fact, that when we got the plane loaded I wasn't sure it would get off the ground. The pilot got out and started the propeller. The engine started, not sounding like any jet I'd ever been on. What jet do you know of that goes "putt, putt, putt"?

We started putt-putting to the taxi area. When we got on the runway, we started putt-putting down the runway. When we got about halfway down the runway, all of a sudden it hit me—"This is nothing but a Volkswagen with wings!" I could tell we were in bad shape by how quiet Rod was. (Rod is *never* quiet.) As we were putt-putting along, all of a sudden we came to this clump of trees. Right in front of us. We were headed right for this clump of trees!

I looked at Rod and I said, "My momma's going to be mad!" Finally, at the last second, the pilot pulled back on the stick, just clearing the clump of trees. I looked at Rod; he looked at me. We had cheated death again!

We started flying over Oklahoma. I was in the front and Rod was in the back. I was asking all sorts of questions—all about the Oklahoma countryside and the plane's instruments—and Rod asked some too. Then the pilot said to me, "How would you like to fly this plane?" My eyes got as big as two fried eggs. Taking the steering wheel, he moved it right over in front of me.

All of a sudden the plane started into a dive—I lost complete control. It was real quiet in the back where my friend Rod was. Finally I got it under control; the plane was a little shaky, but at least it evened out. We were flying along, doing very well, but Rod was still quiet.

We approached a big cloud bank. I had learned in eighth-grade science about clouds, vaporized water all condensed there together. I kept thinking, "cloud, cloud, cloud, cloud," but my subconscious mind was saying, "wall, wall, wall, wall." Rod and I began to talk about how it would feel to be a grease spot down there on the mountain.

I asked the pilot, "Obviously, you want us to go over this? Under this? How about to the right? The left? What? *Straight on through?*" I flinched, knowing in my heart of hearts that we were going to clobber ourselves. We headed into it, and it really was a cloud! If you've ever been in a cloud, it's a little foggy in there. It's cloudy in a cloud. You couldn't see the left wing. You couldn't see the right wing. You couldn't see the nose. And then—I lost complete control of the plane. In the corner of my eye I could see Rod grabbing for the puke bag. Obviously, we didn't die, or I wouldn't be talking to you. But a not so obvious fact is that Rod—miraculously—is still my friend, and a better one from that experience, too.

I want to ask you this question: Why do we need to build friendships? Why did David need Jonathan and Jonathan need David? Why did I need Rod? Why did he need me?

Let me suggest some reasons. First of all, friends are encouragers. Ecclesiastes 4:9–10 says this: "Two are better than one, because they have a good return for their work: If one falls down, his friend can help him up. But pity the man who falls and has no one to help him up!" Have you ever been in a situation that you knew you couldn't handle alone, and you needed to talk to someone but no one was there? That's a lonely feeling, isn't it? We need friends just to be encouragers.

Also, we need friends to give us counsel and advice. Proverbs 27:5–6 says this, "Better is open rebuke than hidden love. Wounds from a friend can be trusted, but an enemy multiplies lies." A lot of times, the friends who are closest to us will risk being honest with us. When they do that, it's real proof of their friendship. We need friends who will be honest enough with us to tell us the truth even when we don't want to hear it.

Thirdly, we need friends because friends challenge our potential. Proverbs 27:17 says, "As iron sharpens iron, so one man sharpens another." Friends sharpen our awareness of others and of ourselves, helping us to open up and forcing us to grow physically, emotionally, mentally, and spiritually.

Now the question is: "Do you have friends who are encouragers, who are counselors, and who are challenging you to reach your potential?" God wants you to have those kinds of friends from the body of Christ so that you can not only know him better, but also so that you can know *yourself* better.

So, how do you make friends? Let's read 1 Samuel 18:1–5 together to find out.

(Read text.)

We've got two people involved in this friendship—Jonathan and David. Jonathan was a great warrior and killed thousands of Philistines. (I know, so far he doesn't sound very friendly, but stick with me.) Not only was he a great warrior; but he was also courageous. Once he and his armor-bearer came upon twenty men who were going to kill them, but he and his armor-bearer took them all on and won. Jonathan was dynamic, a good person to have as a friend.

On the other hand, you have David, the shepherd that turned into the hero when he single-handedly fought the Philistine giant, Goliath. Because of his courage in that fight and in succeeding battles, David was the man that the Israelites felt should be their next king.

Now that's very important in his relationship to Jonathan because the king of Israel at that time was Saul . . . and Saul was Jonathan's father. Technically, that means Jonathan should have been Israel's next king. One would expect Jonathan to feel anything but friendly towards David. After all, how would you feel if someone took your throne away from you?

Let's say, for example, that you're going to be a senior this year and football season is just around the corner. You notice that a certain sophomore, who last year was a 90-pound wimp, has blossomed into a 220-pound dynamo. You're supposed to be the star running back, and he comes in and takes your place. Would that tick you off? You bet it would. Potentially, that guy could become your most bitter enemy.

Or let's say that you're Cherry Cheerleader, and you've been cheering since you were in fourth grade. A girl moves in from another town about one week before cheerleader trials start. She tries out, beats your pompoms off, and before you know it, you've lost your place on the squad. Does that tick you off? You bet your pompoms it does.

That was the same sort of situation that Jonathan was in. David was the hero. Jonathan was the "who's he?" Instead of identifying David as a bitter enemy, Jonathan loved him as his closest friend. That still leaves us with the question of how he went about developing a friendship with a potential enemy. How did that happen?

There are four steps that Jonathan took in building a friendship with his potential enemy—four steps that we also can take to build a friendship with someone who might otherwise be an enemy.

1. The first step is *attraction*. 1 Samuel 18:1 says, "After David had finished talking with Saul, Jonathan became one in spirit with David . . ." David and Jonathan were in contact with each other and, through that contact, they were attracted to one another. Acting on the initial attraction, Jonathan took the initiative for building the friendship.

I remember that with my friend Rod. The first time we ever met, I was recruiting students at the university he was attending. We walked into the same room and our eyes met, so we shook hands, smiled at each other, and talked for just a minute. But in that short minute both of us knew we were going to be friends because we were immediately attracted to each other.

Let me tell you two or three ways that you can develop that initial attraction to another person. First of all—and this is a profound one—say "Hi." Can you say that with me? "Hi." Ever notice how, when you're walking the halls of your school, nobody speaks to anyone but those who are already their close buddies? So everybody walks around alienated from everybody else, and if you're not in my group, I don't speak to you.

One way to begin a relationship is just by saying, "Hello, how are you doing? My name is so-and-so." Yet for some of us, that's a hard thing to do— we are too insecure to say "Hello."

That's why people don't speak at your school.

Do you realize that everytime you pass someone in the hall at school, that is a potentially divine encounter in which God can use you to affect that person's life? That's phenomenal. But the only way that divine encounter can happen is for somebody to take the opening step and say "Hello." Do you speak to people at school or do you alienate yourself by not speaking to people in your classes or in the halls?

After you've met someone, remember his or her name. That's a tough one, isn't it? Let me give you a classic example of how *not* to do this. At one of my former jobs, I got a new secretary. I was introduced to her and talked with her for a few minutes, calling her Margaret. For two weeks I called her by what I thought was her name, but she wasn't responding very well. After two weeks, I realized that there was some problem with her responses—I would call her Margaret and she wouldn't say anything. Eventually I realized that her name wasn't Margaret; it was Wanda. I had been calling her by the wrong name!

When you're introduced to someone, just repeat their name back to them. They say, "Hello, my name is Dan," and you follow with, "Hello, Dan. It's nice to meet you, Dan." Make it stick in your mind. When you remember a person's name, they know that you think they are important.

How do you develop that relationship if the attraction stays? Very simply—start a conversation by asking questions. You can meet all kinds of people and find out all kinds of things about them if you just ask them questions—questions about their friends, their interests, their needs, their relationship to Christ. Questions communicate interest in the other person.

Making friends isn't really that hard to do, so why doesn't it happen more often? Because people fear rejection. We don't initiate conversation or friendships because we are afraid that people are going to turn us away. So we hide within ourselves and our little group of friends with whom we are already comfortable.

However, if we realize that no relationship is more significant than our relationship with God, and if we realize that God accepts us as we are, we can put any rejection in perspective. Then we can speak to anyone knowing that no matter how they respond to us, we're never going to be rejected.

2. After attraction comes *affection.* The last part of 1 Samuel 18:1 says that "[Jonathan] loved [David] as himself." Jonathan and David moved from the phase of attraction and contact to a place of affection and friendship. As you read about David and Jonathan, you see that Jonathan's father was trying to kill David out of envy, while Jonathan was trying to keep David alive out of loyalty. David and Jonathan grew closer because they had a common goal—to keep David alive.

Friendship is built on common experiences and common goals. For example, in 1972 Rod and I worked in a camp for high-school students. We were new to the job and were just one step ahead of the kids. One afternoon, we took a bunch of kids to a ghetto to work with the kids in the neighborhood. We arrived in our car to find our bus stuck, its bumper caught in an embankment, a tree limb snagged in the window. The kids we had come to help were throwing rocks at the bus. After we shooed the little kids away, rescued our bus driver, pulled away the tree limb, and dug the bus out, we finally got away from there without anyone getting hurt too badly!

Friendships are made up of experiences when people are working together for a common goal. These experiences force us to trust each other and depend on one another, and as that happens, we begin to grow in affection. That means we need to seek out those with whom we share common goals. If you're dating a guy or a girl who's going in another direction from the way you're going, you will never develop the closest friendship with that person because you're both moving toward two different goals.

We develop affection by sharing common goals, and as we pursue those goals, we will share common experiences. My friend Rod and I were taking four carloads of kids across the country one summer. After a ten-hour drive, we arrived at Jackson, Mississippi, where we ate supper and presented a program to the youth group. By that time—about ten o'clock—we were totally exhausted. We were supposed to spend the night with the local youth minister, so we followed behind his car in our van. We must have been twenty miles out of Jackson when this supposed youth minister pulls into his driveway, stops, and gets out of his car. We get out at the same time—and see some strange lady standing by the car, looking at us funny. We had followed the wrong car for about fifteen or twenty miles!

This didn't seem special then, but friendships are built around those kinds of experiences. We were trying to take some kids across the country. We had a common goal, a common purpose for which we were working side by side, and the experiences we shared along the way ended up knitting us together as brothers.

3. From attraction and affection we go on to *accountability*. We read in verse three, "And Jonathan made a covenant with David." In those times, a covenant was serious business. Several things happened when you established a covenant with someone: The two people involved in the covenant exchanged the one item that they valued most in life. Then they exchanged blood, cutting themselves and mingling their blood as a symbol of the fact that they were in a covenant relationship, that they were accountable to one another.

How do you develop an accountable relationship with another person? How do you develop that close, intimate, covenant relationship with one of your friends? Here are some suggestions:

Be open with the other person about your needs and desires. In other words, openly share with that person who you are and what your needs are. Make yourself vulnerable to them. Then, *be willing to learn about your friend's needs and desires.* Don't be concerned only for yourself, but find out about your friend's needs and desires too. That leads to the third step in building an accountable relationship—*striving to make the other person happy.* This will involve some sacrifice, some servanthood, and some compromise, but that's the part of the covenant symbolized by the exchange of valuables. It says, "I'm willing to pay a price for this relationship."

I remember how Rod and I entered into a covenant relationship. When he came to work with me as an intern, I told him, "Anything I have is yours; you can have it." He said, "Barry, anything that I've got is yours, and you can have that."

We were willing to sacrifice for one another.

And frankly, there were times when we had to call upon that promise of commitment—we had to put up or shut up. One night I needed something that was being delivered at the bus station, and I needed it badly. Rod stayed at the bus station all night long just to pick up that package for me. Then there was the night I helped Rod move his furniture—in the freezing rain. That's what you call being committed to another person.

Do you have any friends like that? You and your friend could hold each other accountable for consistently spending time alone with God. Or you could hold each other accountable in your dating life so that you don't do anything stupid. You could hold each other accountable to study, so that your grades can improve. That's what accountability is all about—helping your friend to be the best person he or she can be.

The last phase of friendship—after attraction, affection, and accountability—is *agape love.* Look at 1 Samuel 18:4. "Jonathan took off the robe he was wearing and gave it to David, along with his tunic, and even his sword, his bow and his belt." Jonathan was willing to give *everything* to his friend David in *complete* friendship. Jonathan knew David's life was at stake, and he also knew that he would be in danger if his father found out that he was helping

David. Despite that risk, he was willing to help his friend.

To develop that kind of a complete friendship, you must *go through joys and pains together*. Proverbs 18:24 says, "A man of many companions may come to ruin, but there is a friend who sticks closer than a brother." Some people just pretend to be your friends. The first time you do something that crosses them, they're no longer your friends. The first time you do something uncool, they ignore you. Your true friends, on the other hand, will stick by you, loving you just as you are. With them you're able to share joys and pains, strengths and weaknesses.

One night Rod, myself, and some other guys talked about our strengths and weaknesses. They told me about my stubbornness. Without real friendship and agape love, I couldn't have heard them out. But I valued them because they were willing to risk our friendship to tell me the truth about myself.

An agape love relationship also involves two friends' willingness to endure conflict. Any time you're in a close relationship over a period of time, there's going to be conflict. It's inevitable. You do something that ticks them off; they do something that makes you mad. If you're not ready to deal with that conflict, your friendship may disintegrate.

Many times I had to go to Rod and say, "Rod, I was wrong, and I need you to forgive me." Rod also had to ask my forgiveness a number of times. Conflict is inevitable, but complete friendship overcomes conflict.

One last thing: The ultimate friendship says, "I'm willing to die for you." No one loves you with agape love as unconditionally and unswervingly as the God who made you and who knows you even better than you know yourself. He loves you no matter what. He accepts you for who you are. It's not conditional; it's not because you do good things; it's not because you're cool. God loves you in spite of yourself. That's where agape love originates, and when it develops through a friendship and into an ultimate friendship, two people can say, "I love you enough to sacrifice my life for you." Turn over to John 15:13, where you can see that kind of love up close: "Greater love has no one than this, that he lay down his life for his friends."

When you're willing to lay down your life for someone else, then you're also willing to live for them on a day-to-day basis. Rod went through about three years of living on a minimal salary because he was committed to me and committed to working with me. That's complete friendship.

Who are your friends? Who are the people who really care about you and who do you really care about? Have you moved from attraction to affection, from affection to accountability, and from accountability to the ultimate—agape love? God wants you to have at least one friend who will be the kind of friend that Jonathan was to David and David was to Jonathan. Through Christ, you *can* attain that ultimate commitment.

Trivial Pursuit

Mark 10:17–22

Kim Talley

This will be a good evangelistic talk based on the story of the rich young ruler. There are several options for opening this talk: You may ask questions from the trivial pursuit cards, or you may ask local trivia questions, e.g., nicknames, who is dating whom, etc. This might even be a good team game in which contestants are divided up by grades. Give points for correct answers and allow the winning team to see a slide show of Leviticus!

As you move through the talk, it will enhance your message to use an overhead projector or flannel-board system in which you can visualize each of the categories in the game Trivial Pursuit. Introduce each category by adding one more "piece" to the picture of a "pie," so that as you cover each category, the pie gets filled in. Leave the center part of the "pie" empty until the conclusion of the talk when you can add the name "Jesus" right in the middle.

For outline, see page 227.

How many of you have ever played the game Trivial Pursuit? Let's see how good you are at the game.

(Use one of the options mentioned above.)

Trivial Pursuit, because it's so much fun and is such a novelty, has become one of the best-selling board games in the country. The game may be new to us, but there's a certain man who played his own version of Trivial Pursuit over two thousand years ago. Jesus had an unusual confrontation with this trivia player that we will read about in Mark 10, starting at verse seventeen:

As Jesus started on his way, a man ran up to him and fell on his knees before him. "Good teacher," he asked, "what must I do to inherit eternal life?"

"Why do you call me good?" Jesus answered. "No one is good—except God alone. You know the commandments: 'Do not murder, do not commit adultery, do not steal, do not give false testimony, do not defraud, honor your father and mother.' "

"Teacher," he declared, "all these I have kept since I was a boy."

Here's an earnest young man with a valid question: What must I do to have eternal life? He seems to have it all together. In fact, if we take the areas of his life and compare them to a game of Trivial Pursuit, I think you'll see what I mean.

First let's take the category of geography. The blue *(at this point, you may hold up the blue piece from the game, or use the overhead in the way discussed above, or use a blue wedge of flannel for a flannel board)* can represent geography, land, or real estate. Let's call this category wealth. This guy had it made—he probably owned many things and came from a wealthy family. Mark calls him a rich young ruler.

Let's look at some of the other categories. In the area of entertainment *(hold up the pink wedge)*, he certainly lacked nothing. Someone with his status could never be short of "friends" to party with; after all, he could pay for any pleasure, any delight. No doubt about it, he had this category pegged too.

(Hold up the yellow wedge.) But what about history? What was his heritage, his family name? We can tell from his back-

ground as a ruler that he was in a royal family, and with such a lineage his history was probably impressive. So his history category was all wrapped up.

(Hold up the green wedge.) Let's call this next category, science and nature, the area of knowledge. Again, because of his wealthy background, there is little doubt that the young man was trained in the best of Jerusalem schools. He was probably in the top ten and who's who of Jerusalem High. So he could chalk up yet another category.

(Hold up the brown wedge.) How about the next area—art and literature? Back then, students would have studied the Torah, the Old Testament law. Any rich young ruler who was a Jew would have been well-versed in these sacred scriptures. Trained by the Pharisees— the religious rulers—he would have known the Bible backward and forward. In fact, when the rich young ruler asked Jesus what he must do, Jesus said, "You must keep the commandments." And this rich young ruler, with his careful religious upbringing, said, "I have done all these things since I was a boy." He was probably one of the most religious guys in the neighborhood and had this category in the bag too.

(Hold up the orange wedge.) The last category in the game is that of sports and leisure. We'll think of this area as the physical dimension of life. The Bible says that he was rich and young, and a ruler.

He may well have been handsome and athletic, the "G.Q." dude of Jerusalem. I imagine this guy was physically *fit*, so we'll give him a piece of the pie in that category too.

No doubt about it—this guy has all the bases covered. He has the family history. He's bright. He's got religion. He has the body, the looks, and the friends. He knows how to throw a party, and he's wealthy. What more could he ask for? Any way you look at it, this guy was winning the game. He had all the categories covered. But think back to the rules for Trivial Pursuit—you don't win once you have all the pieces of the pie filled in. No, you still have to go to the middle! You have to make the last move and get the last answer right to win.

The rich young ruler had one last move to make. Oddly enough, even with all the categories covered, he still had doubts. So he came to Jesus and "showed" him his little pie. He asked Jesus, "What must I do to have eternal life?" In a sense, this guy was saying, "Hey look, I've got every area covered, but it's still not happening for me. What's the last question? How do I win at the game of life? How do I make the last move and win at this game?"

The Bible says in verse twenty-one, Jesus looked at him and, loving him, told him what he had to do for the last move. "One thing you lack," he said. "Go, sell everything you have and give it to the poor, and you will have treasure in heaven. Then come, follow me."

Jesus saw that the rich young ruler had everything on earth that he needed—he had all the categories covered. But Jesus told him that the way to win at the game of life is to lose. "You are winning at the wrong game," he said to the ruler. The ruler was winning in a game that he could afford to lose, but he was losing the game that he needed to win. Jesus explained to him that the way to win the game is to give up all the other categories and follow him.

(Take the pie holder and dump all the pieces out. Show the empty holder.)

In another place Jesus said, "Whoever wants to save his life will lose it, but whoever loses his life for me will find it" (Matt. 16:25). Jesus had to tell the rich young ruler that the only way to win at life was to dump every other category in favor of, first and foremost, following Jesus.

How did the ruler respond to Jesus' suggestion to drop everything and follow him? He carefully considered the alternatives, looking at his life with all the categories filled in, and then looking at Jesus. He had to decide between the life he knew and the abundant life that Jesus offered. He knew that Jesus was an extraordinary person, but he didn't know that Jesus was God in the flesh, nor that Jesus would die on his behalf and be raised from the dead, giving all those who followed Jesus eternal life.

Mark tells us that the man's face fell when he heard Jesus' words. After thinking it through, figuring the choices and considering the options, he decided he just couldn't make the sacrifice. The Bible says, "He went away sad . . ." Instead of following Christ in faith, the rich young ruler chose to stick with what he could see—his "filled pie."

Observing him, Jesus said to his disciples, "How hard it is for the rich to enter the kingdom of God!" This guy wanted to win at the game of life. He had all the categories covered, and when he asked Jesus what he had to do to win at life, Jesus said to give it all up and follow him. What an unreasonable request! It seems to make no sense. But even though this man had all the categories of his life filled, he still couldn't fill the God-shaped vacuum in the middle of everything. So his life turned out to be just one big game of Trivial Pursuit. He decided he wanted to win at the game of Trivial Pursuit, but in doing so he lost at the game of life.

We can't be too hard on the rich young ruler because you and I tend to do the same thing. Most of us are hotly competing in the game of "Trivial Pursuit" and are missing out on the game of life.

(At this point, go back to your game *pieces or props and work through the "pieces of the pie.")*

Let's take geography, for example. Some of us are working hard at this category. We're chasing after wealth and money, the right car, the right stereo, the right clothes. We want to be like Madonna's "Material Girl" who says, "The boy with the cold hard cash is always Mr. Right" or like a T-shirt I saw that read, "The one who dies with the most toys, wins." We think that if we can get this category of wealth filled in then we'll win at the game of "Trivial Pursuit," and life will work for us.

Some of us are working at the entertainment game. We are party animals. We party till we puke. We party naked. Our theme song is "Girls just wanna have fun" or as Eddie Murphy sings, "My girl wants to party all the time." We think that if we can get as high, stoned, or smashed as possible, we can forget what's bothering us. If we can be party kings or queens of the high school and live for spring break or senior week or the prom or a New Year's Eve party, then life will come together. Some of us are working hard—overtime—on this category.

How about the category of history? Some of us are working pretty hard on that one too. We think that if we could just change our past, or if we were born somewhere else, or in another family, or if we had a different mom or went to a different school, then life would be the way we want it to be. If we could just start over, then life would be great. But the truth is: Life doesn't work that way.

There are some of us who spend a lot of time working on the category of science and nature—or knowledge, as we called it earlier. We think if we can get the best education, graduate top in our class, score high on the SAT, go to the best schools, or get the best jobs, then we'll have life wired—we can win this game of Trivial Pursuit. And let me say, there's nothing wrong with being smart and pursuing academic excellence. It's great! But, some of us put all our eggs into that one basket, and it won't satisfy us forever. Life sooner or later asks us some questions that the best textbooks in the world can't answer. That's when you turn away from the software and start looking for the hard answers.

Then there's the world of art and literature, the brown area. We labeled this the religious area. Some of us, like the rich young ruler, are very religious—maybe even religious fanatics. We think that if we go to the right church on Sunday, or go to every Bible study, Young Life, youth group, Youth for Yahweh, or Brownies for Buddah, then we'll have it all figured out. We think that religion is going to be the answer.

Next comes sports and leisure—the physical category. We think, "If I could just have the right body . . ." or "If I just pump a little more iron . . ." If we can keep ourselves skinny enough, change our hair, or get our nose fixed—if we can be sexy enough or look good enough—then our lives will be all we want them to be. But no matter how hard we try, we never seem to be content with the physical category.

Some of us major in one or two of these categories or in all of them. We're hung up on our possessions, being a party animal, shedding our past, being smart, being good-looking, being religious. All of us work on some of these categories thinking if we can just fill that category, we'll be winners at life.

Tragically, some of us will spend our entire lives trying to fill in these categories, and one day Jesus is going to say to us the very thing he said to that rich young ruler. He's going to say, "My friend, to win at life is to lose at the game of Trivial Pursuit. What good is it if you win the game but lose your soul?" That's why the Bible says in Matthew 6:33, "But seek first his kingdom and his righteousness, and all these things will be given to you as well."

The way to win at life, when it's all said and done, is to be able to fill in the hole in the middle of everything. Jesus says, very simply, to put him in the center of our lives. When we make him number one in our lives, he promises to meet our needs in all the other areas.

(At this point, as you talk about each category and how Christ can meet that need, take the category off the board so that at the end, the only piece left is the one that says "Jesus Christ.")

As far as possessions, Philippians 4:19 promises, "My God will meet all your needs according to his glorious riches in Christ Jesus." Jesus says, "Do not worry about your life, what you will eat; or about your body, what you will wear" (Luke 12:22).

In the area of entertainment, Christ says in John 10:10, "I have come that [you] may have life, and have it to the full." When we know Jesus Christ, he shows us how to enjoy life more than we ever could before. That doesn't mean there won't be difficult times, but it does mean that through it all, you will have a deeply embedded joy in the knowledge that God loves you and is in control.

Addressing the history category, Psalm 103:12 says, "As far as the east is from the west, so far has he removed our transgressions from us." Jesus gives us a whole new history. He makes us new creatures.

In the area of knowledge, Christ says, "I am the way and the truth and the life" (John 14:6). In John 8:31, he proclaims, "If you hold to my teaching, you are really my disciples. Then you will know the truth, and the truth will set you free."

In the area of religion, John 1:12 says, "Yet to all who received him, to those who believed in his name, he gave the right to become children of God." When we know Christ and put him in the middle of our lives, we're not just being religious. Through him we come to know God in an intimate way—we don't just hear about him, we *know* him!

What about the physical? Christ says he knows the very number of hairs on our heads. He knows us better than we know ourselves, and he loves us not for what we look like on the outside, but because of who we are—his creation. He wants us to take care of our bodies. The Scriptures say that our bodies are temples (not pimples). That means that our bodies should be a place in which people see God at work.

If we put Christ first, he takes care of everything we need. So many of us are winning at the game of Trivial Pursuit, but like this young man in Mark's story, losing at the game of life. We've got the right answers to all the wrong questions, and the wrong answer to the only right question: "What must I do to have eternal life?"

Pursuing Jesus is not trivial. It is a calling. It is a challenge. It is life abundant. I wonder what sort of story Mark might have written if he described our meeting tonight with Jesus. Having heard the words of Jesus, how will we respond? For some of us, this can be an opportunity to ask Jesus to fill that vacuum in life. But I'm sure others who are loved by Jesus just as the rich young ruler was will say, just as he said, "The price is too high. I'm going to keep playing the game." Like the rich young ruler, those people will go away sad.

It's your choice. Hold on to your trivial pursuits, and you will lose. Give up your trivial pursuits, and you will live.

Involvement

Matthew 25:31–46

Todd Temple

This talk challenges teenagers to serve and shows them that they can serve in ways they can't even imagine. As you give the speech, substitute examples of kids from your own youth group who have found some creative ways to serve. Or draw from the collective experience of your youth group to make this talk even more encouraging.

The talk begins with an "Agree/Disagree" discussion. You can have the kids vote by moving to one side of the room or the other, or by simply raising their hands. But, before you move on to the next question, ask some of the students why they have voted the way they have. Allow this time to stimulate their thinking about the theme "involvement."

For outline, see page 230.

I'm going to make some statements, and I want you to listen closely and then tell me whether you agree or disagree. Some of them require a lot of thinking.

"Most unbelievers stay that way mainly because of the behavior of their Christian friends." Vote. There's no middle ground.

(Allow time for feedback from students.)

"Non-Christians look at Christians who do the same bad things that everyone else does and say, 'Why should I become a Christian when the Christians are no different from me?'"

(Again, allow time for feedback.)

Next question: "Most people give money to needy causes because they feel guilty." Vote. Disagree or Agree?

(Ask students to give some explanation of why they voted one way or the other.)

I asked you those questions to see how willing you are to commit yourself to an opinion, because in this talk I will be challenging you to commit yourself, to take a firm stand. For example, would you consider doing something more than you are presently doing if you felt you could make a positive change in the world? Or if you heard of something that you needed to do in your life, would you be willing to make a commitment to do it?

When I was in high school, the expression, "Go for it!" meant pouring yourself into something. "Go for it" to my high school diving team meant doing a two-and-a-half forward somersault off the high dive. And everytime I went for it, I'd kill myself. In the middle of the dive, somebody would scream, "Go for it!" and I'd come out early and—smack! I'd never even sink into the water—I'd just lay there on top.

There are all sorts of ways to "Go for it." Going for it is staying up late and reading a three-hundred-page book for a report. Going for it is returning a touchdown kick off return from deep in your own end zone. Going for it is when you type a ten-page report before first period. Every one of you knows what it's like to "Go for it" in some area. You see a cute guy or a girl that you want to go out with, and going for it means that you work up enough guts to ask that person out.

Do you know what "going for it" means in terms of the Christian life? It's pouring yourself into projects that bring glory to God. It's *involvement*. That's what I want us to talk about—giving your all to things that glorify God.

The first area that we can pour ourselves into is the church. Some of you are going, "Oh, I know the church." And in your mind you have this view of what a church is: the steeple, or the building. Wrong view. Some of you have another view of the church; it's spelled this way: R-U-L-E-S. Others of you would spell the church, "Z-Z-Z-Z." But that isn't the church either.

I'll bet that if I asked you to draw a picture of the church, very few would have the most realistic view: a view of a party. You wouldn't draw streamers and party hats and punch and confetti. Yet Christ told us to party. He said, "I have to leave, but I'm coming back, and I want you to party until I get back so people will know that I'm alive and I'm not still stuck in that grave."

I may be paraphrasing, but I think that's what church is—a party. And who are the party-goers? Us. We're the life of a two-thousand-year-old party. Because of us, the squares out there, the ones who don't party, will realize that God is still alive. In fact, in John 13:35 Jesus said, "By this all men will know that you are my disciples, if you love one another." The love that we have for each other and the times we spend celebrating that love show the squares that God is still alive.

We need people that are party-goers. A person who says in a monotone voice, "Sure, God is alive," is not a partyer. A partyer enthusiastically says, "God loves me." The church doesn't need a bunch of party poopers; we need people to be the *life* of the party.

Everybody knows that high-school kids are party-hearty. They know how to make things happen. I know, because I've had some of them in my youth group. Take Cheryl, for instance. Cheryl has the gift of gab. She stands in the back of the room and as people come in, she greets them and even starts a conversation. I can't do that, but Cheryl, this sophomore in high school, can. It's no big deal if a leader talks to a new kid, but when Cheryl does, you can bet that kid will be back next week. Cheryl shows that she really cares and in that way she keeps the party cooking.

Other kids at the party take the cards. ("You guys play cards? What kind of a party do you throw?") Actually, when people come that Cheryl doesn't recognize she'll say, "I haven't seen you around here. Are you new?" And she'll say, "Fill out this little card so we can send you junk mail." Then, when the new kids have filled out the cards, they return them to a group of kids who divide them up: "Here, you call this guy and I'll call this guy." All the party initiates then get a call from someone in the group. They come back, and the party gets bigger and bigger and bigger.

Jim is another one: total partyer. Jim can't talk to somebody to save his life. But to keep the party going he sets up tables before church. There's a table for coffee. There's a table for mission announcements. There are tables everywhere. And those people who pick up the missionary leaflet and say, "I'd like to sponsor a child" fill it out on that table that Jim set up. Jim keeps the party going.

I could go on and on. There are many ways to be the life of the party. All you have to do is go for it, get involved, pour yourself into the church, and then watch your party percolate!

Friendships are the greatest way of getting involved. You all know how to minister in friendships. You may not know how to preach. You may not know how to teach Sunday School. You may not know how to feed people. But you *can* be a friend by giving to people what they need.

I know six things that everybody needs. Give your friends these six things, and you will change their lives.

1. Your friends need your time. How can you have a friendship without investing time? Time is our measuring stick: The more time someone has to spend with me, the more they care about me. If they don't have time for me, they don't care that much about me. We need time to talk, to get to know each other, to enjoy each other.

2. They need you to listen. I have a friend, Mark, who calls me up once a month to tell me how bad life is. I won't say a word; I'll just go, "Uh-huh, uh-huh." Then at the end of the conversation I'll say, "Hang in there, Mark. I know you're going through struggles, but I know you're tough and you'll make it." Mark is pulling his life together after being hooked on drugs and spending time in jail. He can't say, "I've been saved, and now I have no problems." He's growing slowly, as we all do, and I remind him of that. He may say three thousand words to my two words of encouragement, but it's the listening that helps him, so that's what I do.

3. The third thing you can give your friends is transparency. Transparency is being open and honest with people. If you're a Christian, you have one strike against you—friends may expect you to be perfect. You need to be honest with them, letting them know that you struggle too, so they can see your Christianity *at work.*

I used to think that I had to be perfect for people to want to be a Christian. Now when I see Christians struggling with their weaknesses, I respect them, because I realize that they can relate to me and understand my struggles. I like transparent friends who let me know that they struggle with sexual sin, that sometimes they're tempted to get wasted, that sometimes they gossip.

I like friends who will tell me those things, because I realize that they're just like me.

4. A fourth need your friends have is to be held onto. If you're having a hard time at work, you quit, or if you don't like a class at school, you drop it. If you don't like your boyfriend or girlfriend, you dump them. We live in a disposable world where we can get rid of whatever we don't like. In sharp contrast to that is the Christian relationship of involvement, where we squeeze ourselves out like a tube of toothpaste and there's no putting the stuff back in. We pour ourselves into our friendships, never giving up on them.

When a friend is totally blowing it, wasting his life on drugs, we say, "I can't stand to see you hurt yourself like this, but let me tell you something—I love you and I'm not letting go of you no matter what you say. Never!" Can you imagine having a friend like that? Can you imagine *being* a friend like that? That's what it means to be held onto. If you hold on to them, they'll never let go. They'll start to grasp what you mean by the unconditional love of Jesus Christ.

5. Your friends need prayer. I can't say enough about this. You need people to pray for you because you're not going to make it on your own. Your friends need your prayers for the same reason, so pray for them. Take out your date book and pray for one of your friends every day—not a long, incredible prayer on your knees, but maybe just a quick prayer.

6. Finally, your friends need your laughter. If your friends know that you are capable of laughing, especially at yourself and at your own mistakes, they'll cling to you because nobody likes people that don't know how to laugh. This world has enough pain in it; we need some laughter.

I had a friend in high school who did all the things I just told you about. He would sit there and listen to me as I told him all the stupid things I was doing. He'd find out all my horrible secrets, but he'd hold on and never let go. He kept praying for me. He laughed with me. He told me his problems. He was my friend all the way through high school and to this day, ten years later, he's one of my greatest friends. If you can be that kind of friend to somebody, you will probably change that person's life.

Make a difference in the world. It's a big, bad world out there. If you're like me, you say, "There's nothing I can do—the world is messed up beyond all comprehension. And I'm just one person." There's a cartoon that shows hundreds of people standing around. Every one of them is thinking (in the little bubble above them), "But what can one man do? What can one woman do?" I'll tell you what one person can do. With Christ, we can do a lot of things—it only takes some initiative. Here are some ideas.

I know a high-school girl named Laura whose sole means of income is through babysitting. She only receives about $30 per month, yet she spends $21 of that money to sponsor a child in South America who lives in a hut without concrete floors, has little in the way of clothing or shoes, and walks two miles to get to school. She is being fed, clothed, educated, and evangelized through Laura's generosity. Laura spends two-thirds of her own money to keep this girl alive and well and learning about the Lord. Is she crazy? No, she's pouring herself into a project that glorifies God. If that's the only thing she does, she is saving a life!

Here's another one—John. John is a squirrelly kid, but every year he participates in the "Run for Hungry Children." Once a year he bugs everybody on his street to sponsor him for this run. John runs, walks, crawls, and does whatever he can to get through the three-mile course. He usually raises $300, which goes to an infant feeding program in Haiti. That $300 keeps a newborn alive for one year. Here's John, who has never changed a diaper, keeping alive a newborn four thousand miles away!

A pastor of a church in Mexico asked a youth group to help him build an orphanage. The kids said, "We'll try to help. We can't do squat, but we'll try." Three weeks later they piled into a van en route to Mexico to build an orphanage. What did they build that orphanage out of? Cement and mud! And it only took three weeks for a bunch of junior highers who had barely graduated from playing with Legos to build an orphanage.

There are so many ways you can get involved: You can write letters to prisoners. You can go downtown and find houses to fix up for old people who can no longer do hard work themselves. Or you can teach in Vacation Bible School. As you work, you'll be amazed at the difference you can make in people's lives.

Let me close with a story from Matthew 25:31–46, where Jesus talks about what will happen after we've left this party to go to the ultimate party in the sky. God, after gathering everyone together, says, "Okay, sheep here; goats over there; people that are on my side here; people that are not on my side over there." Then he takes all the sheep, the people who did something (they don't know what, but they're about to find out), and he puts them all on one side. He says, "Welcome, my friends, and thank you. When you were on earth, and I was hungry, you fed me. When I was thirsty, you gave me something to drink. When I was naked, you clothed me. When I was sick, you came and visited me. When I was in prison, you visited me."

Meanwhile, all these people are saying, "Come on. When did we see you hungry and feed you? When did we see you thirsty and give you something to drink? When did we see you naked? Now that's something we'd remember, Lord. When did we see you sick or in prison? What did you get imprisoned for? I thought you were supposed to be a good guy?" And Jesus replies, "Whenever you did any of those things for the least of these, my people, you did it for me."

Then Jesus takes all the goats over to the other side and says, "Hey, gang. I'm going to have to kick you out of this party, because when I came to you while you were on earth, I was hungry, and you didn't feed me. When I was thirsty, you couldn't care less. When I was naked or sick or in prison, you shunned me."

They're stunned. "What? Certainly we would have noticed you. I mean, the robe, the glowing face? We sure would have noticed the halo, right?"

But he says, "Look, whenever you didn't do it for one of the least of my children, you didn't do it for me."

I bet those people were thinking, "If only we'd known before—we should have looked a little more carefully." Do you know what? We *do* know it beforehand. We have just seen a sneak preview of something that's going to happen in the future, so now we can prepare for it. How? Whenever you do something, do it for the Lord—pour yourself into a project for God's glory. Also, realize that *every person* you come in contact with is Jesus. When you're on the freeway and you cut somebody off, that's Jesus you cut off. When you flip somebody off, that's Jesus. When you don't feed somebody, or you don't clothe somebody, or you don't visit somebody, or you don't take time to spend with a friend, those are things you're doing to Jesus.

You may interpret that differently in your Bible, but it seems very clear to me. "Whatever you do to the least of these, my children, you do to me. And whatever you don't do, you don't do to me." We need to start thinking about what we do, how we do it, and for whom we do it. It changes the reason why we do things. Don't pour yourself into projects for your own glory—"I'm such a nice guy; I stayed up late to help my friends with their homework. I built an orphanage. Yo, me, right here. I'll take autographs later." That's the wrong motivation.

Secondly, don't pour yourself into projects for pity's sake. Don't say, "Oh, those poor people. I'm so nice to help them. I just feel so rotten because I have so many nice things, and they have nothing. Here, let me share a little with them."

There's only one true reason for doing any of this stuff—to glorify God. As you give of yourself to help others, you'll find that you are giving yourself to God himself. Whatever you do to the least of these children, you do for him. So let me challenge you, folks, to "Go for it!" Get involved—in your church, in your friendships, in the community—and you'll change the world.

Playing Favorites

Romans 15:7

Dan Webster

This is a talk that addresses issues like snobbery, cliquishness, and spiritual pride. Narrate it like a story, or use a drama during the latter part of the story when the main character leads the two "punk" kids into the youth meeting. At this point in the story, lead in some kids dressed as punk rockers whom your youth won't recognize.

If you can pull it off, you could also ask someone to attend the meeting who will dress or act differently than the others. He should be someone the group doesn't know, and he shouldn't overplay the part, yet he should have some visible differences. After giving this talk, identify this person and ask him how he felt he was treated by the group. Then ask the group about the way they treated this person.

For outline, see page 233.

This is a special night for you. You've been attending your youth group for months and have hoped to gain some respect in the eyes of the leadership. It's "Bring a Friend" month and the emphasis is on getting new kids to attend your youth group. Your youth pastor has been putting some pressure on you to bring the "sharp" kids from your school—Klondike High. So you've been pestering two of your friends to come. (Well, they aren't really friends, more like acquaintances.) You are hoping that *Larry Linebacker* and *Patty Popular* will come.

You've asked them a number of times, and they have seemed interested. Larry even told you today at lunch that they would probably come tonight if nothing else came up. You are excited! Man, if they come, you'll finally get the respect you deserve. Not only that, but you've often thought about how God could *really* use people like them—I mean, they know the whole school and everyone looks up to them.

It's 7:30 and you're waiting for them in the room where the youth group meets. The other kids are already in the meeting listening to a guy sing a song with his guitar. One of the youth sponsors has told you to hang around out front and direct any new people to the right place. You gladly volunteer, not telling him about Larry and Patty. You are hoping to surprise everyone if they show up.

You asked one of your friends to save three seats for you—great seats, right near the front, with easy access to the refreshments afterwards. These are perfect seats for people like Larry and Patty! Great seats for people to notice whom you are sitting next to. Great seats because your youth pastor is sure to see whom you are with.

So here you stand out front—waiting. They told you that they probably couldn't make it until 7:30, so you are still hopeful. You stand gazing out the window and are just about ready to go sit down—then you see them drive up in Larry's new Bronco. Right behind them, pulling into the parking lot, is the ugliest car you've ever seen. You probably wouldn't have noticed except for the fact that both doors of the car were different colors from the body. You wonder what losers are in that car and feel a

bit sorry for the kids from their school who will have to sit with them.

You push those thoughts out of your mind as Larry and Patty approach the door. Man, they look good—Larry's wearing his letterman's jacket, and he's got more medals on it than General MacArthur. I mean, you can barely see the "K." And Patty, ooohhh, does she look fine . . . looks like she just stepped out of *Seventeen*. You quickly straighten your letterman's jacket and try to keep your composure—not wanting them to think you are *too* thrilled that they came. You lead them through the back of the room and realize you can't seat them yet. The song is over, but your youth pastor is giving an announcement. You figure that you will wait, and then, just before the next song, you'll escort them down front and everyone will be sure to see you with them. It seems like the announcements are going on forever.

Your mind is rushing with excitement, knowing that now, maybe now, you'll get the respect you deserve. Your youth pastor will be impressed with you . . . your friends will know that you're important. In the middle of your thoughts you get a brainstorm—you think, "Yeah, it's risky, but it might be cool—maybe even an act of chivalry. I should treat her like the lady that she is. Patty is a class lady and should be treated so."

Your idea? Offer her your arm (not

to keep, of course) so that you can escort her to her seat. Larry would understand; he's not threatened by you. A girl like Patty should be treated like royalty. It would be like seating guests at a wedding. Nice touch! Imagine leading the most popular girl in the school down to the front on your arm. Ooohh, would the guys be impressed!

A poke on your arm awakens you out of your little daydream. Larry asks you, "Where's the bathroom? Patty has to go." You tell them there's one just down the hall on the left. You tell them that you'll wait just inside for them and that you've got some great seats picked out. As they walk away, you begin to think about the asset these two could be to the reputation of your youth group on campus. If they came to your youth group, people would see the group as a cool place to go.

All of a sudden, you're overcome by a strange aroma. You wonder what it could be—then you notice who has snuck in the back door and is standing next to you. It must be the couple from that lovely three-tone sedan. Check them out! Punkers ... I mean strange ... leather everywhere ... old army jacket ... chains ... earrings ... strange make-up ... crooked teeth ... hair sticking out everywhere ... and that smell. That horrible smell!

They look at you and you try to be nice. They ask you where they should sit, and in your mind you're thinking of some classic answers. But you explain that most of the kids are seated according to schools and ask them which school they attend. When they answer, "Klondike High," your heart stops. That's your school. You can't believe it. You look a little closer at them and realize that you've seen them at school once or twice, usually hanging around the smoking area behind the gym. You and your friends always jokingly call those guys "nicotine lizards" because of the way they slink and slither around the dumpster in back of the gym.

It's a bit strange, but at this exact moment, you have your first serious talk with God for the day. You pray, "Oh God, how can you allow this to happen to me? I don't want to be seen with them. Why do you put me in situations like this?" You look at them, smile, and tell them that you'll point out where they should sit after your youth minister finishes the announcements. You keep looking back down the hall hoping Larry and Patty will hurry back—but not until you can get rid of these two low-lifes.

You know that the announcements are almost over because your youth leader is making some introductory comments on the theme of that evening. He always gives a little "teaser" concerning the topic of the night. He does this to get everyone thinking along the right lines. But tonight he is doing something different in his introduction. He's reading Scripture verses. You're kind of glad that Larry and Patty aren't here for this— you'd hate to have them turned off before things really get started.

Your youth pastor begins his introduction, "Tonight we're going to be talking about playing favorites—partiality—treating some people better than others. It is very easy to favor the pretty people, the beautiful people, and ignore others that are equally important to God.

"'Don't have a faith in Christ that includes an attitude of personal favoritism . . . God is no respecter of persons! Jesus, during his stay on earth, focused his attention on the poor, the needy, the oppressed, the downtrodden, the broken, the underdog. . . .'" And James, the brother of Jesus, continues in the second chapter of his letter, 'Please let there be no discrimination in the church . . . there is enough discrimination in the world (too much). Let the church be the one place on the planet where all economic and clothing distinctions disappear' (paraphrase courtesy of Dan Webster)."

Suddenly you stop and really look at the girl standing next to you. You sense her presence for the first time. You realize, in a quick reflective moment, that there just might be a good reason why she dresses like she does. You remember something that you heard earlier, that often the "rebel," beneath

his or her tough exterior, has pain and hurt inside. You glance at the eyes of the girl standing next to you and notice that they are tense and bitterly angry. You wonder what circumstances could have occurred in her life that would leave her so angry.

You realize that these two probably get hassled everywhere they go. Everywhere, everyday, these two get hassled . . . at school, at home, in public places. They probably get stares that all effectively communicate how much disdain middle-class people have for anyone below their status, anyone second-class.

At this moment, the voice of God explodes in your mind with a very clear message: "It shouldn't happen here. Discrimination shouldn't ever happen in the church—not in this youth group— not in any youth group!" You tremble inside! You realize, with great heaviness, how much of the world's values still live in your heart.

You remember Larry and Patty and look around for them. Then reality strikes you like a cold blast—they left! You see the Bronco taillights go by the front of the building. They probably sized up your group in a few short moments and decided that it wasn't the type of place that would enhance their image or expand their influence, so they left!

At that moment, a new wave of freedom sweeps over your heart. The

Holy Spirit brings to mind some rusty truths from the Bible that you haven't thought about much recently:

"As I have loved you, so you must love one another." (John 13:34).

"Be kind and compassionate to one another . . ." (Eph. 4:32).

"Accept one another, then, just as Christ accepted you, in order to bring praise to God." (Rom. 15:7).

"We do not dare to classify or compare ourselves with some who commend themselves. When they measure themselves by themselves and compare themselves with themselves, they are not wise" (2 Cor. 10:12).

You bow your head, saddened at your immaturity. You realize that you spent more time scheming than praying, finagling than trusting, worrying than worshiping, trying to impress rather than loving. In your heart you mutter a prayer, "O God, now I know what this whole episode is about. Now I know why you put me in situations like this."

You aren't sure about the exact content of the youth leader's message, but that doesn't matter because you've already heard a sermon in your heart. The message has gotten through: The people standing next to you are very important people that matter a great deal to God. They are Jesus' kind of people! In this moment of sober sanity you realize that while God loves Larry and Patty, God and his work doesn't need them. They need God. You realize that God's work is not dependent upon the Larrys and Pattys of the world.

You look once again at the girl standing next to you, and you decide that you are going to treat her just like Jesus would treat her. You change your game plan of ditching these two near the back of the room and decide to go right ahead with the processional. Right now, you decide that you are going to escort this precious child of God on your arm down the center aisle of the meeting room like a proud father escorts his firstborn down the aisle to the marriage altar. You hope every head will turn!

You pray quietly, "God, turn their heads—and please, Holy Spirit of God—do a work in every heart here. Touch my friends as you've touched me. Minister to them. Break them down. Soften them up. Oh God, may the church, our youth ministry, be the one place on the planet where cold stares stop and where warm embraces abound! . . . Where genuine handshakes are offered and where people are seen as people. And God, I know that's the kind of fellowship that is going to make people take notice of our group—because everybody, even the Larrys and Pattys of the world, more than anything else want to be loved."

Zaccheus

Luke 19

Mike Yaconelli

This talk, especially appropriate for non-Christian and unchurched kids, brings some new insights to the familiar story of Zaccheus. The Zaccheus song can be a fun introduction—especially if you teach it to the other leaders before you give the talk and have them serenade the rest of the group!
For outline, see page 235.

I want to read to you from Luke 19 the story about a little man named Zaccheus.

Jesus entered Jericho and was passing through. A man was there by the name of Zaccheus; he was a chief tax collector and was wealthy. He wanted to see who Jesus was, but being a short man he could not, because of the crowd. So he ran ahead and climbed a sycamore-fig tree to see him, since Jesus was coming that way.

When Jesus reached the spot, he looked up and said to him, "Zaccheus, come down immediately. I must stay at your house today." So he came down at once and welcomed him gladly.

All the people saw this and began to mutter, "He has gone to be the guest of a 'sinner.'"

But Zaccheus stood up and said to the Lord, "Look, Lord! Here and now I give half of my possessions to the poor, and if I have cheated anybody out of anything, I will pay back four times the amount."

Jesus said to him, "Today salvation has come to this house, because this man, too, is a son of Abraham. For the Son of Man came to seek and to save what was lost."

Here we have an itty-bitty tax collector, a crook despised by everyone, standing up in a tree. Jesus walks by. Stops. Points to him. Invites him to dinner. Everybody else gets ticked off. A story like that could make a movie—or an episode on 'General Hospital'!" It could even be a song. In fact, it is a song! Some kids in a youth group in Rhode Island (Barrington Baptist Church youth group, 1979, youth minister Duffy Robbins) wrote a song about Zacchaeus. You sing it to the tune of "Five Foot Two."

> Five foot two,
> Was a Jew,
> And a tax collector too.
> Zacchaeus was a tiny man.
> Jesus was
> Passing by,
> All the others stood too high.
> Zacchaeus was a tiny man.
> So he climbed a tree,
> Thinking he
> Might see the Lord.
> The Lord looked up, looked around,
> Said, "Zacchaeus, come on down."
> At your house
> I must stay.
> That is why I'm here today.
> Oh, Jesus was a hungry man.
> Crowd saw them
> Head for dinner,
> Disapproved 'cuz Zac's a sinner.
> But Jesus was a hungry man.
> Well, Zacchaeus said,
> "I'll return
> All I have stole.
> If I have cheated anyone,
> I will pay them back four-fold."
> Jesus said,
> "Today's the time.
> Life is yours and you are mine."
> Zacchaeus isn't tiny,
> His life is bright and shiny,
> Zacchaeus is a "new-born" man.

Zacchaeus was not exactly your everyday nice kind of guy. Just look at him—he worked for the same government that had placed the Jews under heavy oppression. He was a traitor to his own countrymen. He cheated and stole money from them. Everyone hated him. Yet Jesus came by and invited him to dinner.

Now the reason I've decided to tell you this story is simply this: The more we learn about the Christian life, the more some of us say, "There is no way I can measure up to what God wants of me. I'm not a great Christian, and I'm not reading my Bible like I'm supposed to. I know I'm supposed to believe that God loves me and cares for me no matter what, but I begin to wonder—if Jesus was sending out dinner invitations, I have a strong feeling that I wouldn't be invited. If Jesus suddenly showed up in America, I know Billy Graham would be up at the top of his guest list. Not me. I would be on the bottom somewhere, or probably not even on it."

Deep inside it's hard for me to believe that Jesus would want me to show up at his place for dinner. So it blows me away to read that Jesus chose—of all the people in that crowd, all the religious leaders, all the really good people—he chose Zacchaeus. That's good news for everybody here. That means if Jesus showed up in this room, he'd invite all of us for dinner.

And all the religious, super-nice people would be sitting out there wondering what's going on.

That's the good news—Jesus is always seeking you out. He follows you around, asking you to come over, wanting to talk to you. Even when you say no to Jesus, even when you turn your back on Christ, he's right behind you, following you around.

I always used to think that meant he was out to get me, lurking around the corner, waiting for me to make a mistake so he could pounce on me and clobber the sin right out of me. I go and neck with my girlfriend all night long. Next morning I wake up—no lips. Jesus followed me around and when he saw that kissing, he dissolved my lips!

Of course, that's not the way it is. This is a really shallow example, but it's like when you meet somebody who is absolutely gorgeous and all you can think is, "There's no way this person would even *look* at me. I'm scum. I'm not even good enough to pick up their garbage. If I went up and said, 'Hello, would you like to get acquainted?' they would look at me like, 'Ugh, Yuck.'"

When you meet Jesus—the most gorgeous person alive—and you say, "Um, excuse me, Jesus? Do you have a couple of minutes?" he won't look at you like "Ugh." No, his whole face will light up, and he'll say, "I've been watching you, hoping that you'd notice me—and now you have!"

So you bask in the glow of being wanted and loved for a while. But then, like Zacchaeus, you have to do something. When Jesus said, "I want to go to dinner with you," Zacchaeus couldn't very well sit up there in the clouds and say, "Who me? Oh, wow, that's incredible. Thank you very much." He had to get out of the tree and go to dinner with Jesus.

How you respond to Jesus is important–*very* important. Even though God loves you no matter what, even though God is all-powerful, he will never, ever violate your will. He will not shake you and say, "You're going to believe in me or else." If you say, "No, I'm not ready," he won't say, "Oh yes, you are!" God doesn't slap people into believing in him. He follows you around, but you have to choose him.

Because your "no" can even stop the God of the universe, that makes your "yes" all the more important. When you say "yes," you are using your will to respond to God and to actually choose to follow God. God will not violate your will. Instead, he watches and waits for your "yes."

You need to understand, however, that saying "yes" isn't some big religious deal. It's not saying, "I'm saved. Okay, tomorrow I fly over to India to work with lepers." Somehow we get the idea that when we say "yes" to God, the trumpet sounds, the angels flit about rejoicing, and we suddenly are driven to do some incredibly religious thing. Look at what Zacchaeus did—he just went to dinner!

You don't need to do anything spectacular when you say "yes"; you just need to do *something*. After all, "Something is always better than nothing." You may decide to pray thirty minutes a day. So you make a list of all the people and all the problems that you can think of to pray for, and you start praying like crazy. You stop. You're finished with your list. You look at your watch—three minutes.

Disgusted, you shrug your shoulders and say, "Since I can't pray thirty minutes, forget it—I'm not praying at all." But try to pray just fifteen more seconds, only fifteen more than you prayed yesterday. Don't apologize for starting small. Don't apologize for whatever you give to God, because God can take whatever it is and use it.

One day a mother called me and said, "I would like to know if only popular kids can come to your youth group." I said, "No, no. Anybody can come." She said, "I want my son James to come. But I can't invite him; you're going to have to get somebody to invite him."

When she said "James," I thought to myself, "This guy sounds like he's a little different." She said, "He plays chess and rides his bike to school. And he wears big, thick glasses." I said, "No problem. We'll take care of it."

So I call a gorgeous girl in my youth group and say, "Shannon, I want you to invite this kid named James to come to Young Life." I wish I could tell you she said, "If God wants me to invite James, then of course I will." She invited James, but she wasn't too thrilled about having done so.

James came to youth group every week after that, and even signed up for a mission trip to Mexico. But he would sit in the corner, never talking or socializing. Finally, one night, as everyone was leaving, James went up to Shannon and tapped her on the shoulder. She was with a bunch of guys and didn't want to talk to him, but he looked at her and said, "Shannon, I want to thank you for inviting me to come to this group because it's the greatest thing that's ever happened to me."

Shannon was floored. She had changed his life, and she hadn't even wanted to! God had used her in a small way—her inviting James to the youth group—to accomplish great things. In the same way, God will take your two bits of talent or effort or resources and multiply them over and over. If you read your Bible for only five minutes this week, God will take that five minutes and use it. You don't have to spiritualize it and you don't have to make it into a big deal—all you have to do is offer every little bit of yourself for God to use.

God can even use you in some dull, everyday class—like German. I once read a story about a boy named Richard whom God used in German class.

Richard's German teacher was exactly what you'd expect of a German teacher—she was a battle-ax, an Attilia the Hunness, a regular Hitler in drag. One of her students, named Margaret, was on this woman's hit list. Margaret became so paranoid of this teacher that everytime she tried to translate any German, she'd mess it up. The teacher would then stand right in front of her desk, looming over her like the angel of death, and say, "Margaret, how could you be so stupid—can't you *ever* translate anything correctly?"

Richard, on the other hand, *always* translated everything correctly. He was brilliant, so he had no trouble with an especially difficult assignment that the teacher gave. He came to the class on the day they were to go over the assignment, cool and confident. But the rest of the class was terrified of being called on; they kept their eyes glued to their assignments, as the teacher prowled the room, and hoped against hope that she wouldn't pounce on them. Finally, after a long, taut silence, she stopped in front of Margaret's desk.

"Margaret," she barked out. Marga-

ret's head shot up. "Stand up and translate the first sentence."

Slowly, Margaret stood, clutching her paper, and slowly, she read the sentence. She had studied hard—she really had—but her translation was totally wrong. When she got through, the teacher yelled at her, telling her she was an idiot and should never have taken German. Margaret sank back into her seat and covered her face with her hands. Then the teacher turned to Richard and said, "Richard, stand up and translate the same thing."

So brilliant Richard, Richard the Brain, got up. All eyes were on him, knowing that he would do it correctly and show Margaret how stupid she was in comparison. But as he began to read, those close to him could see he wasn't reading his paper, but a script in his mind. Richard repeated Margaret's translation, word for word.

The class stared. The teacher ranted and raved. But Richard looked at Margaret, and Margaret looked at him. Richard, who actually wrote this story, (Richard Selzer, *Mortal Lessons*, Simon & Schuster 1978, pp. 202–205) said, "It was more than just exchanging looks. We had formed a bond together and nothing would ever be the same again."

A little thing like that rescued Margaret from all the pressure she faced alone. A little thing like that can change someone's whole world. We don't have to do big, unbelievable, incredible things—all we have to do is let God use the little things we do.

Now let's go back to the story of Zacchaeus and look at Jesus' final words to Zacchaeus: "For the Son of Man came to seek and to save what was lost." That sounds very religious, as if it ought to be up on some revival tent. But when Jesus talks about seeking and saving lost people, he's not talking about people who are hiding out in a bar. He's not saying, "You bar hoppers are the *bad* people; you're the people I came to seek." What he's saying is, "I've come to seek and to save those who are in the wrong place." What Christ was saying to Zacchaeus was, "Zacchaeus, it's not that you're hanging around in bars. It's not that you're in a horrible porno movie. The thing that's wrong with you is that you're in the wrong place." Jesus came to put us in the *right* place.

Some time ago a young boy took his own life by hanging himself from a tree in his front yard. Before he died, he nailed a note to the tree that said, "This is the only thing in this family that has roots." There are hundreds and thousands of kids all around this country who feel the same way. They feel isolated. They feel alone. They don't feel attached to anything. Their folks are so busy with aerobics and racquetball and into being kids again that they don't have time for them. And the kids begin to wonder, "Does anybody care? Is there anything that connects me with what's going on? Do I really, in fact, have a place?"

The great news is that Jesus gives us a place—a home. He connects us with the universe and with God himself. When you and I make Christ a part of our lives, no matter who we are, we are significant and important.

Jesus had dinner with Zacchaeus, and when they were done, Zacchaeus was a totally changed man. Jesus didn't tell him what he had to do. Jesus just began to talk with him, began to relate with him, and began to identify with him. Zacchaeus saw that this Jesus he had heard about loved him and cared for him, and after having experienced that kind of love, Zacchaeus *wanted* to change his life-style—he wanted to respond to that kind of love.

I would like to close with a story that I think illustrates Jesus' love for us in a way that we can understand. Imagine this . . . You are a beautiful woman who has been happily married four years. Then a tumor is discovered in your face, and the doctor says, "I'm going to have to cut that tumor out, and there's a good chance that if I do, I'll cut a nerve. I'll do everything I can to avoid that. But if I do have to cut the nerve, the whole left side of your face will droop down and you will look palsied and distorted for the rest of your life."

The woman had the surgery, and the doctor who did the surgery describes what happened (Ibid. pp. 45–46):

I stand by the bed where the young woman lies . . . her face, post-operative . . . her mouth twisted in palsy . . . clownish. A tiny twig of the facial nerve, one of the muscles of her mouth, has been severed. She will be that way from now on. I had followed with religious fervor the curve of her flesh, I promise you that. Nevertheless, to remove the tumor in her cheek, I had cut the little nerve. Her young husband is in the room. He stands on the opposite side of the bed and together they seem to be in a world all their own in the evening lamplight . . . isolated from me . . . private.

"Who are they?" I ask myself . . . he and this wry mouth I have made, who gaze at and touch each other so generously. The young woman speaks. "Will my mouth always be like this?" she asks. "Yes," I say, "it will. It is because the nerve was cut." She nods and is silent. But the young man smiles. "I like it," he says. "It's kind of cute."

All at once, I know who he is. I understand, and I lower my gaze. Unmindful, he bends to kiss her crooked mouth. I am so close, I can see how he twists his own lips to accommodate hers, to show her that their kiss still works.

Jesus, like the young husband, twisted his body for you to let you know that "the kiss still works." And the Jesus who called to Zacchaeus, hiding up in a tree, is looking for you, calling you by name. You may feel that you're too little, that you don't have much to offer, that you're too horrible for Jesus to want, but that's because you don't know how much your God loves you. Today—right now—he's asking to stay in *your* home.

WANTED:
More Hot Talks!

Attention youth speakers! We need *your* Hot Talks for the next edition of this book.

Send us your best youth talk and—who knows?—it might be featured in the next Hot Talks book. Send it to the address below, and we'll let you know whether or not we'll be able to use it. It can be on any topic and of any length.

Our next book will feature more Hot Talks, plus a great selection of short illustrations, stories, and object lessons that can be incorporated into any talk. If you would like to contribute to the next Hot Talks book (and earn some money as well), send your ideas to:

Hot Talks Editor
Youth Specialties
1224 Greenfield Drive
El Cajon, CA 92021

Outlines

Freedom in Jesus

I. Introduction
  A. Articles of clothing and how they symbolize the meaning of freedom
  B. The common belief that freedom is good
  C. Limitations on freedom
    1. Requirements of others
    2. *U.S. News and World Report* quote on stress and depression of adolescence

II. Body
  A. Ways of dealing with a perceived lack of freedom
    1. Running away
    2. Escape
      a. music
      b. fantasy
      c. drug/alcohol abuse
  B. We are copies of the culture and people surrounding us
    1. Example of chameleon blending in with environment
    2. We are slaves to our basic humanity (sin)
      a. John 8:31–36
      b. a slave is one who has absolutely no control over personal life
      c. we are made slaves in three ways
        (1) the lust of the flesh—desire to do
          (a) food
          (b) sex
        (2) the lust of the eyes—desire to have
          (a) material possessions
          (b) money
        (3) the pride of life—desire to be
          (a) reputation

III. Conclusion
    A. Freedom comes through obedience to Jesus Christ
        1. Example from government of England
            a. Queen is most visible
            b. Prime Minister has most power
        2. Freedom is acknowledging Jesus Christ as Lord and Prime Minister of our lives

Encouragement

I. Murphy's Law
  A. Need for encouragement
  B. Words can hurt

II. Youth group as a body of believers in Christ
  A. Hebrews 10:24–25
  B. Reason why encouragement is different
    1. World gears us to isolation.
    2. However, God created us as social creatures
  C. Three ways to encourage one another
    1. Verbal encouragement
      a. saying something nice
      b. writing a short note
    2. Material encouragement
      a. James 2:15–16
    3. Emotional encouragement
      a. presence
      b. hugs
      c. eye contact

III. Challenge to encourage someone in group
  A. Three ways to end talk
    1. Writing note of encouragement to someone
    2. Thanking God for someone in the group through prayer
    3. Reading "A Warm Fuzzy Tale" by Claude Steiner

Forgiveness

I. Introduction
   A. Results of a survey of things that really tick people off
   B. Acknowledgment by speaker of audience's individual hurts and disappointments

II. Discussion of why it is so hard to forgive others
   A. Three reasons why it is so hard to forgive others
      1. We enjoy holding a grudge.
         a. pleasure in resentment
         b. silent treatment—only hurts grudgeholder in the end
         c. story by Robert Louis Stevenson of two sisters who lived together but never spoke to each other
         d. unforgiveness may be fun for a while, but only causes division in the end
      2. We feel insecure
         a. hanging on to the power position
         b. interaction with mother who has power over the child
         c. this becomes a vicious cycle where unforgiveness breeds insecurity
      3. We are angry
         a. we want revenge
         b. unresolved anger leads to bitterness
         c. Ephesians 4:32
         d. bitterness leads to broken relationships
   B. Three thoughts concerning forgiving others
      1. Forgiveness takes time
      2. Forgiving someone doesn't always mean the other person will change
      3. God can help us not be controlled by hurt or revenge after we show forgiveness

III. Story of Nancy Warnath (taken from Prison Fellowship Newsletter, *Jubilee*, July 1986)
   A. Counsels prisoners at Montana State Penitentiary after murder of her son, Jack
   B. If we do not forgive others, we will be held accountable before God

IV. Ways to end talk
   A. Silent prayer
   B. Writing wrongs done to us on slips of paper and cutting them up or throwing them away
   C. An act that will signify a willingness to forgive

Dare to Dream

I. Story of Laconians
   A. People who lived with ball and chain around feet
   B. Tommy, who knew relief of release from the ball and chain, was outcast from the group
   C. Tommy moved to a distant land and lived happily every after

II. High school kids are similar to Laconians
   A. John 8:36
   B. People settle for second best and carry around heavy burdens
      1. peer pressure
      2. sexual temptation
      3. making money
      4. pressure in school and at work
      5. pressure in relationships
      6. pressure with attempts to be religious
   C. High school graduation and ten-year reunion
      1. Settling for second best in high school continues throughout life
   D. Choose to be the man or woman God desires you to be

III. Account of paralytic beside the pool of Bethseda—John 5:2–11
   A. Paralytic settled for second best by making excuses as to why he couldn't get to the water
   B. Jesus offered him healing

IV. Jesus offers us healing as well—do we really want to be made whole?
   A. Story of the eagle who thought he was a prairie chicken
   B. Challenge to be men and women who are part of the solution in this world rather than merely offering excuses
   C. Isaiah 40:28–31

How To Know If You Are In Love

I. Introduction
   A. Girls on beach checking out lifeguard
      1. Love is not infatuation—there is a difference
   B. Speaker's first crush on a girl named Geri
      1. Infatuation is a normal part of life
      2. Difference between real love and infatuation is that real love stands the test of time
   C. Speaker's relationship with wife, Cathy
      1. Attraction
      2. Commitment
      3. Caring
   D. Statistically speaking, teens "fall in love" about five times between ninth grade and their sophomore year in college
II. Practical guidelines in deciding whether or not a particular person is "the one"
   A. Are you willing to give 100% of yourself to your spouse?
      1. True love is selfless love
   B. Do you like the other person?
      1. Scene from movie, *Shenandoah*
      2. Liking the other person's personality and behavior
   C. Are you transparent with each other?
      1. Open communication
   D. Are you and your special friend too dependent on each other?
      1. I love, therefore I need—good
      2. I need, therefore I love—bad
   E. Is your love self-centered?
      1. Getting rather than giving—counterfeit love
      2. Self-giving, self-sacrificing as God loves us—agape love
   F. Do you have a mature love for Jesus Christ?
      1. Good relationship with God individually and together as a couple

III. Love as described by Paul in 1 Corinthians 13
    A. Qualities of love as described in verses 4–7
    B. These qualities can help us honestly evaluate our love for another person
IV. Conclusion
    A. Time will help in distinguishing between love and infatuation
    B. In the meantime
       1. Deal with six questions
       2. Study ideals of love in 1 Corinthians 13
       3. Trust God to show you his will for you

A Fresh Look at God's Love

I. Speaker's personal story
   A. Compulsion to make Christian life work
   B. 2 Corinthians 5:14
     1. Thinking he had to work at loving God more to be a good Christian
     2. However, God's love for us should be our motivation to live a Christian life

II. Five characteristics of God's love
   A. God's love for us is passionate
     1. God seen as cold and calculating
     2. Example of Creation—Genesis 2:8–9
     3. God made variety and beauty with passion
     4. God's response to Adam and Eve was pained
     5. God is an active, passionate God alive in the universe
   B. God is very, very tender
     1. Tender means doing whatever possible to meet a need in the most sensitive and penetrating way
     2. Example of Jesus in John 8:2–11
       a. He took the focus off of the woman and placed it on himself
     3. God understands and cares about us
   C. God is the greatest fan in your life
     1. Personal story of a football game where speaker's dad was cheering for him
     2. Jesus is alongside of us cheering for us
     3. Romans 8:31
   D. God's love is unconditional (absolute, without exception)
     1. Example of Peter
       a. his denial of Jesus
       b. Jesus' complete and total love for Peter
     2. Example of Tom and his three-year-old son, Brandon, who got a glass of milk for Tom to go with his cookies

E. God enjoys us
1. Example of Tessa, who wanted to know if the speaker really liked her
2. Jesus having a wallet with all of our pictures in it
3. Psalm 139
4. Example of Brennan Manning, whose life was saved in Vietnam by a man in his combat unit
   a. Jesus died for us to prove His love for us
III. All that God has done for us and the ways he has shown his love for us give us the motivation to live a Christian life

Fit for a King

I. Christmas account from Luke 2:1–7
   A. God's humble beginning on earth as a baby
   B. Jesus comes to most humble places
      1. He was most comfortable with outcasts
      2. He always looked for humble "manger types"

II. What mangers (places or relationships where we think Jesus may not fit) exist in our lives?
   A. Friends
   B. Family
   C. Dating

III. Jesus wants to enter the "mangers"—the tough, awkward, uncomfortable places—in our lives
   A. Jesus Christ can understand how we feel through his birth, death, and the fact that he lives today to identify with us
   B. Don't hold back on "mangers" in our lives

IV. God still invades our "mangers" today

Our Deepest Need

I. Personal story of the sled race
   A. Crashing into wall
   B. Concern with damage to sled rather than himself
   C. Blood on his face was pointed out to him by others
      1. Condition of sled—what he could see
      2. Condition of his face—what he couldn't see
   D. It took someone else to show him what his biggest need was

II. Account of paralyzed man to whom Jesus gave a bigger perspective of his real need—Mark 2:1–12
   A. Man saw physical need
   B. Jesus saw the man's need as being one of forgiveness for his sin
   C. Sin is our rebellion against God's rightful authority in our lives
   D. The result is a self-inflicted separation from God
      1. Romans 6:23
   E. God takes sin seriously and is deeply offended by our sin

III. Story of the Hollywood star who had cancer
   A. Saw the little blemish as being nothing
   B. We must deal with sin as cancerous growth which leads to a slow death.
   C. Jesus is the Great Physician
      1. We need to take care of our deepest need by allowing Jesus to forgive us
      2. Then Jesus can take care of our other needs

The Only Solution

I. Introduction
  A. The Good News is that we can have a personal relationship with God through Jesus Christ
  B. The only solution to our separation from God is Jesus Christ
II. Three questions to ask
  A. Why Jesus Christ as the only solution?
    1. He said it himself—John 14:6.
    2. Other evidences
      a. Jesus Christ was born of a virgin
        (1) Speaker gives account of Mary telling Joseph that she is pregnant
      b. Jesus Christ was sinless
        (1) The people with whom he lived testified to this
        (2) What would be the result of interviewing our friends as to whether we ever sinned?
      c. Jesus Christ performed incredible, supernatural miracles
        (1) Account of Jesus raising Lazarus from the dead in modern-day terms of raising a guy named Harry from the dead
      d. Jesus Christ is the only person ever to predict his own death and to have raised himself from the dead
  B. Why did Jesus Christ have to die?
    1. He died to pay the penalty of our sins
    2. Description of crucifixion from *Hey, Who is That Man?* by Barry St. Clair
    3. Analogy of receiving a fine for a speeding ticket that someone else offers to pay
    4. God's plan—in order for the human race to be forgiven, God's Son had to pay the penalty of death
    5. The physical pain which Jesus experienced was not as traumatic as the emotional and spiritual pain of having God turn his back on the sin on Jesus at the cross

C. Why did Jesus rise from the dead?
    1. Scripture said that he would and he did—1 Corinthians 15
III. Conclusion
    A. "One Solitary life" by Peter Marshall
    B. Question—Are you ready to apply the only solution . . . Jesus Christ?

The Legend of Eric the Hairball

I. Eric wakes up to discover that he has another head, a growth with a big mouth, growing out of his head
  A. Eric goes to school embarrassed by the growth, but realizes that everyone else has a similar growth on their heads
  B. Eric's friends at school tell him of a psychiatrist who can cure the growth

II. The four cures—for $15 each
  A. Pretend that the growth is not there
    1. Growth gets bigger
    2. Pain becomes severe
  B. Blame the existence of the growth on others
    1. Growth continues to get bigger
    2. Pain becomes excruciating
  C. Cover up the growth
    1. Stocking caps and top hats
    2. Growth now has its own head and hands and has grown down into Eric's internals
    3. Pain is unbearable
    4. Growth will not stop talking—both quietly and loudly
  D. Dress it up and enjoy it
    1. Eric decides to dress up growth and enter show business

III. Amid his success, Eric meets an old school friend who tells him of a doctor who can cure the growth
  A. Eric goes to doctor who tells Eric that the only cure is so expensive that the only way Eric could afford it would be to admit he has a need and accept the money from a foundation established long ago by the wealthiest person who ever lived
  B. Eric is insulted because he has already earned much money and he leaves the doctor to go out and earn even more
  C. Eric returns to the doctor two more times to buy the cure, but the doctor refuses and repeats that Eric must accept the money from the foundation

D. Eric refuses the doctor's help and the money from the foundation and dies

IV. The moral of the story
   A. We all have a growth inside of us—sin
   B. We were created to have God at the center of our lives, but we rebel against Him and decide to run our own lives—disease
   C. We deal with this disease in the following ways
      1. We deny that it exists
      2. We convince ourselves that it is not real
      3. We enjoy it
   D. This disease leads to spiritual death
      1. Total separation from God, his power and his joy
      2. Think of the loneliest moment in our lives and multiply that by infinity
   E. What John, one of Jesus' best friends, had to say
      1. If we refuse to admit that we have sin, we live in illusion
      2. If we admit our sin, we will find truth
   F. Jesus will thoroughly cleanse us if we admit our need and accept God's free gift of the cure which is found in his Son

Taking on Temptation

I. Introduction
   A. Divide into groups with one person being the "tempter" and the rest "temptees "
   B. Situations
      1. Tempter has answers to a test that the rest of the group did not study for
      2. Tempter comes up to the rest of the group at a party with a few beers for them
   C. It is much more difficult to resist in real situations
   D. Other situations
      1. A person visits boy/girlfriend even though parents have said no and lies to parents as to his/her whereabouts
      2. A person is with boy/girlfriend until late at night and sexual temptation becomes great
   E. These are considered to be the four "biggies"
      1. partying
      2. cheating
      3. lying
      4. sexual immorality
II. There are other temptations which may be more socially acceptable but cause as many problems as the big four
   A. The temptation to be impatient
      1. Two examples from speaker's high school experiences
   B. The temptation to be uncaring
   C. The temptation to be physically beautiful
      1. Example of speaker's brother
   D. The temptation to gossip
      1. Passing on news that is not helpful
      2. Example of girl about whom a rumor was spread that she was pregnant

E. The temptation to be respected
  1. Money as a means to gain respect
    a. guys at football game cheering about money
    b. Madonna's "Material Girl" song
F. The temptation to judge
  1. Being proud of not sinning as others do
G. The temptation of power
  1. To have control over others
  2. Example of girl whose boyfriend would not allow her to go to camp
H. The temptation to be cool
  1. Hiding the real you for fear of disapproval by others
III. Defining temptation
  A. Temptation is . . .
    1. potential
    2. a choice set before us
    3. making ugly that which could be right
    4. a reality we will never escape
    5. James 1:2
      a. we will never get away from temptation
      b. temptation is not the same thing as sin
        (1) illustration of girl on the beach
          (a) saying yes to temptation and allowing mind to play with fantasy is sin
  B. How do we keep temptation from becoming sin?
    1. Sex is created by God
    2. Temptation is an opportunity to choose—making a choice
      a. Should I save sex for marriage or go for it now?
    3. Love is created by God
      a. Example of a high-school girl falling in love with a married man
        (1) opportunity to choose
  C. Temptation is a choice between whether to sin or not
    1. We all have basic desires
      a. The desire for a man or woman is actually the desire of wanting to be loved
      b. The desire to drink is actually the desire to be accepted
    2. Normal, healthy desires can lead us to make bad choices

IV. Dealing with temptation
    A. The worst way to deal with temptation is to try to fight it alone
        1. We need a group of peers where we feel comfortable in expressing ourselves
            a. Example of a man's marriage being saved because he was able to confess to his peers who encouraged him
            b. Example of Scott who was a former drug-pusher
    B. 1 Timothy 6—flee from youthful lusts
        1. Don't allow ourselves to get into situations that put us under pressure or make us vulnerable to temptation
    C. Build a group of friends that put us under positive peer pressure
    D. Make decisions ahead of time
        1. Example—decide now to care for others
    E. Jesus battled temptation by knowing Scripture and through prayer
        1. He could then know what was right to do
        2. Prayer gives strength
    F. Know how to refuse temptation with grace, courtesy, and firmness
        1. Ideas concerning cheating, drinking, and gossiping
V. Conclusion
    A. Temptation is a struggle, but it is also a great promoter of growth and enables us to become stronger Christians

Resisting Sexual Temptation

I. Introduction
   A. Society's view is that sex is all-important
      1. The pressure to be sexually active surrounds us
         a. movies
         b. magazines
         c. T.V.
         d. billboards
   B. Church's view sometimes is that sex is dirty, wrong, sinful
      1. Speaker's experience at a Christian camp
   C. Sex is neither
      1. A sexual relationship is one that has been designed by God to be enjoyed by a man and woman within the context of marriage
         a. analogy of goldfish which survives only in the context of water

II. Joseph as an example of someone withstanding sexual temptation—Genesis 39
   A. Background information on how Joseph came to be Potiphar's slave
   B. Four principles for resisting sexual temptation
      1. Verses 6 and 7—everybody is handsome in form and appearance to somebody
         a. all of us will inevitably face sexual temptation in one form or another
      2. Verses 8 and 9—set your standards ahead of time
         a. Joseph immediately refused Potiphar's wife
         b. Joseph had adopted what the Bible has to say about sex as a standard for his life
         c. we must follow Joseph's example
         d. our relationship with God must be priority
      3. Verse 10—avoid contact with temptation
         a. Potiphar's wife persisted
         b. sexual temptation is powerful—don't hang around
         c. before going on a date think of the following

   (1) where to go
   (2) what to do
   (3) whether to "park"
   (4) whether to pursue a good night kiss and how long
  4. Flee
   a. Joseph ran from Potiphar's wife
   b. get out of the situation—2 Timothy 2:22
   c. this may be hard to do, but it needs to be done
   d. Joseph was thrown in jail for attempted rape
    (1) consequences are not always easy
    (2) speaker's personal story about the time when his college friends learned that he was a virgin
III. Conclusion
 A. God will be with us to help us set up standards for ourselves and to keep them

Understanding the Opposite Sex

I. Introduction
   A. Imagine earth with only guys or only girls
   B. Electricity of coming in contact with the opposite sex
   C. Frustration and confusion in attempting to understand the opposite sex
   D. Picture in your mind relationships you are involved in right now as we go through the talk
   E. Give girls a chance to call out characteristics of guys
   F. Give guys a chance to call out characteristics of girls
      1. These lists are full of stereotypes
   G. Four ground rules
      1. Some say that differences between girls and guys are biological while others say the differences are cultural
         a. The fact is that the sexes are different—Genesis 1:27
            (1) God created us for a purpose
         b. To understand the differences between girls and guys, you must want to understand
            (1) "I can't understand" equals "I don't want to understand"
            (2) To understand how to relate is fun and important
         c. All differences are not necessarily due to our sex
            (1) Morning versus night people
            (2) Neat versus messy people
            (3) Our definition of masculine is all wrong
               (a) It is not to be everything that is unfeminine—Rambo
         d. We are here to learn and have fun, so let's get into the study

II. Areas to look at
   A. How the sexes relate physically
      1. Research
         a. Guys are ten times more likely to be color-blind
         b. Girls are five times more likely to cry
         c. Guys have thicker skin
         d. Strength
            (1) Guys primarily have their strength in their upper body

(2) Girls develop strength in their lower body
B. How the sexes relate mentally
  1. Men are not necessarily smarter than women
  2. Woman are not necessarily smarter than men
  3. Research
    a. Guys are more curious about objects and tend to excel in math and mechanical skills
    b. Girls talk earlier than guys and excel in foreign languages and verbal skills
    c. Girls have better memories
  4. It is not a matter of one group being better than the other, but a matter of different groups possessing different strengths
C. How the sexes relate emotionally
  1. We all need to know that other people like us—that we are important
  2. Our self-image is largely determined by what others think of us
  3. Girls and guys develop self-worth in different ways
    a. Guys develop theirs by building a positive reputation through personal accomplishments
    b. Girls develop theirs through relationships where they know that people love and understand them
    c. Ephesians 5
      (1) . . . love wives
      (2) . . . respect husbands
    d. Hint to girls
      (1) To make a guy feel good, pay attention to things he does well—compliment him
        (a) Guys are insecure
    e. Hint to guys
      (1) Need to want to understand girls
      (2) Seek to know and to sympathize with feelings that girls have
        (a) Personal example of wife's work with computers and her wanting him to understand that she had a lousy day
    f. We need to understand each other and know that we have feelings
D. How the sexes relate socially
  1. Guys relate to girls in one way, while girls relate to guys in a completely different way

        a. Guys get together when they have something to do—problem solving and task-oriented

        b. Girls get together to talk

           (1) Slumber party

           (2) Guys don't know how to talk to other guys

               (a) Guys stand next to each other facing out

               (b) Girls stand face to face

           (3) Girls should help guys out by asking specific and helpful questions about how they feel

           (4) Guys should open up and tell girls how they feel when asked such questions

           (5) Girls should keep asking questions when guys give lousy answers

  E. How the sexes relate sexually

    1. Guys can hardly relate to girls without it being a sexual encounter because sexual feelings are tied up with who they are

    2. Presupposition is that God's design for sexual intercourse is that it should be kept to a committed marriage relationship

    3. Guys are turned on by what they see

        a. Media caters to this

    4. Guys are not necessarily discriminating

    5. Girls are discriminating

        a. Need and want a sexual relationship

        b. Is an emotional experience

        c. Are turned on by compassion and understanding

    6. Girls should realize that their clothing communicates strongly to guys

        a. Think about what you are saying with your clothes

    7. Guys should be careful about casual touches

        a. What are you trying to say?

III. Break into small groups for three minutes

  A. Girls with girls and guys with guys

  B. What would you like to say to the opposite sex about your own?

  C. Allow for girls' and guys' responses

IV. Summary

  A. Philippians 2

Choose Your Own Adventure, Part One

I. *The Dragon's Den*
  A. Introduce the book
    1. Explain the concept by which the plot develops
      a. The plot develops according to decisions made by the reader
  B. Read the book and allow for decision-making
  C. Doing this is fun
    1. You can go back and do it again if you don't like the first ending
    2. Your decisions really count in the unfolding of the plot
  D. Problem is that, in real life, you can't always go back, and so we need to make good decisions

II. Today's culture forces many decisions and choices
  A. Research by supermarket chain
    1. We pass by 6–10 items per second in a grocery store
    2. 235 new items were introduced on the market in one month's time
  B. Choices among products
    1. Ice cream
    2. Lipstick
    3. Chicken
    4. 9-Lives cat food
  C. Decisions are a part of our everyday lives

III. Three critical life-shaping decisions that must be made by teens
  A. A *Master*—who or what will be the most important person or thing in your life?
  B. A *Mission*—what are you going to do with your life?
  C. A *Mate*—who will you marry?

IV. Ways of coming to decisions
  A. "Close your eyes and pick" method
  B. "Eeny-meeny-miney-mo" approach
  C. Two different models of decision-making are demonstrated by Abram and Lot
    1. Read Genesis 12:1–4; 13:8–16

      2. Abram was faced with a decision—*go* where God said or say *no* to God

V. The first step in making good decisions
  A. Abram made a firm *decision of allegiance*
   1. Example of saying "Pledge of Allegiance" in elementary school
   2. We live out the conscious and unconscious decisions of allegiance daily
    a. language
    b. dress
    c. music
    d. friends
    e. homework
    f. calories
  B. Abram's firm decision of allegiance was to God
   1. 12:1—"go"
   2. 12:4—he went
   3. It was a firm commitment
  C. Abram's firm decision of allegiance to God meant that he was willing to give up former allegiances
   1. Saying yes to new directions from God means saying no to old directions we choose for ourselves
   2. Example of marriage as a pledge
   3. James 1:7–8
   4. UPI newspaper article
    a. Problem of double-mindedness
    b. Double-headed snake
  D. Abram's firm decision of allegiance to God was a "go-for-broke" decision
   1. Abram banked everything on God
    a. Verses 1 and 2
    b. All hinged on God—there was no back-up strategy
    c. Example of disciples following Christ
   2. It's a tough thing to do
   3. It means that we must say no to old habits, lifestyles, relationships
   4. One decision of allegiance affects every other decision made
   5. Lot never made a go-for-broke decision for God

        a. His was a half-baked commitment

        b. He followed Abram

           (1) Verse 4

        c. Many make half-hearted decisions to follow parents or friends

    6. This shows up sooner or later

        a. Abram and Lot—Chapter 13

           (1) Problem—not enough room on the same land for both

           (2) Solution—split up

           (3) Abram offers first choice of land to Lot

               (a) 13:9

           (4) This shows Abram's decision of allegiance to God because he couldn't lose

           (5) Lot chose what he thought was the best land for himself—selfishness

               (a) 13:11

        b. When the heat is on, the lord of our lives comes through—God or ourselves

    7. The irony is that, in the long run, Lot's decision led to disaster

VI. Conclusion

    A. The choices we make now determine options and choices faced later

    B. Making good decisions now is so important

    C. Start by making a firm decision of allegiance to God

Choose Your Own Adventure, Part Two

I. Introduction
- A. Story from newspaper in Albany, New York
  1. A woman who volunteered to work a kissing booth at a M*A*S*H Bash Benefit for the March of Dimes was found to have hepatitis
  2. Those who had paid $1.00 for a kiss now had to pay $5.00 for a shot
  3. Things are not always as they seem
  4. Something that looks so good can potentially be deadly
     - a. Hidden cost
     - b. Pain
- B. The problem with making decisions based solely on appearances is that appearances can be very deceiving
- C. Bad decisions based on the way things look cost much more than ever guessed and can cause pain

II. The Lesson that Lot Learned—Genesis 13:8–16; 19:15–30
- A. Background information on Abram and Lot and their split
  1. Abram's decision of allegiance was to God
  2. Lot's decision of allegiance was to himself
- B. Lot demonstrates second key to making good decisions—don't be fooled by the *deceit of appearances*
  1. Genesis 13:10—"like"—things are not always as they seem
  2. It looked *like* that before the Lord destroyed Sodom and Gomorrah
  3. Lot selfishly chose his homestead in a land so evil that God would totally destroy it in later years
- C. One of Satan's greatest strategies is similarity—what looks and seems *like* the real thing
  1. Examples
     - a. love—lust
     - b. Christianity—formal religious game
     - c. worthwhile goal—relationship—we get burned
- D. Making decisions is risky
  1. Many people in our culture will lie to you
  2. Our culture is unbelievably gullible

      a. Teens are the main target
        (1) They have more discretionary spending money
        (2) They make more decisions based on appearances
          (a) Example of Smirnoff ads
          (b) Example from *Philadelphia Inquirer*
    3. Many never look behind images or appearances
      a. Example of Eve in the Garden of Eden—Genesis 3
  E. We need to look at Abram's style of decision-making
    1. Lot chose by sight
    2. Abram chose by faith by leaving choice in God's hands
      a. Verses 14–16—God will bless Abram's faithfulness

III. How this applies to us today
  A. When you choose by sight, you are trusting in your own judgment and that is risky
  B. We need to stake decisions on the judgment of God
    1. Trust God
    2. Choose by faith
  C. Consider the risks of making decisions based on our own insight
    1. Genesis 19:15–30—picture of consequences
  D. Wise decisions come when we avoid the deceit of appearances
    1. Example of the California ad for a boa constrictor
    2. The same can happen to us—we can make costly, deadly decisions because we are fooled by the deceit of appearances
  E. Summary
    1. Begin with a decision of allegiance
    2. Continue by avoiding the deceit of appearances
    3. Proverbs 3:5–6

Choose Your Own Adventure, Part Three

I. Horse Trading Problem
   A. According to the problem, did the speaker make money, lose money or break even with the horse and how much?
      1. Allow for answers
      2. Vote on answers
   B. Problems which appear so simple can really be much tougher
   C. It is tough to know whom to listen to
   D. One of the hardest parts of making good decisions in your life is choosing carefully whom you will side with

II. The third factor in making good decisions is the *discernment of alliances*
   A. This involves choosing good friends
      1. Some people who you thought were allies may be telling you lies
         a. 1 Corinthians 15:33
   B. Lot as an example of what not to do—Genesis 13:8–13
      1. Background information on Abram and Lot
      2. Chapter 14—the land of Sodom and Gomorrah was on the verge of war between two kings
         a. Bera, King of Sodom
         b. Birsha, King of Gomorrah
         c. War took place in the Valley of Siddim
            (1) 14:10—the valley was full of tar pits
            (2) The armies were locked in hopeless defeat
      3. Notice what has happened in these passages—it is subtle, tricky, and very important
         a. Example of cheering for bad guy in a movie without realizing it
      4. Lot moved into Sodom knowing of evil that existed and, as time went on, his whole value system was turned upside down and he saw the bad guys as being good
         a. 14:13
      5. Lot fights on the side of wickedness
         a. Lot makes a half-hearted decision of allegiance with his move to Sodom

        b. Lot became confused by the deceit of appearances by becoming comfortable in Sodom

        c. Lot lacks discernment in alliances by making friends and choosing the wrong crowd to live around

  C. The same thing can happen to us

    1. Hanging around a group of friends

    2. Sharing in their daily lives

    3. Sharing in their thinking

  D. Kids who are neutral towards God

    1. Begin hanging out with a crowd into sin

    2. What little faith and morality they had goes

    3. They come up with answers that are totally off-the-wall

  E. If you haven't made a firm decision of allegiance to God, you are fair game

III. The end of the story for Lot

  A. Bera, the King of Sodom, was defeated

    1. The enemy army moves in—verse 12

    2. Lot becomes the prisoner of a hostile army

    3. How many of us make this mistake?

    4. Lot can't even make his own decisions anymore

  B. One of Lot's servants escapes and runs to Abram—14:13

  C. Abram comes to Lot's rescue—14:16

    1. Abram meets two different kings—Genesis 14:17–23

      a. Bera, King of Sodom

      b. Melchizedek, King of Salem

        (1) Genesis 14:18–19—description of Melchizedek

    2. Abram must make a decision between two kings and kingdoms

      a. Bera + = wickedness.

      b. Melchizedek + = righteousness

        (1) Salem + = "shalom" + = peace

        (2) Priest of Most High God

        (3) Reference to Hebrews 7

      c. A decision between the promise of God (the riches of God) or material gifts (the riches of men)

    3. Abram shows us how to make good decisions

        a. He uses discernment and chooses his partner carefully by faith

        b. He knew that Melchizedek was his priest and Bera was his enemy

    D. This same scene happens today, and so we need to choose our alliances carefully

IV. The only way to make right decisions

    A. Make a clear decision of allegiance to God

    B. Follow up that allegiance with choices based on faith and not on sight.

    C. To maintain clear thinking, be discerning of alliances made

    D. Check yourself

        1. Who are you like in patterns of decision-making?

           a. Abram or Lot?

           b. The Kingdom of God or the kingdom of evil?

The Wall

I. Nehemiah learns that the wall of his hometown, Jerusalem, is torn down
  A. A high-school friend visits Nehemiah at Galilean Community College and tells him about the wall
    1. Nehemiah 1:3
  B. Nehemiah is extremely upset about the wall in his hometown
  C. City walls were very important
    1. They protected against enemy attacks—physical strength
    2. They were an indication of the spiritual condition of the people—righteousness
  D. Nehemiah requests time off from his employer, the king, to return to his hometown

II. Nehemiah returns to Jerusalem to rebuild the wall
  A. He publicly announces the formation of a volunteer construction company
  B. The neighboring governors, Sanballat and Tobiah, hear of the work and set about to thwart the construction plans
    1. They do this because, as long as the wall is down, they can influence the people of Jerusalem to wickedness and their own political views
    2. They begin with verbal insults
    3. Nehemiah warns his men not to stop
    4. Sanballat and Tobiah decide to use arrows and stones on the crew
    5. Nehemiah responds by having half his men act as guards while the other half continue to build the wall
    6. Sanballat and Tobiah realize that God's armor can not be penetrated

III. Sanballat and Tobiah come up with a master plan
  A. They offer refreshments to the construction crew
    1. Nehemiah tells his crew not to stop for anything
  B. They invite Nehemiah and the crew to a special dinner
    1. Nehemiah tells his men not to be sidetracked
  C. They offer Nehemiah a coaching position for a Jerusalem team in an inner-city basketball tournament.

        1. Nehemiah thinks it is great to bridge a gap with neighboring communities

        2. God reminds Nehemiah that the most important thing is to get the wall rebuilt

    D. They forge a letter from the king offering Nehemiah a seat in Congress

        1. Nehemiah is ecstatic

        2. God reminds him that the best thing right now is to rebuild the wall of righteousness

        3. Nehemiah's response to Sanballat and Tobiah is, "Why should anything sidetrack me from doing God's will?"—Nehemiah 6:3

IV. The construction crew completes the wall in 52 days

    A. They do it by being consistent

    B. Nothing sidetracks them from doing the will of God

 V. How do we build a wall of righteousness around our lives?

    A. Read the instruction manual

        1. We need to follow his instructions on a daily basis

    B. Follow Nehemiah's example

        1. He realized the importance of each individual

           a. What we do for God matters

           b. We all have an important part in building the kingdom of God

        2. He realized the importance of wearing the armor of God

           a. Ephesians 6

           b. We need to spend time with God and gird ourselves with his protection

        3. He realized the importance of determination

           a. We cannot allow ourselves to be sidetracked

           b. We must determine to lay spiritual bricks day after day

    C. Verse from Ezekiel

    D. God looks for those who will discipline themselves on a daily basis to build a wall around their lives through Bible reading, consistency, and doing his will

    E. Are you building that wall?

What Kind of Person Does God Choose?

I. Goliath
    A. Characteristics of Goliath
        1. Was 14 feet tall
        2. Wore a 76" belt
        3. Throat was so big he could swallow a McDonald's meal whole
        4. Never used deodorant
        5. Collapsed locker at school every time he threw his books into it
        6. Would cut through both frog and table in biology class
        7. Was a nightmare of a man
    B. Characteristics of David
        1. Was talented with a slingshot
        2. Gave this skill and committed his life to God
    C. It doesn't matter how much ability we have, but how much availability
    D. David was consistent with his availability
        1. He gave his talent to God and made it available on a daily basis
        2. God spent a lifetime preparing David to face the giant
    E. What is God preparing you for?
        1. Commit everything to God and make yourself available and he will equip you with everything you need to face giants
        2. God chooses to use the person with availability

II. Daniel
    A. Characteristics of Daniel
        1. Chose to be consistent in his prayer life
        2. Made himself available to God
        3. God used him to turn his nation around
    B. Availability is the key issue—not ability
    C. God uses ordinary people to accomplish fantastic tasks

III. Moses
    A. Characteristics of Moses
        1. Made many mistakes
        2. No one wanted him as a leader
        3. Had a lisp

    4. However, he was available

    5. Probably looked like Herman, the vacuum cleaner salesman

    6. God chose Moses

    7. Had a walking cane as his only material possession

       a. God asked for control of the cane

       b. God took that ordinary piece of wood and transformed it into a dynamic instrument full of power

  B. God will do exciting things in our lives if we let him

  C. Does God have 100% control of your life, material possessions, skills, and abilities?

  D. He wants 100%

IV. Jesus and the Five Thousand

  A. Dilemma of how to feed so many people

  B. Andrew knows of boy who is willing to give what little he has

  C. Jesus performs miracles and feeds five thousand

  D. The little boy gave all he had—he was available

V. Conclusion

  A. Summary of people God used when they gave everything they had to him

  B. Are you available?

  C. Now is the time to become available 100% to God

  D. Give each teen a small dowel to symbolize the rod of Moses as a reminder of what God can do with ordinary things

    1. Label one side with "I am available"

    2. Label other side with the date

How to Make and Keep Friends

I. Introduction
   A. Importance of friendship
   B. David and Jonathan
   C. Personal illustration of friendship

II. Why we need to build friendships
   A. Friends are encouragers
   B. Friends give counsel and advice
   C. Friends challenge our potential
   D. Question: Do we have friends like that?

III. How do we make friends?
   A. David and Jonathan's friendship
      1. Jonathan
      2. David
      3. Their problem
      4. Illustration
   B. Attraction
      1. Illustration
      2. How do we begin a relationship?
         a. Say "hello"
         b. Remember names
         c. Ask questions
   C. Affection—based on common goals and/or shared experiences
      1. Common goals
         a. Illustration
         b. Christians dating Christians
      2. Common experiences
   D. Accountability
      1. How do we develop accountability?
         a. Openness
         b. Willingness to learn friend's needs
         c. Sacrifice for friend's happiness
      2. Example of accountability

    E. Agape love
      1. 1 Samuel 18
      2. Going through joys and pains together
      3. Willingness to endure conflict
      4. Willingness to die for your friend
        a. God loves like this
        b. John 15:13
IV. Conclusion—God wants us to experience this kind of friendship

Trivial Pursuit

I. Trivial Pursuit
  A. Choose a method to begin talk
    1. Ask questions from Trivial Pursuit cards
    2. Ask group local trivial questions
    3. Divide into groups for a team activity
  B. Trivial Pursuit is fun and is the fastest selling board game

II. Trivial Pursuit played 2,000 years ago—Mark 10:17–22
  A. Jesus had an encounter with a rich young ruler who asked, "What must I do to have eternal life?
  B. This man seemed to have it all together in all areas of his life
    1. Geography (blue)
      a. Wealth
      b. This guy had it made in terms of money and possessions
    2. Entertainment (pink)
      a. He had plenty of friends
    3. History (yellow)
      a. He had a heritage and a family name
      b. He was from a royal lineage
    4. Science and nature—knowledge (green)
      a. He was trained in the best of Jerusalem's schools
    5. Art and literature (brown)
      a. He was well-versed in the sacred Scriptures (the Torah)
      b. He had been trained by Pharisees
      c. He had kept all the commandments since his youth
    6. Sports and leisure—physical dimension (orange)
      a. He was probably very handsome
  C. This man had everything life could offer
    1. He was winning the game
    2. He had all areas covered
    3. However, he had to go to the middle in order to win
  D. The man came to see Jesus
    1. "What must I do to have eternal life?"

        a. How do I win game of life?

        b. How do I make the last move?

    2. Jesus' response—verse 21

        a. "Go, sell everything you have and give to the poor, and you will have treasure in heaven. Then come, follow me."

        b. The way to win the game is to lose

        c. The man was winning at the wrong game

        d. The way to win the game was to give up all other categories and follow Jesus

    3. Man's response

        a. His face fell

        b. He considered the alternatives

            (1) Jesus could offer eternal and abundant life because of his death and resurrection

        c. He could not make the sacrifice, so "he went away sad"

III. Many of us compete in the game of Trivial Pursuit, but we are losing the game of life

  A. Geography

    1. Chasing after wealth and material possessions

  B. Entertainment

    1. Partying

  C. History

    1. Changing our past

    2. Wanting to start over

  D. Science and nature—knowledge

    1. Best education

    2. Highest GPA and test scores

    3. Best job

    4. There is nothing wrong with pursuing academic excellence until you become totally wrapped up in it

  E. Arts and literature—religion

    1. Fanaticism

  F. Sports and leisure—physical

    1. Obsession with our looks

  G. We major in these categories

  1. Matthew 6:33—The way to win at life is to fill the hole in the middle
  2. Put Jesus in the center of our lives
IV. How Christ meets our needs in each category
 A. Possessions
  1. Philippians 4:19—God will supply all our needs
 B. Entertainment
  1. John 10:10—an abundant and joyful life is found in Christ
 C. History
  1. Our sins are gone
  2. Jesus gives us a new history
 D. Knowledge
  1. Jesus is the way, the truth, the life
  2. John 8:31—we shall know the truth and it will set us free
 E. Religion
  1. We are the children of God
  2. We get to know God in a personal and intimate way
 F. Physical
  1. He knows us best and loves us
  2. Our bodies are his temple
V. Conclusion
 A. If we put Christ first, he takes care of all our needs
 B. Pursuing Jesus is a challenge and is life abundant
 C. We have a choice
  1. Start following Jesus
  2. Keep playing game

Involvement

I. Introduction
   A. Agree/disagree discussion
      1. Ask questions
      2. Allow kids to vote
      3. Allow time for feedback
   B. We need to see how willing you are to take a firm stand
   C. Would you be willing to make a commitment to something if you felt it would make a positive change in the world?
   D. The expression, "Go for it!"
      1. This means anything into which you really put your all
      2. In your Christian life, it means pouring yourself into projects that bring glory to God
      3. In a word, it is involvement

II. Areas into which we can pour ourselves—be involved
   A. The church
      1. Views of the church
         a. A building
         b. R-U-L-E-S
         c. ZZZZ . . .
         d. A party!
            (1) Church is a party, a celebration
            (2) It is a 2,000-year-old party and still going strong because of us
            (3) Why have this party?
               (a) The church is evidence to the world that God is alive
               (b) John 13:35
            (4) We need people who are party-goers
            (5) Examples of getting involved in the party
               (a) Cheryl had the gift of friendship and would welcome new people into the youth group
               (b) Chris would set up all the tables before church
      2. Pour yourself into the church to God's glory
   B. Friendships

      1. Give people what they need
        a. Someone to spend time with them
          (1) Time is a measuring stick of caring
        b. Someone to listen
          (1) Example of Greg who calls speaker once a month to talk
        c. Transparency
          (1) Open and honest with people
          (2) Let them know that you struggle as a Christian
        d. Someone who will hold onto them
          (1) Our world is disposable
          (2) Christian involvement means pouring ourselves into relationships and not giving up
        e. Prayer
          (1) Everyone needs prayer
          (2) Use an address book or calendar to pray for friends
        f. Laughter
          (1) Have fun
          (2) Laugh at your own mistakes
          (3) Example of the friend who helped the speaker through high school—he did all six things
      2. You can make a difference in the world by pouring yourself into relationships
    C. The world
      1. What can we do?
      2. It takes initiative
        a. Example of Laura who babysits to support a child
          (1) Some of you could sponsor kids
        b. Example of Josh who runs once a year to raise money for hungry children
        c. Example of group who built an orphanage in Mexico
        d. Other ideas
III. Conclusion
    A. Read Matthew 25:31–46 where Jesus tells a story concerning the end times
      1. God gathers everyone together

  a. Sheep—those who did something, those who are his
  b. Goats —those who didn't do anything, those for whom the party
   is over
 2. Since we now know beforehand, we can be sheep
  a. Whenever you do something, do it to the Lord
  b. Pour yourself into projects for the glory of God
  c. What you do to others, you do to Jesus
B. Two things not to do
 1. Don't pour yourself into projects for your own glory
  a. Think about what you do, how you do it, and whom you do it for
 2. Don't pour yourself into projects for pity's sake
C. Our one motivation and one reason for doing anything should be for the
glory of God
D. "Go for it!"

Playing Favorites

I. This is a special night
   A. You are hoping that the leadership of your youth group will notice you
   B. You have invited Larry Linebacker and Patty Popular to "Bring a Friend" night at your youth group
     1. Now you will get the respect that you deserve
     2. God could really use these two in your group

II. The meeting starts
   A. You are waiting around the back upon request of a youth sponsor to direct new people to their right place
   B. You have saved three great seats up front for Larry, Patty, and you
   C. You wait anxiously
     1. Larry's new Bronco pulls in
     2. It is followed by a three-tone piece of junk
   D. Larry and Patty look terrific
   E. However, you must wait until the announcements are over to seat them
     1. You daydream about how you will offer your arm to Patty and escort the two of them down the aisle
   F. Larry and Patty go to the bathroom
     1. You continue to daydream about how much of an asset they will be to the reputation of your youth group on campus
   G. Suddenly you smell a strange aroma
     1. It is the two punkers who came in the ugly car
     2. They ask where to sit
     3. You find out that they are from your school
       a. "How can you allow this to happen to me?" you ask God
       b. "Why me?"
   H. You keep them waiting hoping that Larry and Patty will return soon

III. The leader begins to read Scripture
   A. You are glad Larry and Patty aren't back yet because they might not like this part
   B. The leader says in his introduction that the topic that night will be playing favorites, partiality, treating some better than others

C. The leader reads from Scripture
    1. God is no respecter of persons
    2. Let there be no discrimination in the church
D. You realize that the girl standing next to you may be a rebel because of pain and bitterness in her life
E. You realize that these two probably get hassled everywhere they go
F. You realize that Larry and Patty have left
G. You experience a new freedom
    1. The Holy Spirit brings Scripture truths to mind
      a. John 13:34
      b. Ephesians 4:32
      c. Romans 15:7
      d. 2 Corinthians 10:12
    2. You are sad at your immaturity
      a. Scheming instead of praying
      b. Finagling instead of trusting
      c. Worrying instead of worshiping
      d. Impressing instead of loving
    3. Now you know why God put you in this situation
      a. These two people are very important and matter a great deal to God
      b. God's work is not dependent on Larry and Patty
H. You escort the two punkers up front, offering the girl your arm
I. You pray that others in your youth group would be softened by the same message and see people as people

IV. Ending suggestions
  A. Have two punkers arrive late in the story and be seated
  B. Have someone attend who is new to the group and ask them to share at the end their impressions as to how they were treated

Zaccheus

I. The Story of Zacchaeus
 A. Read the story of Zacchaeus from Luke 19
 B. This is an incredible story
 C. Sing the Zacchaeus song
 D. Characteristics of Zacchaeus
  1. He was a traitor
   a. He worked for a government which heavily oppressed the Jews
  2. He was small
  3. Everyone hated him
 E. The reason for telling this story is that we tend to say that the more we learn about the Christian life, the more we say that we will never measure up to what God wants

II. Good news from the story of Zacchaeus
 A. Jesus would invite us to dinner
  1. He seeks us out and follows us around
   a. Not in the sense of waiting to punish our mistakes
   b. Example of going up and talking to a gorgeous person who says, "Ugh," to us
 B. However, Zacchaeus had to do something about Jesus' invitation
  1. He had to get down out of the tree
  2. God will never violate our wills
  3. When we say "yes" to God, it means so much
   a. However, it does not mean that you must become a missionary
   b. But you must do something
  4. Principle—something is better than nothing
   a. No matter how small, God can use and multiply it in your life
    (1) Example of Shannon inviting James to the youth group
     (a) It changed his life
    (2) Example of the German class
     (a) Richard takes teacher's ranting and raving on himself for Margaret
 C. "I have come to seek and to save those who are lost"

1. This means that Jesus came to seek and to save those who are in the wrong place
2. Jesus came to put us in the right place
   a. Example of the boy who committed suicide
   b. Many kids feel isolated, alone, unattached to anything
      (1) They wonder if anyone cares
3. Jesus gives us a place because we are significant and important
4. Jesus related and identified with Zacchaeus so much that Zacchaeus wanted to change his lifestyle

III. Conclusion
   A. Example of woman whose face drooped after surgery
      a. Her husband still loved and kissed her
   B. Jesus twisted his body for us
   C. Jesus is looking for us
   D. We can receive him joyfully